On Democratic Politics

A Selection of Essays by
Norbert Lechner

Edited by **Velia Cecilia Bobes**
and **Francisco Valdés-Ugalde**

Translated by **Victoria Furio** and
Mariana Ortega-Breña

LATIN AMERICA
LASA ■■■■■ **RESEARCH COMMONS**

Published by
Latin America Research Commons
www.larcommons.net
larc@lasaweb.org

Cover design: Estudio Entre
Cover image: Philippe Gruenberg (born Peru, 1972), *Ejecutivo. Los poderes del Estado* serie, 2002, silver copy on Baryta paper, 120 x 200 cm. Lima Museum of Art, gift of Deutsche Bank donation. Photo by Daniel Giannoni.
Print version typeset: Lara Melamet
Digital versions typeset: Estudio Ebook
Copy editor: Melina Kervandjian
References: Elvira Cevallos
Bibliography and index: Lisa Rivero

ISBN (Paperback): 978-1-951634-37-7
ISBN (PDF): 978-1-951634-38-4
ISBN (EPUB): 978-1-951634-39-1
ISBN (Mobi): 978-1-951634-40-7
DOI: https://10.25154/book12

Suggested citation:
Bobes, Velia, Cecilia and Valdés-Ugalde Francisco, eds. *On Democratic Politics. A Selection of Essays by Norbert Lechner*. Pittsburgh: Latin America Research Commons, 2023. DOI: https://10.25154/book12
License: CC BY-NC 4.0.

To read the free, open-access version of this book online, visit https://10.25154/book12 or scan this QR code with your mobile device:

*Obra editada en el marco del Programa de Apoyo
a la Traducción para Editoriales Extranjeras de la División
de las Culturas, las Artes, el Patrimonio y Diplomacia
Pública (DIRAC), de la Subsecretaría de Relaciones
Exteriores de Chile.*

Work published within the framework of the
Translation Support Program for Foreign Publishers
of the Division of Cultures, Arts, Heritage
and Public Diplomacy (DIRAC) of the Ministry
of Foreign Affairs, Chile.

DIRAC
Ministerio de
Relaciones
Exteriores

Gobierno de Chile

Table of Contents

Foreword

The German-born, Chilean author Norbert Lechner (Karlsruhe, 1939–Santiago, 2004) remains one of Latin America's most prominent and creative social scientists. Throughout his career as both a researcher and thinker, Lechner greatly contributed to our understanding of issues relating to the state, democracy, and political order. His early work—which reflected his concern for the specific characteristics of the Chilean state as well as that of other countries in the region—resulted in powerful examinations of the political and social phenomenon of authoritarianism, problems concerning the constitution of political order and consensus, and democratic theory. During his later years he undertook what are possibly his major contributions to Latin American political thought: his reflections on politics and the subjectivity of individuals, both in Chile and across our regional societies. His theoretical input regarding these topics garnered him international recognition.

Although Lechner's oeuvre remains resonant and influential throughout Latin America, his texts are rarely translated. This book gathers some of his writings in an English language translation with the purpose of disseminating his work to a larger audience, one that is academic as well as general. The texts included here are an extremely relevant contribution to the field of social sciences, for Lechner's thought is both consistent and current, as well as widely recognized. The translation of his work is also important to the propagation of Chile's culture and its international image.

The dark period encompassed by the rise of Latin America's military dictatorships led to, among many other things, a pause in the construction of regionally specific theoretical paradigms with which to understand our territories. Thus, if the 1950s and 1960s were steeped in these debates and in the rise of a literate urban culture that determinedly sought to fashion the necessary tools to address Latin America from a local perspective, the military regimes of the 1970s and 1980s stifled support, shut down think tanks, persecuted social scientists, and exiled Latin American thought both literally and symbolically. In this gloomy scenario, Lechner's work offered new theoretical keys with which to understand the novel realities facing our countries.

This anthology, which includes the first translations into English of three of his most outstanding works—the introduction and epilogue to *The State and Politics in Latin America* (1981), as well as *The Inner Courtyards of Democracy* (1988), a volume planned and edited by Lechner himself which gathered work by notable Latin American authors, and *The Shadows of Tomorrow: The Subjective Dimension of Politics* (2002)— can guide our readers, like Ariadne's thread, through the intellectual output of this great thinker. It should also be said that these writings contain some of the most intellectually stimulating approaches to political sociology written in Latin America. Published between the 1980s and the first decade of the 2000s, the texts cover a span of more than thirty years during which the author developed a very personal vision as he sought to understand politics in a different way.

Lechner's work is indebted to the intense debates regarding theories of modernization, developmentalism, and dependence that took place in Latin American intellectual and political circles. These theoretical sources were present as a cognitive horizon in his essential writings, and many of the central concerns that enlivened his oeuvre arose from his intellectual immersion in these deliberations. If the confrontations with the revolutionary discourses of the 1960s informed his vision of the Latin American state, his experience with authoritarianism led him to pose a question that would become central to all his output: What does it mean to do politics, and what does it mean to do democratic politics?

To answer these queries, he suggested we view politics as the work and construction of all involved actors; he also stressed the importance of attending to the imaginary-symbolic components of power and the problems inherent to its legitimacy, bringing them to the foreground. Without ignoring the relevance of the institutional dimensions of democracy or extant pacts on the rules of the game, Lechner drew attention to the need to reflect on "styles of doing politics," the values and beliefs of participating actors, and the diverse interpretations of reality present in the democratic game. His considerations regarding these "new ways of doing politics" evidence the connection between institutions, actors, and subjectivities, an approach that, in turn, makes way for the analysis of non-state or partisan actors the likes of which have, in many cases, played major roles in Latin American politics.

His work is defined by two aspects that we believe constitute his main contributions as a thinker: First, he grants theory a central place in the realm of democratic practice—we can think about politics based on close observation of its mechanisms and extant problems without foregoing the vision of an ever-fluctuating future. Second and concomitantly, we can recover the subjective and symbolic dimensions of politics—the presence and motivation of national and regional cultures in shaping the imagination of the future.

The current volume has been drawn from the author's collected works, published as *Obras* by Facultad Latinoamericana de Ciencias Sociales México and Fondo de Cultura Económica and edited by Ilan Semo, Francisco Valdés-Ugalde, and Paulina Gutiérrez. Readers interested in perusing the breadth of Lechner's writings should refer to that edition.

We would like to thank FLACSO Mexico and Paulina for their support in the publication of this book.

Velia Cecilia Bobes and Francisco Valdés-Ugalde

Mexico City, July 2023

Translated by Mariana Ortega-Breña.

Acknowledgments

The publisher would like to thank FLACSO Mexico and Fondo de Cultura Económica for providing the original versions in Spanish of *Presentación de Estado y política en América Latina*, *Los patios interiores de la democracia: subjetividad y política*, *Las sombras del mañana*. and *La dimensión subjetiva de la política*, which were published together for the first time in *Obras* by Norbert Lechner. And thanks also go to Andreas Schedler for sharing the translation of "The Erosion of Political Maps," published in *The End of Politics? Explorations into Modern Antipolitics* (UK: Palgrave Macmillan, 1996).

The State And Politics In Latin America

First published in Mexico, Siglo XXI Editores, 1981
Translated for this volume by Mariana Ortega-Breña, 2023

Foreword

Contrary to tradition and healthy editorial policy, this book does not set out to fill a gap but, rather, to create it. Indeed, these past years we have witnessed an explosion in studies regarding the topic of the state in Latin America.[1] We have plenty of empirical studies on the state and agrarian or educational reforms, the state and trade unions, the financial bourgeoisie and the state, etc. However, taken all together, these leave us with an ambiguous feeling. Beyond the valuable contribution they make to the knowledge of a given society, I have the impression that they often take for granted some concept of the state itself. By not making it explicit, they turn the state into a residual category to designate a colorful mix of government, power structure, class domination, public policies, legal framework, ideological direction, etc. However, the very practical question of what the state in Latin America might be cannot be resolved by defining, a priori, a concept of state. On the other hand, the theoretical problem posed by such conceptualization is not bypassed by direct access to reality. In short, an analysis of the state cannot start from a given definition that could only be deployed in its historical concreteness, nor from an evident and tangible presence that would only require naming.

The difficulties in specifying what and how the sui generis capitalist state is in the region reveal a "theoretical deficit" that contrasts with the lively political struggle. Precisely because conflicts in Latin American societies always involve the state, their insufficient conceptualization ceases to be an academic matter. I presume that recent political crises are not alien to a crisis of political thought. Political theory not only guides us

---

1   Norbert Lechner prepared this edition and wrote the foreword and epilogue reprinted here.

in the solution of problems, proffering instruction on the selection, classification, and combination of "data" (both real and causal) but is itself part of the problem. In an epilogue to this book I try to describe some of the current problems that call for an urgent renewal of Latin American political thought. I dare say that if there is something positive about the new authoritarian regimes, it is that they have shown us the inadequacy of our conceptions regarding the political aspect. Their pretense of creating a tabula rasa with accumulated experiences should not impel us—by simple denial—to cling to the usual interpretations. Rather, it seems that now is right time to undertake a critical review.[2] Such a revision could start by addressing the paradoxical fact that the "inflation" of research on the state is occurring in a notoriously anti-statist era. The anti-statism now in vogue[3] partially stems from an intellectual "fashion," partially from dramatic everyday experiences. On the one hand, the current Latin American vision of the state is increasingly marked by the violence exercised by dictatorships in Southern Cone and Central America rather than the expectations of socioeconomic development that focused on government activity years ago. Now, this more or less direct experience is intertwined with a world opinion that is averse to state omnipresence, both in those countries characterized by "real socialism" as well as in the capitalist countries of the welfare state.

The current suspicion toward the state and politics can be based on the Western theoretical tradition. To the extent that the topic of the state was incorporated into the field of political science and, specifically, into the North American renewal of the discipline, this was reduced to the government and the political system.[4] Here the state phenomenon

---

2   Cf. Guillermo O'Donnell's presentation at the CLACSO assembly held in Quito in 1975 on the State Commission (in *Latin American Research Review* 12:2, 1977, 109 ff.). One of his lines of work addressed the theory of the state and politics, and it is to this vein that this anthology seeks to contribute.

3   Lechner writes at the time of what he himself termed the "neoconservative" strategy that initiated a process of dismantling the old European welfare state. [—Ed.]

4   For David Easton, one of the founders of the systemic approach to politics, the concept of the state was insufficient because "It describes the properties not

vanishes beyond the apparent concreteness of institutions. The prag-
matic interest in governability overcomes the anti-statism of liberal
philosophy without rethinking the problem. Moreover, Marxist currents, having overcome economistic reductionism, have not managed to
develop a positive determination of the state. And it seems unlikely they
will as long as they continue to affirm that the goal of the process of social
emancipation is the extinction of the state and politics. Finally, we have
the suggestive contributions of Foucault and others to study the state *in
actu*. However, and in this case, the dismantling of everyday processes
and the subcutaneous mechanisms of power also feed on an anti-statism
that, as in the case of the other currents, like to think possible a degree of
social cooperation that can dispense with a unifying principle.

It is paradoxical—and significant—that despite the anti-state and
anti-political discourse of the liberal and Marxist tradition (and even of
the new authoritarian strategy), concern for the state remains in force.
I suspect that the research is motivated by more than the cognitive-instrumental interest that its titles proclaim. The state seems to awaken
that strange mixture of fascination and horror provoked by the sacred
(and the transgression of all foundational interdiction). If so, the study
of the state in Latin America requires a much broader inquiry than that
which characterizes our usual political analyses. The "enlargement"
of the capitalist state taught by Gramsci does not refer as much to the
extension of state functions that did not previously exist (though this is
also the case) as to an extension in conceptualization. We have a much
too narrow (instrumental) conception of what the state and politics are.
It is not a question of adding a few more tiles to an extant mosaic, but
of rethinking the political-state phenomenon as a whole. Rather than

---

of all political phenomena but of only certain kinds, excluding, for example,
the study of pre-state societies; it stands overshadowed as a tool of analysis by
its social utility as a myth; and it constitutes at best a poor formal definition."
From this perspective, systemic analyses set aside the problem of the state
and dispensed with the study of constitutions and law, focusing their analysis
on the concepts of behavior, groups, systems, and processes. David Easton,
The Political System: An Inquiry into the State of Political Science (New York:
Knopf, 1953), 108–109). [—Ed.]

develop already established lines of thought, we should construct our research subject.[5]

Thanks to a couple of dear friends—Francisco Delich and Guillermo O'Donnell—I turned that initial intuition into a project. They prompted me on an adventure: prepare an anthology on the theory of the state and politics in Latin America.[6] I use the word "adventure" because dissatisfaction regarding our present situation did not translate into a positive statement about the approaches and issues to be developed. Distrusting categories in use no longer implies an alternative approach. We can speak of a theoretical deficit precisely because of the absence of an established body of problems around which the accumulation of knowledge can crystallize. Nor is there any general hypothesis in recent literature that presents itself as an "obvious" starting point. Verifying a theoretical deficit means, therefore, acknowledging the necessary multiplicity of what have been, for quite some time, heterogeneous and heterodox efforts.

Acknowledging the facts does not imply accepting them. I thank Nita Manitzas and Richard Dye, from the Ford Foundation, for having managed a small grant that made it possible to organize this work. Their support is all the more appreciated given it was not possible to define the content in advance—this was a work of theoretical reflection

---

5   With regard to the European and North American discussion, see, among others, the anthologies edited by H. R. Sonntag and H. Valecillos, *El Estado en el capitalism contemporáneo* (Mexico: Siglo XXI Editores, 1977), and E. Moyano and F. Rojas, *Permanent Crisis of the Capitalist State* (Bogotá: Sociedad de Ediciones Internacionales, 1980); see also the special issues of Archives Européennes de Sociologie 18:2 (1977), especially C. B. Macpherson's article, "Do We Need a Theory of the State?," and *Daedalus* (Fall 1979).

6   The authors and texts contained in the book edited by Lechner are E. Laclau, "Teorías marxistas del Estado: debates y perspectivas"; S. Zermeño, "Las fracturas del Estado en América Latina"; E. Torres Rivas, "La nación: problemas teóricos e históricos"; F. Rojas, "Estado capitalista y aparato estatal"; O. Landi, "Sobre lenguajes, identidades y ciudadanías políticas"; G. O'Donnell, "Las fuerzas armadas y el Estado autoritario del Cono Sur de América Latina"; A. Przeworski, "Compromiso de clases y Estado: Europa occidental y América Latina," and F. H. Cardoso, "Régimen político y cambio social." [–Ed.]

(something usually understood as "abstract," if not "useless") and because the topic itself is foreign to North American culture, characterized by a low stateness.

In April 1979, I sent a summons to the authors here gathered. My invitations were informed but arbitrary. Without intending to provide a representative sample on the state of the discussion, I requested the collaboration of some colleagues whose theoretical reflections I found most stimulating. Subjectivity aside, I took care to ensure a certain geographical and generational distribution to accommodate different concerns and contexts. The collaborators' task was not easy: I suggested a general framework and possible topics to be addressed, but no agenda based on common agreement was established. The essays were written during 1980 specifically for this anthology. The readers will decide if the collection is more than the sum of its individual contributions; that is, if this multifaceted vision allows them to better "grasp" the problem. I thank each of the collaborators for their dedication to this endeavor. Despite their multiple other obligations, they did not grow impatient with their coaxing editor and generously helped get this ship out to sea. The future will tell if can brave the storms and, above all, if there is a shore to be found on the other side. Due to its porous and fragmentary nature, this anthology opens gaps. Providing a free platform raises new questions and opens paths without delimiting this *terra ignota* in advance or getting reduced to an *x* in an otherwise familiar equation. It provokes argumentative confrontation, prompts us to establish relations between one paper and another and, in short, to participate in an inconclusive debate. Giving up a final conclusion or solution is the privilege of intellectual discussion. It, however, does not discharge the editor from his duty to sort out the texts. I confess immediately: there is no "logical order," no "Ariadne's thread" to guide the reader through the different inquiries. This is an unscripted itinerary. However, I think it is possible to pinpoint some of the "landscapes" traversed by this book.

Theoretical Notes on the State and Politics in Latin America would undoubtedly be a more accurate title. There are, according to the Real Academia, the governing body of the Spanish tongue, different meanings for the term "to note": "[1] To point with the finger or in any other way toward a specific place or object. [2] In writing, notice or point toward something using a line, star, or any other mark, so it may be found easily." Here what we have is not a question regarding a specific object but, on the contrary, the issue of determining the subject of research. And it would be an act of arrogance to maintain that we will easily find said subject. Here is another meaning: "[3] to start affixing and temporarily place something, as when someone begins nailing a board or canvas without riveting the nails." We are facing outlines, ongoing inquiries, more concerns than results. These are texts that express and point toward an activity, not to a closed system. In this sense, we are engaged with theoretical notes.

Theory has fallen into disrepute for different reasons. Because of the vacuity inherent to the blind application of "imported" categories and exegetical works that only obscure our understanding of concrete experiences. And—in the name of such intimate subjectivity—because of the current fashion for killing "master thinkers." There seems to be a (Western) "crisis of reason" as the questioning of the foundations on which the social order rests is paralogized. However, justified criticism of "systems" and, more generally, of the excessive pretensions of science should not lead to a cult of irrationalism or the comfortable cultivation of supposedly objective data. The search for truth is ultimately not a logical procedure but a historical practice. However, social practices baffle us inasmuch as they imply the elaboration of an alternative order.[7] There is a tendency to oscillate between an acquiescent realism that surrenders to "the force of things" and an illusory triumphalism awaiting final victory. Both positions are entangled in an idea of revolution as maturation as well as the ultimate and definitive resolution to objective contradictions. In the absence of such redemption, every effort at reflection is abandoned or gives way to an act of faith. There is a reluctance to accept the tearing of reason to confront what is versus what could/

---

7   The critique of "real socialism" is not new, neither is the proposed revision of Marxist theory. "'The truth' is a moment of right practice," Horkheimer said in 1935, "but whoever equates it directly with success ignores history and becomes an apologist for the prevailing reality." Regarding this immediacy of positivist thought, we can affirm with Claude Lefort that "There is a crisis of reason to the extent that we fear addressing a question to which we have no a priori answer" (*El Viejo Topo* 47, August 1980).

should be. This requires imagination. Without fantasy, Marcuse said, all theory is attached to the present and lacks a future.

A limitation of thought in Latin America resides in the lack of "spiritual fathers" (such as Hegel or Croce) who can bring the current order into their concept. It is they who provoke (and facilitate) a radical critique of existing conditions. The absence of a conceptual synthesis, elevating Latin America to a "universal" plane, is not accidental. Sergio Zermeño and others point toward some of the fragmentations, overlays, and juxtapositions of structures and processes in our underdeveloped capitalist societies. Their forms of capitalism hinder not only the development of systematic regularities, but also of norms of communication. And these diffractions stand up against the imperatives of coherence and the aesthetic demands of logical thinking.

There was always the view (on both the right and the left) that underdevelopment was only a "delay" in the course of inexorable progress. Hence the temptation to superimpose categories constructed in metropolitan capitalist societies on Latin American particularities. The situation has changed in recent years with processes of inter- or trans-nationalization that are not merely economic. As the discontinuities of capitalist development become more present in everyday experiences, a new notion of contemporaneity emerges. The topicality of problems and tasks takes on a global dimension. I insist: the discovery of this simultaneous discontinuity covers all social relations; it also concerns the state and politics. Finally (and thankfully!) proffering the first synoptic exposition of the Marxist discussion in Europe, Ernesto Laclau does not present "information" to broaden our horizon; he addresses our problems. We are contemporaries of those debates reviewed by Laclau in his introductory essay. In fact, we set goals and appoint tasks on a universal plane (according to an international standard), although their feasibility and accomplishment depend on particular (national) forms. For this same reason, the book is characterized by a certain cosmopolitan temper. Its purpose is not to complement the empirical diagnosis of the different Latin American societies but to elaborate a perspective. The theoretical effort lies both in the novelty of posing new problems, and in rethinking problematics from a new perspective. Our perspective is Latin America (just as Italy, its division and unification, was Machiavelli's perspective).

The democratic state in Latin America is the perspective from which we shed light on certain issues and ignore or displace others.

I have grouped the essays around three problems that (even though they reflect subjective inclinations) may suggest new lines of research.

I. Social Division

Sergio Zermeño explicitly thematizes what, in the end, constitutes the common reference to all modern approaches to the state: social division. The question of what the state is also entails the question of the social division it produces and to which it refers.

I do not know whether social division is no richer than Fernando Rojas presumes in his determination regarding the form the state takes depending on capitalist relations of production. I wonder if the Hegelian distinction between language, instrument, and family is not more appropriate. These categories would designate three equivalent patterns of consciousness—symbolic representation, work process, and interaction—that need to come together in order to grasp the "spirit," i.e., social development. This multiplicity of mutually irreducible relations has been suggested by recent political anthropology studies regarding the emergence of state-organized societies.[8] These works can help us review the historical production of the concepts through which we think about the state phenomenon. A historical-materialist approach, indeed, cannot dispense with a historical analysis in order to explain the specificities of the capitalist state and, consequently, the possible aims of its transformation.

---

8   Cf., for example, the works of P. Clastres, *Vivre contre l'État* (Paris: Minuit, 1974); M. Gauchet, *La dette du sens et les racines de l'État*, vol. 2 (Paris: 1977), and K. Eder, *Die Entstehung staatlich organisierter Gesellschaften* (Frankfurt: Suhrkamp, 1980). On the Hegelian discussion, see J. Habermas, *Technik und Wissenschaft als "Ideologie"* (Frankfurt: Suhrkamp, 1968) (the chapter on "work and interaction").

This is not about historicizing the present or updating history. I prudently limit myself to outlining three dimensions present in the evolution toward "societies with a state." In pre-Columbian America, there had been a sedentary population for approximately 5,600 years; around 1,500 BC we got a combination of pottery, urban life, and food production. In some cases, a transition to "classical cultures" took place: those of Mochica and Tiahuanaco in the Andean region, as well as Teotihuacan and Monte Albán in Mexico. Here arose the first political centers with royal palaces and temples, long before the Inca and Aztec empires. How did these populations come to organize themselves statewide? It seems that such a mutation was a "response" to demographic-ecological pressures and to certain organized violence (war). Some "stateless societies"—such as the one described by Clastres[9]—that could not or did not want to innovate, ended up in collective suicide. Populations that evolved into "state-led societies" survived and expanded. The emergence of the new organizational principle advanced in a triple manner: 1) Technique: mastery over external nature; that is, the production of tools to always satisfy new needs. Innovations in the material production of life modified the notions of space and time, of reality and causality. However, it is not possible to reduce the evolution of social organization to cognitive changes, objectified in technique. 2) Kinship: it is through the definition of kinship and its institutions (filiation, marriage) that the first patterns of interaction are built. The norms of inclusion/exclusion and the rules of reciprocity and dependence have to be redefined with the establishment of a new organizational principle. By splitting the authority structures of kinship relations, a new formalization of social relations is elaborated. 3) Morality: the selection and stability of accepted social relations is ensured by the symbolic-normative order. It evolves from ritual, aimed at restoring a status quo ante, to conventional regulatory norms, open to innovation. Through an increasing formalization of this symbolic communication and religious norms, power relations are consolidated. The figure of the chief-judge is

---

9   P. Clastres, *Investigaciones en antropología política* (Barcelona: Gedisa, 1981), and *La société contre l'État* (Paris: Les Éditions de Minuit, 1978). [—Ed.]

detached from kinship structures to act as an integrative nucleus on the basis of an abstract idea.

These notes are not intended to outline the debate on the historical origin of the debate. Still, they are suggestive enough to introduce the assumption that the development of a proper instance of power and hierarchical social structures, as well as the principle of a political organization of society, are necessary (i.e., rewarded) innovations not reducible to the evolution of the social division of labor. I do not propose replacing the latter with another "definitive" principle, but to draw attention to the combination of different mechanisms and processes.

Sergio Zermeño finely highlights the complexity of divisions in Latin American societies. Following his tracing of the different diffractions, I perceive the need to approach our research in more sociological terms. Political analyses generally begin with preexisting "actors" and study the relationships between them. On the other hand, Zermeño's essay draws attention to the multidimensionality in which the subjects are constituted. We will return to this recurring topic throughout this book's contributions. To say that economic structures are necessary but insufficient to determine subjects is perhaps commonplace nowadays, but it is worth repeating: there are no objective class positions prior to the class struggle. That is, the struggle between certain "actors" is in turn the product of struggles over the formation of such actors. Zermeño's study helps us visualize the multiple divisions/struggles in Latin American societies in order to reconstruct the social conditions in which historical subjects are made, undone, and remade. This line of research raises doubts on whether the usual contrast between civil society and the state remains a satisfactory framework for analysis. It is probably more fruitful to approach the state as a moment of society's production.

II. The Social Synthesis in the Form of the State

Divisions in society imply an integrating moment. How much and how does a divided society cohere? Liberalism held the market to be the integrating force. The capitalist market promotes functional interdependence but proves incapable of absorbing social inequalities. Faced

with the limits of market ideology (freedom of private property, equality of fair exchange), liberalism itself fosters integration through political democracy and the welfare state. Even the current neoconservative
project reinforces the "free play of the market" with disciplinary strategies and, even so, fails to unite what it has created as atomized masses.
On the other hand, and while emphasizing the division in bourgeois
society, Marx too affirmed that only political superstition can believe
that the state is what holds society together. If civil life holds the state
together, then the political is ultimately futile.

Both approaches privilege the social over the political. Politics is sub-
limated in the functional organization of social relations. Assuming a harmony (already in existence or to be achieved) between specific interests
and the general interest, the union of social life would then be founded
on "society itself" as a pre-state sphere. The state would be nothing but
the external guarantor of an already extant social cooperation already
in force or a coercive integration of its mutually isolated producers that
disappears along with the re-establishment of a direct association.

A second leitmotif of the anthology is the revaluation of the work of
synthesis carried out by society in the form of the state.

The classical-modern expression of society's state integration is
the national state. Its formation is more than a territorial-administrative unification that claims sovereignty "outward," monopolizes power
against state privileges and local autonomies "inward," and organizes
the processes of capitalist accumulation. Therefore, it is not enough to
see the obstacles encountered by the full development of a national state
in the structural heterogeneity of Latin America and its late and dependent insertion into the world market and the international system. It is
not that this framework is not important, but it places too much attention on the state apparatus. It would not explain how a national project
arises and is imposed against the state apparatus. Edelberto Torres Rivas
studies in detail the highly complex mediations in which the distinction/
border between the national and the international is made: nation-class,
nation-state, nation-democracy, nation-people, nation-culture. Analyzing in depth the discontinuities of these mediations in the historical
conformation of Latin American societies, Torres Rivas addresses the
difficult articulation between the "national question" and the "social
question" that takes place in Latin American revolutionary processes,

especially in Central America and the Caribbean. The experiences in Cuba and Nicaragua forbid reducing nation-building to administrative centralization or economic homogenization; Torres Rivas's reflection makes us think of a "social regeneration"[10] that transforms all of the previous order and, in particular, the implication between collective identity and "universal" history.

The historical and political analysis of the national refers to a more conceptual reconstruction of this process of social self-production. Both Zermeño and Torres Rivas warn us against an ahistorical study of the state; but this does not invalidate Fernando Rojas's effort to thematize the "state" form. The problem posed by Rojas is the state as a form through which capitalist society produces and reproduces itself. Why does "something" like the state exist in every capitalist society? A historical description or typological classification of its development is not enough; Rojas attempts a logical reconstruction of the capitalist state. His question regarding the state points to the constitution rather than the organizational forms of the state. There is a state form regardless of the various possible political regimes. Politicians, Marx already suspected in 1844, usually look for the cause of social ills in a certain state regime that they try to replace with another. They do not question the principle of the state; that is, "the actual organization of society of which the state is the active, self-conscious, and official expression."[11] It is by returning to Hegel's preoccupation with the state as an abstraction that Marx comes to seek the state's *raison d'être* in "social evils." But it would be wrong to maximize his polemic against Hegel to the point of visualizing the state merely in terms of economic structures. Attempts to explain the capitalist state by its functions and deduce these from the process of accumulation are unsatisfactory. Categorically speaking, the state cannot be reduced to an actor that fulfills certain roles in and for capitalist economic development.

---

10 The expression is by José Aricó, *Marx y America Latina* (Lima: CEDEP, 1980).

11 Karl Marx and Friedrich Engels, "Critical notes on the Article: The King of Prussia and Social Reform. By a Prussian," in *Marx-Engels Werke (MEW)*, vol. 1 (Berlin: Dietz, 1958), 392.

It is not about minimizing the importance of state bureaucracy and government activity. That said, just as the enterprise is more than an aggregation of "factors," so too is the state more than the sum of coercive, economic, and ideological apparatuses. In order for Cardoso's practical interest—what to do with and in the state?—to be more than the concern of a bureaucrat only engaged in administering what is already there, we need a conceptual (and not merely historical) analysis of the process of objectification of social power under the state form.

A merely historical analysis of the process of centralization and the concentration of state power usually understands this process of objectification as alienation. The emergence of the modern state appears as the expropriation of a power proper to society and, therefore, as mere domination. Such an approach assumes that individuals could live in society without externalizing their own power to an instance outside them. That is, it supposes the effective possibility (not as a concept-limit) of direct social relations. Under this implicit assumption, the representative state is criticized as a usurpation of the sovereign power of the represented, and individuals are therefore seen in need of recovering their own powers; that is, a direct self-management of the social process by the freely associated producers. By thus anticipating an overcoming of social atomization, the problem of the state is reduced to the destruction of a coercive and parasitic apparatus.

Here we assume, on the contrary, that the modern distinction between society and state is not an "organic" split. In truth, the objectification of social power can be thought of as a constitutive relation of social life. This implies accepting that social divisions cannot be abolished but only transformed. Given social division (the "war of every one against every one," according to Hobbes), it can only act and dispose of itself by externalizing the meaning and goal of social coexistence in a place outside of it: the state form. Such ordering of social boundaries is coercive insofar as it is all "doing." Therefore, state power should be thought of less as violence and oppression than as a relation of production: production and reproduction of social life via the state.

Oscar Landi opens the conceptualization of the state in Latin America toward the invisible and intangible, but no less effective, dimension of the political. His reflection on imaginary and symbolic representation points to an extremely fertile approach to understanding the "spiritual" force of the state: Landi allows us to visualize the capitalist state as a "representative state" in a much broader sense than legal representation (popular-sovereignty, government-mandate). We can speak of the state as the representative of society insofar as it is society's representation of itself. That is, the representation in which capitalist society finds its identity. The imaginary is—in Lacan's interpretation—an identifying mechanism of the subjects. That is, since there is no social relation as "pure" materiality (a "society in and of itself"), society recognizes itself (recognizes the "self") in the imaginary order. It appears effectively here in the imaginary object (that is, in the representation of itself). Social relations construct their identity through the duplication/affirmation of themselves in an imaginary-symbolic order. Using Hegelian terms, I would say that civil society gains access to its concept in the state.

The hypothesis that capitalist society does not have an immediate identity (which does not exist in "itself" but in the imaginary and the symbolic) allows us to venture a second hypothesis. There would not be—unlike the classical liberal and Marxist postulate—a societal order prior to state organization. There would be no (natural) economic integration to be "given" political envelopment. On the contrary: only by means of "the political" is the social order organized. If the order of the imaginary and the symbolic is constitutive of a life in society insofar as it traces social divisions, then—in capitalism—such ordering is condensed in the state.

This very personal interpretation of Oscar Landi's research intends to highlight the point in which his approach complements the reflections by Torres Rivas on the national state and those of Fernando Rojas's on the state form. Although these pieces cannot be integrated into a single approach, they would appear to come to the same conclusion: the state as a synthesis of the divided society. Such synthesis does not entail a presumed general interest or consensus, nor the organizational monopoly of physical coercion, but representation in which the subjects recognize and affirm themselves as a "society." In this sense, it could be said that the state is both a product and a producer of social life.

I would like to propose a further step. Indeed, it can be presumed that future society will also be a divided one (without direct social relations) and that, therefore, will require a unifying instance. That is, the principle of the state is possible and necessary even under transformed capitalist social relations. I therefore propose to change the perspective implicit in much of the research and to abandon both the liberal utopia of the invisible hand of the market as well as the Marxist utopia of a free association of producers—that is, the possible extinction of the state and politics. Imaginary and symbolic creation certainly goes beyond political activity. Indeed, it is conceivable that future society will produce other forms of representation and recognition of itself. For now, however, the state and politics remain the privileged stage for the appearance of subjects.

III. The Democratic State

A review of extant research on the state and politics in Latin America reveals a significant change in the analytical perspective that corresponds to a shift in political objectives. If the problematic of the revolution was the main focus of Latin American societies in the 1960s (from, let us say, the victory of the Cuban Revolution in 1959 to Allende's overthrow in 1973), the leitmotif of our current period is democracy.

This is not an opportunistic process of "ebb and flow" that advocates or brackets socialism depending on its assessable feasibility. This would presuppose a fixed "model" of socialism, established once and for all, and waiting for the right conditions. Democracy (formal or bourgeois) would only be the tactical sphere inside which to propose socialism. Such an approach makes the accomplishment of socialism dependent on the unviability of capitalist development; its feasibility would be assured by the collapse of capitalism and revolution would be the only and total rupture. That is, socialism would be imposed by exclusion, not as an alternative.

The question of the feasibility of socialism—as well as the governability of democracy—is valid, but insufficient insofar as it only asks about the "how" and takes the "what" for granted. It is a technical question that does not touch on the fundamental questions: What socialism? What is democracy? These are historical projects that (are not exhausted in one or another governmental program and) arise from certain social practices. It can be said that these produce "radical needs" (Agnes Heller) that come from (but go beyond) the capitalist order. Their actuality lies in being projects produced by current capitalist relations. To the extent that project goes beyond the existing order and aspires to another reality, it is always also a utopia.

Once, the critique of utopia meant vindicating its fulfillment. Later, the defamation of utopia reflected the *horror vacui*, the fear of transforming the established. Today, utopia is the way of thinking about what to do. And perhaps the future, to some degree, can only be determined in a negative way: tomorrow (the day after tomorrow) as a negation of existing living conditions. In rebellions, desertions, even in the failures with which the people resist disciplining, there is a latent advance in the freedom to be attained. The alternative order, however, is not a mere inversion of the present order. To construct an alternative, we need to have an adequate concept of the already extant freedom; this will prevent us from thinking about emancipation as simple negation but, rather, as overcoming.[12] I do not think I misunderstand the authors when I interpret their concerns for democracy from this perspective.

In a final section, I have gathered three works that address the political motivation of the anthology more directly: the construction of a democratic state. The task of elaborating a theory of the state that implies a democratic determination is outlined throughout the book. However, when reflecting on the relationship between the state and democracy, we must address the current authoritarian offensive. Guillermo O'Donnell's text offers a first global assessment on the triggering phenomenon that led to the new problematization of the capitalist state in Latin America (that is, the military implementation of an authoritarian state in the Southern Cone of the region). The military regime of capital (local and multinational) cannot be understood without reference to the previous process of democratization. The progressive and sometimes radical activation of the popular movement was demanding social reforms that, despite their limited scope, reduced the capitalist "private initiative." Despite the importance of the so-called state of commitment in many of our countries, we have paid little attention to

---

12   On the genesis of current "catastrophic" thinking, see A. Wellmer's article "Terrorismo y crítica social," in J. Habermas, ed., *Stichworte zur geistigen Situation der Zeit* (Frankfurt: Suhrkamp, 1979).

the underlying "rationale." Now, in the face of authoritarian reaction, we see with new eyes the incipient welfare state, previously denounced as "reformism," now as "statism."

How is a negotiated redistribution of social wealth made effective in capitalist societies? Adam Przeworski's contribution lies in undertaking a lucid interpretation of a reality discarded by Marxist theory: class compromise. Przeworski elaborates an explanatory scheme of cooperation between capitalists and workers as a rational strategy in certain circumstances. The author does not fail to point out the difficulties faced by Latin American capitalist societies in establishing such a negotiation strategy. Fernando Henrique Cardoso deepens this reflection on the political problems intrinsic to the articulation of interests. Only by taking responsibility for these difficulties is it possible to present an answer to this new authoritarianism. Acknowledging the tension between the theoretical categories and the empirical conditions of the Brazilian experience, Cardoso outlines some of the questions we must address if the invocation of democracy is to be embodied in a collective practice.

A nuanced analysis of the authoritarian "constellation" in Argentina, Brazil, Chile, and Uruguay allows O'Donnell to sketch the specificity of this new type of authoritarianism. To the extent that military governments are relatively institutionalized, their closeness to the neoconservative project being implemented in the capitalist centers appears more clearly. Perhaps it is precisely in the Southern Cone that the various modalities of the new capitalist project crystallize in their purest form.

The "crisis of democracy" would be the result of an excess of political participation that causes such an increase (in quantity and quality) of social demands, that societies become ungovernable. In Huntington's words, "What the Marxists mistakenly attribute to capitalist economics, however, is, in fact, a product of democratic politics."[13] Neoconservatives oppose the kind of statism that suffocates individual freedom. At the same time, they demand a strong government—that is, one indifferent to the demands of the majority. Basically, they struggle against the

---

13   Cf. M. Crozier, S. P. Huntington, and J. Watanuki, *The Crisis of Democracy* (New York: Trilateral Commission–New York University Press, 1975), 73.

political will to collectively determine the material conditions of life. Their aim is to "extirpate" socialism as "the illusion that we can deliberately 'create the future of mankind.'"[14] That is where the right perceives the implications of democracy and socialism sometimes better than the left itself: the constitution of society into the subject of its development.

It is not just authoritarian aversion to a "democracy" of negotiation (Hayek). The left is also characterized by a contempt for political activity. A sign of our times is the displacement of politics by a technical-formal rationality. By reducing the social process to simple relations of means and ends, it is thought we can dispense (in the name of technical knowledge) with the political. The increasingly exclusive concern for what is done or is had conceives social relations only as relations between things. Only the question "who is" allows us to visualize political activity in non-instrumental terms. Here, the Marxist critique of fetishism refers us to the legacy of Greek philosophy. Aristotle understands politics as "the work of man qua man" and defines this "work" as "living well." Such "labor" is not, therefore, the product of labor; political practice, rather than a means to an end, is an "end in itself" as the subject's affirmation of himself.[15] In other words, doing politics is not a "plus" with respect to another "basic" activity, but the properly social relationship in which men recognize each other as subjects.

For this reason, a reply to the authoritarian project that only insists on the antagonism between capital and wage labor ("class against class") seems insufficient. Already in the introductory article by Ernesto Laclau the question arises of how subjects or "classes" are made, undone, and remade. The rejection of essentialism in the current understanding of "actors" is now widespread (except, perhaps, in political parties). It is no coincidence that the concern about "what organizes the political organization" should arise with more urgency precisely in authoritarian regimes, where it is forbidden to do politics. Not hindering efforts at depoliticization, a fundamental question of the political emerges more

---

14   For neoconservative thoughts on democracy, see Friedrich A. Hayek, *Law, Legislation and Liberty* (London: Routledge, 1998), 152.

15   I base this on Hannah Arendt's work, *The Human Condition* (Chicago: University of Chicago, 1969).

strongly: the ordering of social relations. The violent modernization of capitalism today repeats an experience well perceived by Marx: "All fixed, fast-frozen relations, with their train of ancient and venerable prejudices and opinions, are swept away, all new-formed ones become antiquated before they can ossify. All that is solid melts into air, all that is holy is profaned, and man is at last compelled to face with sober senses his real conditions of life, and his relations with his kind."[16] If there are no "natural" relations between men, they themselves must produce the social order. It is they who determine the divisions in society. Isn't that precisely what the formation of subjects is about?

We must still further assess how the constitution of classes implies a continuous disordering and reordering of society that passes through the state. This process includes the aforementioned "crisis of democracy" and, therefore, also the struggle for democracy.

Having said all of the above, I do not intend to draw any final conclusions from the book. The authors acknowledge and express the crisis of political thought in Latin America, and do not propose a happy ending. The common and permanent concern for a democratic state is not the "offer" of a solution. This is a debate to which Ernesto Laclau introduces us in the first text. It is the attempt to theoretically specify a perspective with which to understand and transform national realities. This anthology aims to provoke the need for similar efforts by opening this rift.

Santiago de Chile, March 1981

---

16 Karl Marx and Friedrich Engels, *The Communist Manifesto* (New Haven: Yale University Press, 2012), 77.

Epilogue

The state is a central issue in the political debate and sociological concerns of Latin America. Why? Undoubtedly, the trigger for this recent interest lies in the emergence of a new type of military-authoritarian regime in the Southern Cone. With the studies of Fernando Henrique Cardoso on the Brazilian political model and Guillermo O'Donnell on the authoritarian bureaucratic state,[17] the state stands in the foreground of the analysis of the Latin American reality. However, research on this topic does not date back to yesterday. Reviewing the most modern tradition we can distinguish several approaches. They respond, in part, to the theoretical problems posed by the research process itself. However, this not only serves a certain "research rationale" but also attempts, above all, to respond to the problems posed by the political situation. We have to "read" the different approaches to the state against the background of the strategies around which the political struggle crystallized in recent years. It is not a question of establishing a classificatory typology of theoretical approaches or political strategies, nor even of proposing any correlation. However, the simple confrontation allows us to glimpse some of the extant impasses in Latin American processes. These practical problems are not unrelated to certain inadequacies in theoretical conceptions.

A very schematic critique points to two fundamental problems. First, the tendency to reduce the state to the state apparatus. A lot of the studies concerned with state activity treat the state as an "actor" that fulfills a role. Thus, the state is defined by the functions it performs

---

17   F. H. Cardoso, *O modelo político brasileiro*, Series en Cuadernos, no. 11 (Flacso-Chile–Elas: 1971), and G. O'Donnell, *El Estado burocrático autoritario. Triunfos, derrotas y crisis* (Buenos Aires: Editorial de Belgrano, 1982). [—Ed.]

for or in the context of other "systems." These instrumentalist conceptions assume that the state and society are two independent spheres. Second, we have the liberal claim about the separation of political society and civil society, or the Marxist theorem according to which the basis determines the superstructure. Liberal thought emphasizes political freedom and equality regardless of material living conditions; the materialist tradition perceives the state as an alien and hostile power that is the product of capitalist relations of production and must disappear once these are overcome. Both approaches consider the economy an almost natural process, and therefore identify human emancipation with "rational control" over nature. In both cases, there is an objective reason (a harmony of current or future interests) that unites society as a whole. There is therefore no place for politics visualized as ideological or demagogic alienation and replaced by technocratic knowledge.

On the contrary, we see the political necessity of a theory of the state in the necessity of "doing politics." To do politics is to become a subject, and it is through the state that subjects are constituted. Basically, the theory of the state is therefore about our collective interest and will to determine our way of life, the meaning of social coexistence. I will now suggest some lines of reflection along this perspective.

I. Studies on the State of Latin America

We can schematically distinguish four major lines of research on the state in Latin America.[18]

---

18   The literature review I originally made had to be abandoned due to the number and disparities between studies. These are often more of an application of some theoretical approaches developed in European-North American discussions rather than original theoretical elaborations. On the other hand, they demand a discussion of empirical references that goes beyond the framework of a paper. Finally, and to lighten the text [of the epilogue], no bibliographical indications are included. I here state my intellectual debt to many contributions and, above all, to the collaborators of this book. I thank José Joaquín

A first current emerged in the 1960s, along with the emergence of modern sociology in the region. Under the influence of the theories of "social change" and political development, it thematized the problem of the state from the point of view of democratic participation and its obstacles. Here, the state is usually identified with the political system, and the extent to which it meets the requirements of modern society are addressed. Those attempts have the great distinction of offering a first empirical diagnosis of the socioeconomic structure that is expressed in the form of the state. They thus verify the structural heterogeneity of Latin American societies, but without problematizing the sui generis capitalist character of the state. The uncritical reception of structural-functionalism hinders the possibility of appreciating the state as a his-torical-social product and of addressing the specificities of its constitu-tion in Latin America.

A second line of research emerged at the same time, one mainly linked to ECLAC, and this addressed the state as an agent of economic development. Humbler in its academic ambition, it had greater political impact by turning the state apparatus into the effective subject of the strategy of economic and social development. In this case, the critique of international structures of economic dependence privileges the analysis of "state interventionism." In the absence of a "national bourgeoisie," it becomes the task of the state to "nationalize" the social control over the economy and initiate self-sustained growth by means of structural reforms. This approach has the merit of thematizing government activ-ity (public policies) and capturing the "extension" of the modern state, but at the price of reductionism. It tends to identify the state with the governmental apparatus and treat it as an actor outside class structures.

The stagnation of "developmentalism" shifted interest from inter-national dependence to its rootedness in national structures of domi-nation; instead of a reform of the state apparatus, a revolution of social structures was proposed. The functionalist approach proves incompe-tent when it comes to this new interest in knowledge, which then leads to the academic reception of Marxism. Studies on dependency reframe

---

Brunner and Tomás Moulian for their comments on an initial version of this epilogue.

the issue of the state and politics as an expression of struggle and class alliances in each of the societies. Focusing on the insertion of local economies in the world market and the resulting social structure, it seeks to reconstruct the historical formation of the state. This analytical approach gives a vigorous impetus to the understanding of the particularities and transformations of the state according to the respective socioeconomic formation. And yet, this way of conceiving social classes and of posing the relationship between society and the state, between economy and politics, is not always exempt from a certain class reductionism, which turns the state into a mere "expression" of class relations.

Finally, we can pinpoint a fourth line of research triggered by the emergence of the authoritarian state. Now the state itself becomes the center of analysis. The development of military regimes reinforces the conception of the state as class domination but forces a more nuanced study of the articulation between society and state that considers changes in international relations (economic and political). Precisely because domination is more naked, it becomes evident that the state is "something" much more complex. It is not enough to denounce violence or to uncover and describe the "model" of the new authoritarianism.

The political crisis refers to a crisis of political thought. A certain excessive use of the term "crisis" (political crisis, crisis of hegemony, crisis of the state) is symptomatic of the extant degree of awareness regarding social contradictions. This is a bewildered conscience that can no longer rest easy on an almost theological vision of historical progress. Thinking from a place of defeat implies not only reviewing the interpretations we made of our stories, but also the concepts we used to imagine our futures. Another crisis, the crisis of Marxism, indicates the questioning not only of "realized socialism," but even of the classical (Leninist) theorems of a revolutionary strategy. The daily experience of authoritarianism leads us to question what we really want. And to wonder about the authoritarian state is to problematize an alternative order: the democratic state.

II. Political Strategies

We must now undertake a critical review of the studies that have been carried out, their contributions and insufficiencies. In order not to analyze them "abstractly," we prefer to situate our conceptualization efforts within the main political currents in Latin America. The problems posed by social processes are crystallized in these, for good or ill. A brief sketch of four important political strategies from these past decades allows us to return to some of the issues already highlighted by Edelberto Torres Rivas and Sergio Zermeño.

1. Between 1930 and 1960, *populism*[19] was the main political strategy, which marks, with greater or lesser intensity, the struggle in almost all Latin American societies, especially Argentina and Brazil. The populist strategy responds to the collapse of the "oligarchic state," torn between the contradictory demands of positioning itself "outward" due to its growing insertion in the world market, a liberal order in accordance with the free development of capital and having an "inward" turn given its agricultural export economy as a social base to a landowning oligarchy. The ascending process of industrialization drove the rise of the middle sectors and urban labor groups without the landowning class completely losing their dominance. Although in Brazil we still find strong social heterogeneity and difficult interregional conflicts, Argentina is already characterized by important urbanization and labor unionization, as well as a partisan organization of the middle sectors.

---

19 Following the global crash of 1929 and the deterioration of trade terms in the international market for Latin American countries, several of them experienced internal political and economic crises that led to decisive changes in production strategies and forms of political liaison. Some reactions to this crisis were, as in Argentina, of a conservative nature, which led to the coup d'état of 1930. When Lechner speaks of post-1930s populism that seeks to resolve such state crises, he is referring to what has been termed "classical populism" in Argentina and Brazil. In the first case, Juan Domingo Perón, who was president in 1946–52 and 1952–55; in the second, Getúlio Vargas, who was president in 1930–34, 1934–37, and 1937–45. [—Ed.]

And yet, both countries face the same problem: the development of the national state.

The formation of the Latin American modern state makes its appearance linked to a double demand that, unlike what happens in Europe, does not arise in successive stages. On the one hand, the advance of import-substituting industrialization requires a liberalization of the labor force and an expansion of the domestic market. On the other hand, the decline of the oligarchy requires the mobilization of popular support, and the citizen incorporation of these masses implies, in turn, the capacity to satisfy their economic demands. This gave birth to the so-called state of commitment: commitment between the different social groups and commitment between political participation and capitalist economic development. Due to the precariousness of the state, the compromise required plebiscitary representation.

Populism was the first strategy that sought to resolve the crisis of the state, which began in 1930, in much of the region. It effectively revolutionized politics by advising popular mobilization and participation. It managed to collect and organize the transformations in society, but it was incapable of "translating" them into the construction of a new state. The dilemma of the populist strategy is that the "popular masses" recognize themselves in the figure of the caudillo, but not in the state; while that makes populism strong, it also entails its ultimate failure. Through the charismatic leader, the masses become a new subject. The figure of the caudillo replaces the absent form of the state as a representation of "the generic." But instead of a universal abstraction, externalized by the social struggle, the caudillo represents "the generic" only as the apex of a social pact. The generic referent is, therefore, visibly subordinated to the aggregation of specific interests. The constitution of the masses as a subject is then truncated to the extent that their autonomy is delimited in advance by compromise. In the absence of a hegemonic social force, the populist strategy undertakes democratic demands only in authoritarian forms; it cannot summon and mobilize the masses except within the framework of the existing commitment. The delimitation of popular mobilization to the defense of corporate interests points to the problem of citizen participation—ever since then, this has convulsed the formation of a democratic state.

2. So-called *developmentalism*, which takes place in societies of lesser and subsequent industrialization, also went into a crisis. If populism represents a defensive strategy of political stabilization in the face of the disintegration of the ancien régime, developmentalism is an offensive strategy of modernization. Here, modernization is regarded as the goal, advancing the progress of history: economic development and political democracy. Let us remember that during its heyday in the 1960s (and not only because of the influence of the CEPAL and the Alliance for Progress), development was taken as an objective reason by capitalist approaches; it was nurtured by the postwar economic boom and the global Pax Americana, as well as by communist expectations regarding the development of the productive forces and the leadership of a "national bourgeoisie." This implicit agreement on economic development as the "national interest" facilitated the expansion of democracy. Democratization then appears as the political strategy that channels the structural reforms required by capitalist modernization and is put into practice as a policy of national integration (citizenship) and social integration (consumption). It is also suspended as soon as it can lead to a redefinition of the goals of development and the reforms to be undertaken. This limitation of developmentalism comes from its conception of the state and politics.

It is no coincidence that the developmentalism of the 1960s and its current revitalization would be particularly popular in societies whose export sector is not in the hands of a local bourgeoisie and where, therefore, the government apparatus plays a primordial role in the redistribution of the wealth generated by this enclave (Chile, Ecuador, Peru, Venezuela and, as an exception, Colombia and Mexico). Under these conditions, the state apparatus is visualized as the natural engine of every process of development. The old structure of domination, embodied by the world of finance, is liquidated (agrarian reform) and replaced by public administration. The state apparatus will be the new place of power and the symbol of authority.

The reform of society is based on a reform of the state, which is conceived as the arbiter of political competition and social conflicts but, unlike what happens in populism, no longer as a plebiscitary-personalist embodiment of a social pact. Rather, as a technical-neutral body that executes the imperative goals of development. In fact, it is a question of organizing an efficient bureaucratic apparatus, supposedly not traversed by social struggles, which is legitimized by the effectiveness of structural reforms. That is, the state is identified with the governmental apparatus and the latter with a pre-social rationality.

This proposition leads developmentalism into a dead end. "State interventionism" is based on a supposed objectivity of development, and the government becomes directly responsible for, as well as dependent on, a massive improvement of living conditions when, in fact, government intervention is required and restricted by the development of private capital. At first glance, the failure of the developmentalist strategy is attributed to the incompatibility between a process of social change and a process of capitalist accumulation. It would not be possible to modernize "underdeveloped" capitalist structures while simultaneously guaranteeing the legitimizing principle of private property.

The unviability of capitalism in Latin America was hastily deduced from the developmentalist dilemma: development would be the task of socialism. This analysis (accurate in its critique of situations of dependency in which capitalist relations of production are implanted and reproduced) questions effectiveness, but not the very notion of development. The proposed socialism would be nothing but a more efficient form of development. This suggests evaluating the developmentalist experience as a phenomenon common to different social projects (capitalist modernization/socialist revolution). What seems to characterize "developmentalism" is that it poses development as objective progress entrusted to the state apparatus. Of course, it is not trivial whether such development follows the rationale of capital or whether it refers, at least formally, to the popular will.

But in all forms of statism, life in society appears as a destiny external to individuals, without roots in their daily lives. In a developmentalist strategy, political parties act more as spokespeople for a pre-social "rationale" than as organizers of concrete experiences. Hence, developmentalism (of one or another persuasion) leads to a crisis of representation.

3. The *revolutionary strategy* inherits two problems: the overcoming of capitalist underdevelopment and the constitution of the national state. It must simultaneously resolve the social question and the national question,

each referring to the other. For many years, the "model" was the Cuban Revolution. The technical nature of the Cuban process lies precisely in the articulation of both moments in a single movement: national independence and social revolution. The Cuban example pinpoints two problems. One resides in the democratic postulate: How are the people constituted as the subject of their development? The socialist perspective takes up the naturalist conception of sovereignty: the identification of the sovereign people with the juridical subject. Popular sovereignty is modeled on that of the monarch, taking the sovereign for an individual personification and sovereignty for a subjective right. In such a construct, the sovereign is a subject that, therefore, cannot be in contradiction with itself: identity between the sovereign people and the empirical people. There would be—in Rousseau's terms—a "general will" that fixes, a priori, the "will of all." This shows the strength of the Western idea of One, which tends to suppose an objective harmony of interests. Specific interests would already be objectively predetermined by a "general interest" of which the state would be the executor. If there is a social evolution that obeys an objective principle, how can freedom be conceived?

There is a conception of revolution as the definitive resolution of social contradictions and divisions. If class antagonism had been overcome, there would no longer be any reason for the split between society and the state. The second problem stems from the prospect of the eventual extinction of the state in socialist society. The famous debate of the early 1960s revolved around this possibility; the Cuban insistence on moral incentives and the genesis of a new man does not merely concern the abolition of the market as an ex-post regulation of total social work, but also the eventual need for any externalized instance of social mediation—that is, in the end, the need for a state. The presumed self-regulation of society works as if rulers and the ruled were identical. To the extent that revolutionary strategy preserves this principle of identity as a real goal, it cannot interpret the socialist state except as a consequence of the struggle between the world "blocs" or as a remnant of capitalist relations of production. The perspective of a society without power relations prevents existing power relations from being problematized and ends up hiding them ideologically.

Undoubtedly, the Cuban Revolution was not conceived (unlike a tendency of Marx's) as a mere "political form of social emancipation," a simple instrument for the overcoming of capitalist relations of production. There is an awareness that social liberation, human freedom, are also realized in politics. However, political activity is conceived as the practice of a single subject: the people. The supposed identity of interests limits the political decision-making process: everything lies inside the revolution, and nothing outside of it. What is the limit, and who draws it?

Politics is conceived more in terms of reason than decision, more as scientific knowledge than as self-determination. What is the reason for some inefficiency of popular mobilization, despite the validity of political freedoms? It seems to be an atrophy of the public sphere that tends to camouflage the complex relationship between society and the state, and (on the contrary and against the original intentions) encourages state idolatry.

The other "model" of revolutionary strategy is the so-called Chilean road to socialism. Popular Unity presents an astonishing link between the liberal democratic tradition and the Leninist tradition. On the one hand, its practical organization is based on the public factor as the space where particular people make their appearance, distinguish themselves, and unite. On the other hand, its theoretical perspective takes economics as the real basis of political institutions and ideological positions. Hence its ambiguity toward democracy: it experiences it as an area of its vital development and at the same time distrusts it as a cover that paradigmatically belongs to capitalism. There is also ambiguity toward socialism: it formulates this as an economic reorganization but approaches it as a political process.

Chile's early national integration and relative social homogeneity proffers political activity with a space that did not exist in Cuba. This, however, is a space structured around the state apparatus. In a society such as Chile's, in which economic dynamics depend on a mining enclave and political dynamics stem from an unstable equilibrium between the different social groups, the governmental apparatus appears as the apex of the economic and political process. It is by reference to the state apparatus, bearer of the incipient "welfare state" and its public services, that an amorphous mass is formed and can be invoked as "the people." How can we link this empirical notion of people with the theoretical category of class as a preconstituted subject? Faced with a double and ambiguous referent (theoretical-empirical, political-economic), Popular

Unity oscillates between a class strategy that seeks the destruction of the state apparatus "from below" and a type of populism that mobilizes the masses in support of government policy "from above."

This oscillation also expresses yet another tension between people and class. What is the relationship between the people as the legitimizing basis for an invocation of the generic and class as a particular interest? The problem of Popular Unity lies in its combination of the realization of the specific interests of some social groups with the representation of generic interest. In fact, it operates a reduction. The people are defined economically (anti-imperialist, anti-oligarchic, and anti-monopoly). Assuming an insurmountable economic antagonism, which predetermines political actors, the invocation of the generic can be replaced by an aggregation of related interests, represented by a front of parties. Popular Unity thus poses the struggle in the political field but subordinates it to an economic determination, unable to take charge of the specifically political: that is, the determination of the generic.

4. The *authoritarian strategy* now executed in the Southern Cone shows the weaknesses of the others but, at the same time, fails to become institutionalized. It is not easy to sketch a "model" and its internal tensions given this is an ongoing process with important differences between one country and another. Looking for a common denominator, we come upon the "modernization" of capitalist development. This brings the authoritarian strategy closer to the developmentalist approach, but with two basic modifications. On the one hand, it is inserted into a new international order. The process of capitalist accumulation is no longer based on import-substituting industrialization, nor does it postulate a more or less self-centered development. We have the implementation of a growth strategy via export supported by a partnership between transnational capital and national capital. Because a strong disparity of income, the fall in real wages and salaries, and high structural unemployment are all intrinsic elements of the new economic model, the repressive function of the state apparatus is accentuated. However, this is not the main characteristic of the authoritarian order.

It seems that a change in the very conception of the state and of politics is more important. While developmentalism was linked to the rise of the democratic ideology, the authoritarian strategy corresponds to a "crisis of democracy." The failure of democracy is attributed to an excess of participation (demands) that prevented actual governing. Having failed at the developmentalist goal of increasing the administrative capacity of the government apparatus, it is proposed, on the contrary, to relieve an overtaxed state of all these responsibilities and entrust the "logic of the market" with the satisfaction of social needs. Accepting the impossibility of resolving or, at least, neutralizing the dramatic imbalances of underdeveloped capitalism, the choice is radical de-statism. The state apparatus will no longer be responsible for managing, counteracting, and compensating for the crisis of capitalist development: it will delegate the proper functioning of the economy to the private initiative. The problem of this neoconservative project lies in how to carry out such privatization in societies that have already known an attempted welfare state (and where, therefore, social inequalities are not perceived as natural and inevitable). Along with the strengthening of the market, a resocialization that erases egalitarian values and collective responsibility is required. This necessitates the use of drastic disciplinary mechanisms.

What characterizes the authoritarian strategy is neither violence nor ideology nor mass mobilization. There is, of course, the exercise or pervasive threat of physical coercion and the doctrine of national security as a guiding principle of the military "mentality." But the efficiency of the new authoritarianism seems to reside primarily in the normative force of the factual: a factual conditioning of social reality such that it is recognized as a valid norm for social behavior. Here Foucault's contribution seems relevant: power produces. Power produces not only factual realities but also the way of thinking about reality. To the extent that it determines social practices, it also determines the interpretations that people make of their practices and interests. That is, power not only shapes social reality, it also secretly shapes reason. Along with producing social facts, it produces discourses regarding the truth of those facts. Thus, it is the very power relations that produce and induce consent.

How does this "rationale of power" link to the "rationale of capital"? Through technocracy. It is not my intention to present the fundamentals of the technocratic approach. Let us only recall its postulate according to which social facts are objective facts. If so, technical knowledge can be applied to social processes (What effect does a certain cause have? What cause produces a certain effect?). Having assumed a certain goal—capitalist development—social conditions can then appear as technically necessary. If social problems are transformed into technical problems in this manner, there will be one and only one solution (the optimal answer). Instead of a political decision between different possible social goals, it would be a technical-scientific solution about the correct means to achieve a predetermined end. Public debate therefore becomes unnecessary; a technical fact or a "scientific truth" cannot be put to a vote. The citizen ends up replaced by the expert.

Technocratic efficiency, however, does not solve social integration. It creates strong functional interdependence, but not normative motivation. Herein lies the authoritarianism of the neoconservative project. Unable to offer meaningful rules for consensual integration, it must de facto induce some "sense of order." For the social reality "ordered" by power to acquire normative force, to appear as "the force of things," it is essential to prevent alternative interpretations of reality. Its production and historical-social reproduction must be hidden. However, this freezing of the present seems precarious. The feasibility of a radical functionalization so thorough that it dissolves the individual into a network of roles is doubtful. Despite the evident privatization and compartmentalization of their social practice, individuals refuse full de-subjectivation to simple bearers of functions. The functional interdependence that develops behind men's backs cannot renounce normative legitimacy. Because the market is insufficient as an impersonal mechanism of social order, claims of "meaning" emerge constantly. Such invocations of another possible future question the supposed naturalness and normality of the status quo. Hence the dilemma of authoritarian strategy: to make the "normative force of the factual" effective, it must combat any elaboration of alternative meanings while, likewise and for the same reason, it arouses doubts around "things being what they are." The factual order ceases to be an incontestable fact.

III. Problems of the Juridical-Individualist and Economic-Classist Conceptions of the State and of Politics

The above outline of the main political strategies, though superficial, served to recall and locate some of the problems addressed by research on the state in Latin America. We can now return to the latter and explore how the respective strategies conceptualized the political crossroads. This requires a careful and nuanced literature review, which · goes beyond the framework of this work. We prefer to therefore take another path, one which tries to highlight some more general theoretical implications. Proceeding quite schematically, we will address two main inspiring aspects of political strategies. In the first place, the juridical-individualist conception of liberal origin, which considers the bourgeois individual as the new subject of the social process, the one to which power would belong as a natural attribute. Second, the economic-classist conception in the Marxist tradition, which makes social classes (as personified carriers of the contradictions of the capitalist production process) the subjects of the power struggle. Needless to say, this is not a critical review of liberal and Marxist theories of politics and the state, but only an "ordering," broadly speaking, of some theoretical problems present in the political strategies of the region.

1. The Juridical-Individualist Conception

The conception of an autonomous and rational individual as a preconstituted subject demands a new conceptualization of the state. From Hobbes onward, the problem is to justify the existence of a centralized apparatus of power in a manner consistent with individual autonomy. If power is considered as an individual *potestas*, whose social recognition is the law, the constitution of political power is visualized in an analogous way to a juridical relationship. The logical origin of the state is explained by the social contract, through which the individuals-subjects associate and cede their individual power to the sovereign. The contractual relationship implies a relationship of equivalence; we must therefore dispense with social inequalities and presume an association of free and equal subjects. The fiction of a political society, split from civil society, legitimizes the state as an instance that unites a multiplicity of individuals without interfering with their individual autonomy—that is, without modifying concrete inequality. The triad of civil society, political society, and the state thus allows for the presentation of a central instance of power on the margins and in function of individual economic freedom.

The split between society and the state is theoretically founded on two arguments. The first entails individualizing power in the state through the notion of sovereignty. Sovereignty would then be the place of political power. What is important here is the personalization of sovereignty in analogy to the individual. The sovereign appears as a personal subject, and political power would be the recognized right of the sovereign. The personalization of sovereignty in the figure of the monarch is transferred to the people; the principle of popular sovereignty is modeled on royal sovereignty. The people are sovereign insofar as they are a personified subject. And taking the people as the subject means dispensing with the inequalities that divide them; as a sovereign subject, the people are a subject constituted outside any social relationship. This preconstituted subject would have, like every individual, a single body and a single will, and power can still be thought of as an individual attribute. Only now, the relationship between the sovereign and the performing apparatus is reversed. While the individuality of the monarch absorbed the apparatus that executed the sovereign will, now the exercise of power by the state apparatus leads to it being seen as an individual subject. The state then appears as a sovereign who requests and receives obedience from its subjects. There is a subjectivation of the state whose effect is to transform power into the legitimate rights of the sovereign, on the one hand, and a legal obligation of obedience, on the other. This conception does not change when we speak of a military government in the form of a dictatorship or, in a complementary way, of a legitimate right to resistance. In both cases, power is thought of exclusively as a relationship between sovereign and subject, a juridical-political relationship that hides the processes of power in social relations.

The split between civil society and the state is based on a second theoretical operation, which regulates state interference in civil society.

This is the question of legitimacy itself. Once the sovereign-state is subjective, we must define the legitimate exercise of power. The problem is simple insofar as the reference to the sovereign people is not problematic; any state activity in accordance with the will of the people is legitimate. The problem becomes difficult when the fiction of the people as a personal subject loses its social basis (a people made of proprietors), and the "general will" no longer finds empirical referent. As conflicts and divisions develop in civil society, a new barrier must be erected between the state and society. Staggered legitimacy is built to prevent social inequalities from becoming the object of decisions.

On an initial level we have the formal legitimacy of any political decision validated through legal procedure. The principle of legitimation is the autonomous individual: according to bourgeois anthropology, an unlimited consumer and, therefore, an unlimited accumulator. By proclaiming the bourgeois individual as a preexisting subject to social relations, the processes of production and consumption are excluded from political decision as a datum of nature. Consequently, it is no longer possible to give material content to the general interest; the classic goal of happiness is spiritualized in a private state of mind. By conceiving social relations of production as a natural movement that cannot be judged as good or bad, the popular will can only be legitimized by the way in which it is generated. Legitimacy no longer depends on what is decided but on how it is decided. The same decision-making procedure is the legitimizing norm: legitimacy via formal-legal procedure.

This kind of formal legitimacy does not prevent a legally correct decision from affecting the social relations of production. To avoid any kind of "legal revolution," a second level of material legitimacy is established. The market economy is defined as good (and sometimes explicitly elevated to constitutional status) and any political decision must be legitimized by reference to this criterion. The formal-legal procedure is subject to this basic consensus (call it "spirit of the constitution," "the national being," or, simply, "the rules of the game"). "Legitimacy by legality" operates only within the framework of the basic axiom; any decision that does not respect the established (capitalist) economic order is declared illegitimate despite its formal legality (Allende). In other words, the freedom of the "open society"

(Popper)[20] is subject to the ex-ante definition of individual freedom (freedom of private property).

The liberal perspective treats the phenomenon of the "state" primarily as a problem of legitimacy. The problem of legitimacy is not limited to the a posteriori justification of violence; it deals with beliefs in the legitimacy (as per Max Weber's concept of *Legitimitätsglaube*) of domination and its effect on the type of obedience, bureaucratic organization, and the character of the exercise of power. Let us address some of the angles of this problem.

1. Conceived as the result of a social contract between free and equal people, the legitimacy of the state depends on its representing individuals as particular people. There is a right to command and an obligation to obey when there is harmony between central authority and individual autonomy. If the supposed harmony is evidenced as an incompatibility (de jure or de facto), the transfer of power is invalidated and considered null and void. Even without reaching such an extreme conclusion, the underlying prejudice is to defend freedom (whose exclusive domain would be civil society) against the threat of statist usurpation. This legal conception of freedom inspires an approach to the state in constitutionalist terms: the representative state and the rule of law. The problem of the state appears thematized in the defense of human rights as individual guarantees against state power or in the question of the effectiveness of democracy, understood as pluralistic competition between equals. A concern for legitimacy predominates insofar as it concerns the stability of the juridical order; that is, of the government in its function as non-interfering guarantor of the freedom of the private individual.

The existence of a conflict between central authority and individual autonomy can also lead to a diametrically opposite conclusion: the affirmation of an objective identity between particular interest and generic interest. The emphasis moves from the individual to society. If, in the previous case, society is a mere legal derivative of the preconstituted subjects, in this case society is a preconstituted order over which

---

20   Karl R. Popper, *The Open Society and Its Enemies* (London: George Routledge & Sons, 1947), 152. [—Ed.]

individuals do not have initiative. The individual will is subordinated to the achievement of the supposed generic interest by the centralized apparatus of power. This approach emphasizes a perception of the state as a national unit with regard to centrifugal forces, as an administrative capacity with regard to social crises or as a bearer of national security. The interest in legitimacy also predominates in these cases, although no longer regarding the formal-political procedure but, directly, as the stability of the economic order.

2. The boundary separating political equality from social inequality is not arbitrary. One must consent to the unequal distribution of property in order to be recognized as free and equal. The proper functioning of the economy (that is, the "free play" of social inequality) delimits citizenship; those who do not accept or supposedly would not accept the foundations of the "good order" are excluded.

De jure discrimination becomes problematic under the validity of democratic postulates. Generalized political participation appears as a requirement of formal legitimacy and, simultaneously, as a threat to material legitimacy. To neutralize possible conflicts over the economic system, political participation is linked to a "development strategy." Democratic reforms are based on state intervention which compensates for the dysfunctions of capitalist development, depoliticizing participation in decision-making via participation in consumption. Thanks to the state, the expansion of citizenship is articulated on the needs of economic development. If the formation of such a welfare state is not possible or insufficient, material demands will penetrate the political sphere, where they are usually treated as an (intrasystemic) conflict over wealth distribution, not over the mode of its production. When such demands go beyond political institutions and question the relations of production, a crisis of legitimacy is denounced. It does not address the economic organization of society, however, but its juridical-political institutionality. In short, a crisis of democracy is denounced.

In the legal-individualistic conception of power, participation is analyzed according to the logic of the market; the state would be the area for the negotiation of existing demands and remedies. From the starting point of the producer-consumer as a legal subject, "doing politics" means establishing a contractual relationship around certain available goods. The proclaimed "basic consensus" means that political will is subject to economic facts. We have already observed that, in Latin America, "development strategies" are not only the indispensable complement to democratization processes, but also determine the "limits of democracy." An analysis of the state from this perspective addresses the exclusion or incorporation of citizens only insofar as it adjusts political institutions to economic functionality. Demands for political participation are treated as demands for individual participation in the consumption of goods, services, values, and institutions in which the market's rationale governs (meaning that redistribution takes place ex post, from established production). The excesses of participation are "normalized" by the strengthening of the market, replacing citizen freedom with consumer freedom. In other words, participation does not include the will to dispose collectively of the material conditions of life and to subject economic structures to political decisions.

3. By establishing a split between society and the state, the juridical-individualist conception rejects political initiative regarding the material conditions of life; the free allocation of resources by the market must not be distorted by arbitrary (i.e., political) concessions. However, its very goal—the consolidated reproduction of capitalist relations of production—incites governmental intervention in the economy. How to reconcile the primacy of the economy, conceptualized as individual freedom, with the need to stabilize the confrontation between those private initiatives?

Since there is no organized and planned capitalism, the state is forced to intervene to ensure the reproduction of capitalist relations and is simultaneously obliged not to restrict the freedom of private property. It must articulate a set of economic and social interventions that counteract local crises and the international imbalances of capitalist development without limiting the development of capital itself. By considering the economy as a natural process, the liberal conception fails to conceptualize state interventionism as anything other than external intervention. "Interventionism" thus deepens the crisis of legitimacy. On the one hand, the state has to legitimize (by ensuring the proper functioning of the economy) the capitalist mode of production. State interventionism cushions social contradictions, transposing conflicts from the realm of production to the political sphere. The economic crisis is defused using different and contradictory stabilizing measures. On the other hand, this politicization undermines the legitimizing principle of the state as a representation of the generic interest. Faced with this dual imperative—to politically legitimize the capitalist economy and to respect its own legitimacy as an external guarantor of the "invisible hand"—the capitalist state suffers from chronic legitimacy deficit.

4. As a response to the legitimacy problem posed by state interventionism, new authoritarianism resurfaces. Diagnosing the crisis as a gap between social demands and the administrative capacity of the state apparatus, it proposes a dismantling of the incipient welfare state. However, since the latter is collateral to a political mobilization of society (and its institutionalization in a democracy), the reduction of government activity requires drastic depoliticization and demobilization.

The authoritarian strategy radicalizes the anti-political and anti-state approach of the classical juridical-individualist conception, rescinding the democratic reforms introduced in liberalism. The achievement of freedom is subtracted from political action and handed over to the market, while the latter is entrusted with the task of rationally differentiating individuals and, simultaneously, integrating them into a socially accepted hierarchical order. It seeks to restore supposed economic automatism, detaching social regularities from any normative motivation. However, an impermeable barrier between the market and politics cannot be established. Capitalist labor cannot be entirely privatized (functional integration via the market). Rather, it requires political organization (normative integration via the state). The state reveals itself as more than a service apparatus and includes the meanings and norms of social life.

Authoritarian strategy can effectively rely on conformism induced by disciplinary mechanisms, but it fails to eliminate politics as an intersubjective elaboration of a "sense of order." Except the latter no longer finds mediation structures. The different social groups no longer recognize each other as a common referent. Therefore, the meaning of each specific practice must be determined and articulated. Everything becomes political, but without a public realm in which to build joint (national) representation.

2. The Economic-Classist Conception

This conception, present in many left-wing analyses, comes from a certain "reading" of Marx. Although Marx does not elaborate a proper concept of power, we readily recognize two ideas. One approach places power in the set of individuals united in society; it focuses power insofar as it is social power. Individuals separated from each other by the social division of labor objectify the power they constitute as a society in the form of the state. This objectification is an alienation to the extent that the state is separated from society (from concrete people). The question of power is, therefore, the recovery by individuals of their own potency. The other approach situates the power of a given social group; it focuses power insofar as it is an imposition on others. The inequality that divides society is criticized as an act of violence, which comes from capitalist relations of production where one class exploits another. The state is, therefore, the extension of a power rooted in society and, specifically, in the process of production. The question of power then lies in overcoming capitalist relations of production.

Different interpretations of the two fundamental theorems on the state exist depending on one or another approach. The first theorem states the formation of the state which, according to Marx, falls under the general law of production. This statement can mean, on the one hand, that the state is a human creation, a social and historical product. By separating itself from itself, by abstracting from its real conditions, capitalist society produces the split between civil society and the state, between the atomized society of concrete people and the community of abstract citizens. The social production of the state refers to the constitution of the capitalist state. On the other hand, the affirmation may imply a relationship of determination. The economy as the basis of civil society determines the set of social relations and, therefore, the state. In this interpretation, the social production of the state refers to its causal determination by civil society.

The second theorem deals with the independence of the state: How do people who created the state submit to it? Here too we find two interpretations. One emphasizes the subjectivation of the state with respect to society as a whole; it is a question of accounting for its special existence alongside civil society, as well as outside it, a substantive form in which the whole of civil society is condensed. The other visualizes the state as the executive organ of the common interests of the entire bourgeoisie, as an instrument of capital against labor. It is about criticizing the apparent subjectivation, showing the relative autonomy of the state apparatus.

The point here, of course, is not to summarize Marx's conception of the state, but only to recall its complexity and hint at the difficulties of integrating the different aspects into a single approach. Can the state be conceived simultaneously as a social power split from society and as the affirmative power of a class in society? How to analyze the state as an (illusory) community in which citizens recognize each other as free and equal and, at the same time, as an instrument of repression of one class over another? That is, how are its generic form and class content integrated?

In a highly schematic vision of socialist strategies in Latin America, it is worth highlighting the economic-class conception of the state and politics derived from well-known economism. Due to the historical weight of the state apparatus in Latin American societies, the state is not perceived as a simple reflection or epiphenomenon of economic structures. Still, even when a certain "relative autonomy" of state activity is considered, this is analyzed from and according to the economy. By identifying the material production of life with the economic aspect, the analysis of the state focuses on the functions it fulfills in the capitalist process of accumulation. Again, here we find two currents. One conceives the state directly as an instrument of domination employed by the ruling class; that is, in Marx's words, as the war machine of capital against labor power. The workers' movement would therefore be external and antagonistic to that fortress-state oppressing it. The other defines the state as the extra-economic instance necessary to fulfill the general functions required by the capitalist economy. It is a "left-wing functionalism" that denies the liberal assumption of market automatism, but also affirms the predominance of economic development. It is the inadequacies of the latter (its structural "scarcity") that determine the state's raison d'être.

The conception of the state conditions the strategic goals. In the first case, the idea is to annihilate the state as a repressive apparatus of the bourgeoisie. There is a preference for a militaristic strategy of siege and assault on the fortress-state ("dual power") that destroys the state machinery and establishes popular power. In the second case, an alternative use of the state is intended. Assuming that the state apparatus is a neutral instrument in its form whose class character lies in its content, it seeks to modify the correlation of forces within state institutions in order to use them against capitalist relations of production. In both cases the state is reduced to the state apparatus, and state action to economic functions.

The emphasis placed on the interference of the state apparatus over the economy tends to dampen the postulate regarding the objective laws of the capitalist economy. It is through state power that the contradictions of capital become the object of political will. It is, therefore, through the "seizure of power" that capitalist relations of production can be transformed. Hence the central place revolution plays in socialist strategies. Revolution is the victory of political will over economic laws; both before and after the revolution, politics would be determined by economic structure. The "primacy of politics" is thus circumscribed to the moment of revolution. For a strategy focused on the "conquest of power" as a rupture and definitive resolution of economic development, politics degenerates into a mere technique (the technique of revolution).

The economistic approach to politics as a revolutionary technique or pure power politics allows us to understand some tendencies (implicit or explicit) in the socialist strategies of the region. If all social processes converge and culminate in a single great explosion—revolution—then the militarist conceptions of the political party as the vanguard (*estado mayor*, or the command structure) of the working class and of political action as the accumulation, organization, and mobilization of forces would be justified. We can also understand the astonishing combination of opportunism, which responds to a calculation of efficiency in terms of the power struggle, and technocracy, which administers social practices according to supposed economic imperatives.

This juxtaposition of political voluntarism and economic determinism, which Laclau points out in his contribution, has its theoretical foundation in class reductionism. Following Laclau, we can characterize it via the following features: 1) the identification of classes, conceptually defined by their insertion in the production process, as empirically existing social groups; 2) the paradigmatic ascription of certain political and ideological positions to each social class and, conversely, 3) the reduction of all political-ideological forms to positions derived from a certain class nature.

Such an analysis begins with already constituted subjects, each of which has its corresponding "superstructure." Conversely, every political position and every ideological value would belong consubstantially to one class or another. This approach is encouraged by the facilities it offers for the rapid and controversial classification and qualification of social conflicts and for the effective organization and delimitation of a group identity. However, this reduction in complexity, which successfully draws clear fronts of struggle and opens fields of autonomous action, ultimately leads to simplistic strategies with the usual results.

The fundamental mistake in the economic-class conception lies in considering social classes as preconstituted subjects in the capitalist process of production. The categorial definition of the subject is impervious to the analysis of its empirical development; the subject-classes (with their corresponding political-ideological positions) would exist prior to any social relationship and would not be modified in their social practice. In this case, there is no class struggle per se, only classes in struggle—the struggle being something external and indifferent to the nature of the subject. Understood as a pre-social subject, class becomes a metaphysical notion and, therefore, an invariable actor throughout capitalist development, with nothing to learn from social changes or from its own practice. Nothing would alter class interests and goals; it would be enough to safeguard orthodoxy. If subjects were not constituted via social relations/struggles, history would advance through parallel worlds—bourgeois domination on the one hand and the maturation of the working class on the other—and these would only intersect at the point of revolution. It would be possible to dispense with an analysis of the social problems that trigger struggle of its goals; the very forms of struggle would become irrelevant. This would render a study like Przeworski's on the institutional context and social conditions in which calculations of interests and risks are developed, and in which strategies of conflict or cooperation are constituted, impossible.

A conception that begins with a preconstituted subject with certain objective interests leads to a corporate-particularist strategy. Its best-known form in the region is the vanguard. If the logically prede-termined working class does not "appear" empirically, "false conscious-ness" is denounced. A vanguard will be responsible for filling in for this empirical "deficit" and acting on behalf of that logical subject and its true interests. And this false consciousness of objective interests will also serve as an argument to discriminate against any "class betrayal" and avoid any ideological contamination.

The essentialist conception of social classes also conditions the politics of alliances. Assigning the subjects an ex ante and invariable existence, the so-called accumulation of forces is nothing more than an aggregation of factors. Alliances are approached as a sum of actors whose goal is tallying up power. In other words, a certain "share of power" is attributed to each subject, so that in a zero-sum game the range of alliances would determine the "correlation of forces." Such an operation of addition and subtraction would leave the subject-classes unscathed; political practice then becomes an arithmetic operation.

The critique of class reductionism should be followed by a critique of cognitive-instrumental reductionism. Historical-materialist analy-sis tends to overvalue metabolism against external (technical) nature to the detriment of the social world and internal nature. We lack a deeper study of the fact that social relations are constructed and that such evolution is directed by ritual-religious interpretations. It could be assumed that the mutation of the organizational principles of social life depends on learning processes that advance in different dimensions. One dimension of social learning is the cognitive structuring of the world, delimiting the field of objectifiable knowledge. At the same time, however, there is learning in the dimension of the symbolic structur-ing of the world, ensuring the intersubjectivity of the various possible experiences, and in the dimension of the moral structuring of social practices, which secures the normative order of society. The study of the symbolic-normative dimension of social life appears essential for a renewal of political thought.

IV. Some Topics for Theoretical Reflection

The above observations do not provide us, by mere inversion, with a theory of the state. What we can do as a provisional conclusion is outline some themes for a renewal of political thought and a reconstruction of political activity.

1. Society and the State

We have seen the difficulties extant in a conception that affirms a split between society and the state such that there would only be a relationship of exteriority between the two. This approach does not acknowledge political participation as the way in which society decides and takes initiative regarding its development or state "interventionism" as the way in which society acts on itself. That is, it does not recognize in the state a form of social practice. We have also seen the political consequences of a simple subsumption of the state under society. Whether the state is considered a reflection/appendage of the economy, or the relative autonomy of its apparatus is highlighted, political action in both cases is something subsequent and secondary to the economic "data."

What both conceptions have in common is conceiving of the relations of production as a pre-political relation. If one excludes the political disposition of the economy, the other makes political action dependent on the economy; in both cases, "doing politics" is no longer an intrinsic necessity of human activity.

Let us try the perspective developed throughout this epilogue. We return to the affirmation, shared by all contributors to this book, that there are no "pure" social realities: no realities uncontaminated by political and ideological struggles. Every social practice (even economic practice) is a significant practice. Every social relationship is a process of production and reproduction of meanings. Without this continuous elaboration and articulation of meanings—the true construction and classification of social reality—we would despair in a meaningless world. The production and reproduction of meanings is not subsequent and external to the material production of life but, we insist, a moment intrinsic to it. To do politics is to discover, formulate, and articulate the senses inherent (consciously or not) to social practices.

This perspective is radically opposed to the architectural image of base and superstructure. With capitalism, the state and politics (as well as art and religion) acquire autonomy with respect to economic forms, but without a division of staggered levels. It would seem more appropriate to approach the social process as a whole and study the unfolding of its moments, its internal differentiation, attending to structures of mediation. By mediation we do not understand external combinatorics or a static link, but a relationship of reciprocal implication. Society and state, economic relations and political practices, involve each other. Making a merely analytical distinction, the problem of the state and politics concerns the differentiation and articulation of social practices. Every divided society—as Latin American societies are—produces an ordering instance that compresses and summarizes the set of social relations. More specifically, it is the division in society that creates the split of the state from society. The state is constituted in reference to social division: "The Estates are the synthesis between state and civil society" (Marx). The state form, thematized by Fernando Rojas, would be the place of condensation and structuring of the different moments of the social process, a compulsive instance of differentiation and unification. The issue of the political appears to refer to this state form. It is possible to think that state actions that usually attract our interest (coercion, economic intervention, ideological socializations, structures of legitimation, the use of generic currency) are nothing but mechanisms through which the social order is deployed and imposed in the form of the state. If so, the theoretical effort to elucidate what and how the state is primarily entails the reconstruction of the complex processes and mechanisms through which we elaborate that synthesis of social life and use it to affirm ourselves in our diversity/division.

2. The Constitution of Subjects

The constitution of subjects is perhaps the central topic of a political theory. However, it is usually displaced toward the anthropological assumptions on which the different approaches are based—that is, without problematizing them. This also implies the concept of class.

Returning to Laclau's previous propositions, we could affirm that all practice, insofar as it is significant, is an invocation of meaning that repeats and affirms meanings inherent to social practices themselves, and it is through this interpellation of a common sense that subjects are constituted. Different social practices give rise to different meanings that can be articulated in different ways. Subjects are constituted by means of and alongside with the invocations/articulations of meaning. Instead of approaching politics as a struggle and an alliance of classes as preexisting subjects, we would need to study the constellation of invocations/articulations of meanings through which subjects are constituted.

The class struggle is precisely about the constitution of subjects. It is a struggle to articulate (disarticulate and rearticulate) different meanings around opposing articulatory principles. These articulations involve absorptions and exclusions. Certain meanings are to be excluded because it is through their proscription that the articulating principle is affirmed. That is, for people to recognize themselves in one category they must deny another. When this denial is a simple exclusion, this is a particular-corporate invocation, which does not pretend to have general validity. (Social subjects, such as the feminist or student movement, can be formed around such exclusions.) On the other hand, the constitution of a political subject requires a "state spirit" (Gramsci), the invocation of a tendentially universal sense—an articulation capable of uniting different and even opposed meanings. To achieve such hegemonic action, negation must be "recovered" in the subject's self-affirmation. That is, an affirmation that takes place thanks to the recognition of an "other" and recognition by that "other." This struggle for reciprocal knowledge as subjects demands reference to a "generic equivalent." By means of a general referent, each subject affirms themselves, at the same time recognizing and denying the other. This form of the generic is the state. By means of the state form, each subject recognizes the other subjects and affirms specific particularity. If, on the one hand, each specific subject is only constituted in relation to the general form of the state, on the other, the state is constituted only in reference to the diversity of particular subjects. The state as a generic referent establishes the division between the specific subjects while it unites them; it is simultaneously an instance of particularization and homogenization, of division and synthesis.

Lately, the communicative nature of the constitutive process of the subjects has been reiterated. (The opposite—that is, the mere verification of objective interests—would make solidarity a metaphysical category.) The constitution of the subject is, in Gramsci's terms, that of a "collective will." However, the invocation of a sense through which a social group is recognized and amassed is not a purely ideological process either. If ideological discourse is not a "superstructural reflection" of preexisting interests, neither can it be immanently analyzed outside historical conditions. Both the invocation of meaning and the reception of such interpellation occur under certain social conditions. The distance between the conditions of production and those of reception affects the success or failure of said invocation. To be successful, it must give an account of the conditions and concrete experiences of those whom it is convening. That is, the process of subject constitution also and always implies the interpretation and organization of a certain "daily life." This work on everyday life is, as O'Donnell shows, a privileged field of maneuver for discipline strategies. On the other hand, it is from this daily reproduction of the specific individual, from a rearticulation of the meanings inherent in that daily life, that a "national-popular will" is constituted.

This sketch is not intended to argue any hypothesis but only to suggest a possible reformulation of the problem of the state; to think about the joint constitution of the subjects and the state. The political significance of a theory of the state then becomes apparent. The theoretical reflection on the state is, fundamentally, a reflection on our political practice. If politics is made necessary by the division of society—by the need to order it—it is made possible by reference to the state. Only in the form of the state can society—the set of subjects—organize social coexistence. That is, "order" its division.

3. The State as Mediation

The division of society—the separation of people from each other, without direct social relations—requires structures of mediation between them. This happens via the constitution of the subjects and the state: the two processes are moments in the social self-formation of society. The divided society cannot recognize itself, cannot act on itself directly; it only produces itself, only becomes aware of itself via an *alter* self. That is, society becomes identical to itself through mediation. In the absence of an immediate identity, society objectifies the power and meaning implicit in social practice in a place outside of it and affirms itself through that externalized referent.

In capitalism, this instance of mediation takes the form of the state, and capitalist society also relates to itself in this way. Despite this split and independence from the state, it is not a phenomenon external to society; this mediation structure is, in itself, a social production.

The state form configures a structure of mediation similar to that proffered by religion. Without positing a linear process of secularization and disenchantment, we could speak of the state as the god of our time (sans the salvatory character of the Christian god). The state form is, like the figure of God, the locus for the symbolic representation of the universe, making the regulation of worldly activity concordant with the cosmic order (or, what is the same, the "eternal laws" of human nature). Here is a topic for further exploration: the presence of a religious dimension in politics. The modern "scientification" of politics has made us neglect the effectiveness of myth, ritual action, sacrifice, etc., in politics. These religious forms are not mere remnants of a pre-scientific age. Contrary to a certain positivist conception so in vogue nowadays (on the right as well as the left), we must assume a symbolic-normative dimension. Continuing Oscar Landi's inquiry, it would be necessary to review whether "doing politics" is not essentially a communication (one that constitutes collective identities) and a moralization of social relations (the ensuring of organizational principles). From this point of view, the mediating character of the state could be specified: it would be the externalized foundation of the validity of the normative structures of society.

4. State Idolatry

When studying the state, one of the major concerns is state idolatry. Politics (not only in Latin America) is marked by an almost religious veneration of the state. This has, of course, sociohistorical reasons; in societies of high structural heterogeneity such as Latin America, the concentration and centralization of power "in the hands of the state," which is the main force of social cohesion, reemerges. In the face of socioeconomic fragmentation and disintegration (the well-known coexistence of several "societies" within a country), the state ensures not only territorial-administrative unity, but also seeks economic dynamics, political representation, and the ideological "glue" that links and brings centrifugal forces together. State idolatry, however, is not only the result of a historical situation in which the state is everything in the face of a dispersed and gelatinous society. It is a process intrinsic to the capitalist state that requires a theoretical analysis. The autonomy of the state is presented to the empirical gaze as a historical result, and while this verifies its existence, it does not explain it. Only theoretical reflection can discover the inversion of reality and ask how, from being the producers of the state, the masters of the world and of life, people become slaves who worship the state's seeming power over life and death, its decisions over order and chaos.

State idolatry is a consequence of social division. In the absence of direct social relations, people wonder about the separation between them. Suddenly, there is a need to explain the origin of social life; Why and how they live together in society. This "debt of meaning" (Gauchet) refers to a point outside society, a transcendental referent subtracted from social division/struggle. Idolatry arises from such submission to an exteriority, one on which we feel dependent and see as the force responsible for the existence and operation of society. This is not a simple superstition or mere psychological compensation. That state idolatry persists despite the daily experience of "institutional violence," and that it should not disappear with an explanation of the illusory character of the community of free and equal citizens calls for a more detailed study of the phenomenon.

It is possible to find an explanation of state idolatry in state fetishism. Just as the fetishism of commodities, money, and capital rises over the earthly world of capitalist production, so too does the capitalist state have a "physically metaphysical" nature. To analyze this intangible aspect, we must consider a double process: the spiritualization of the state and the commodification of the people. Let us say that, on the one hand, we have the subjectivation of the meaning inherent in social practices in the form of the state, and, on the other, the commodification of people who submit to the objectified sense as an alien and hostile power. While people believe they have initiative over the state and subordinate it to the will of all, in fact, the fetishized state dictates the norms of their social conduct. The state apparatus appears to react to social stimuli, but behind the institutions hides a "spirit." Like other products, the state is substantive, erasing all traces of its social production. People do not see, therefore, that they themselves, separated from each other by their inability to directly order the division of society, produce the state as the transcendental referent of the social order. They do it, but do not know it, Marx would say. That is why they venerate in the state the "spirit of the laws": the law that is the foundation of life in society.

5. The Transformation of the State

Let us recapitulate the suggested perspective: people in a society objectify the power of taking action over the organization of their coexistence and the meaning of their communal life in the form of the state. This objectification becomes independent and turns against the people as an instance that is both external and "above" them. It is the price people pay for living in a society when there are no direct social relations between them. Only an externalized and substantive instance of mediation can ensure the existence of a diversity of wills without leading to carnage.

People will be separated from each other as long as commercial and domination relations subsist. These relations will persist even when the capitalist relations of production have been overcome. Which is to say, the socialist society will also be a divided one and, as such, will need to recognize and affirm itself by means of a generic referent. Such an instance of society's mediation with itself may take various forms (e.g., religion), but the historically probable one is that of the state.

Any reflection on the socialist state has been hampered by the assertion of its extinction. From such a perspective, the existence of a socialist state can be explained only as a remnant of capitalist relations. That is, it does not arise as a problem of socialist society. It can be presumed, however, that future society will have its own "realm of necessity" and, therefore, the need for a mediating body. If so, upholding a utopian horizon as a feasible goal means concealing existing relations of domination. In fact, proclaiming the extinction of the state in a divided society leads to totalitarianism: the coercive imposition of an identity of interests.

If we affirm the persistence of a divided society, we must abandon the idea of a society without a state and politics. Socialist society also externalizes an instance of mediation and synthesis, but this need not be made subjective behind the backs of the people. The goal is a transparent mediation consciously formed by the people. Instead of blindly submitting to an alien and hostile power, they have power over the organization of society. Division will not disappear in a future society, but it can be determined collectively. This perspective does not solve the problem of "socialism and democracy," but at least it allows us to raise it.

6. The State and Good Order

Finally, the Latin American situation urgently raises a generally overlooked issue: the relationship between politics and morality. A split between moral judgment and political action predominates, and this is developed from the bourgeois distinction between individual duty and public legality. Morality appears as something external to politics. In such a relationship of exteriority, moral efficiency always ends up subordinated to, or instrumentalized by, the efficiency of power (let us remember human rights policy).

Instead of considering morality as an evaluative judgment on a social action, we must conceive it as a symbolic order, intrinsic to all practice. All social practice is, as we said, a process of production and reproduction of meaning, which refers us to the idea of a "good order." The polis, says Aristotle, comes into existence for the sake of living, but continues to exist for the sake of living well. What is the good life? It is linked, of course, to the world of needs. We should not "spiritualize" good order in an act of faith; living well is not something alien to material needs nor a mere "plus," but neither is it reducible to these. Today we already know that liberation from misery and poverty does not per se entail liberation from servitude and oppression. In fact, we currently find a strange juxtaposition: on the one hand, a determination of good order through formal procedures that ensure the representation of individual decisions (democracy). On the other, a more material determination of the Lockean principle of a right to life for all: good order as real universality—but projected onto a utopian horizon.

Both the liberal utopia of good order and the communist utopia refer to the extinction of the state and of any relationship of domination. The paradox of these utopias of Enlightenment, typical of a secularized and anthropocentric era that identifies the good life with removing alienation, is that they are essentially religious conceptions that aspire to a world without necessity and free of contradictions. That brave new world of total freedom repeats religious alienation to the extent that it promises unattainable feasibility. And yet, despite its impossible perfection, it would seem we need utopias, at least as an "Archimedean point" from which it is possible to think about the existing state of things.

Morality was excluded, like religion, by a rationalist conception of politics as a science. There has been no lack of attempts to reintegrate this problematic into political thought, but, in short, an instrumentalist conception currently predominates. This better corresponds to the capitalist "rationale" to the extent that it repeats it. However, the political calculation of its efficiency has made us forget the roots of religious problems in social life itself. Social coexistence requires symbolic-communicative reproduction that (through a set of prohibitions and prescriptions) offers a temporal-spatial horizon to each human activity within the social division of labor and allows us to domesticate nature (external and internal). This self-control of instincts, affections, and passions is imposed and legitimized by the belief in an absolute sense. Politics-calculus assumes the validity of a universal law. It refers to a "last instance" normativity—the purity of the Decalogue. We call for a general principle from which it is possible to establish a clean classification of the world and a final reduction of the complexity of life. However, only one gone mad would take that universality as a norm for practical action. Purity makes for the prophet's critical force but, at the same time, seals his failure as a ruler (armed or not). Humanity is half angel and half beast—and as "animals," we are subject to want.

Both the utopia of the perfect market and the dream of the man who can hunt in the morning, fish in the afternoon, and devote night to criticism, assume a life without limitations, a world lacking order. However, and in the absence of such direct social relations, the social process has to be ordered, classified, and formalized. People must face necessity, and for this, politics is a "basic need." The world of necessity is an impure reality that demands cunning, opportunistic decisions, contaminated judgments, contradictory actions, and, in short, an incoherent practice. That world is—in the eyes of the purity that characterizes beautiful souls—a hell, but, as Machiavelli said, we, who are afraid of hunger, afraid of prison, cannot be afraid of hell. That is, we cannot submit to a morality that is external to the problem of poverty and power. In other words, freedom cannot be thought of as the absence of needs but as something in tension with them.

We cannot renounce impure politics because that would be ignoring needs, or pure morality because that would be abdicating our ordering action over them. Law and transgression are equally indispensable. The paradox is well summed up in the maxim: obeyed, but not fulfilled. This is the fundamental principle of "corruption." There is no social life, no politics possible without "corruption." It is the subtle adaptation of the general law to the world of needs (an incorrupt order would strike terror into the very concept). And yet that does not mean that corruption is morally acceptable. It must be recognized as a vice, even if it functions as a virtue. In this tension, transgression mediates between politics and morality. Morality is neither external nor reducible to politics. Even if excised and in contraposition to practice, it produces universal norm as the ordering referent of what this concrete work implies, in contradiction and dissonance regarding the needs that make politics.

Possessed of a greater religious sensitivity or being, simply, more cynical, the right has always cared much more about this problem than the left. This not only develops the casuistic morality that makes it possible to reconcile crime with the law and legitimize the exercise of power as a moral duty. The history of the "reason of state" indicates a refusal to abdicate the representation of the generic; more than deny, transgression reinforces the invocation of a good life. Good order is not a utopian projection toward the future (a universality to be realized on the day the state is extinguished), but a transcendence made directly effective via the state, because the state is already a transcendent referent, the depository of an idea of universality. The right does not forget that the state is a "mortal God" (Hobbes).[21] Its anti-statism is opposed to the (collective) political disposition over the economic process, not to the form of statehood. On the contrary, it invokes the general form of the modern (capitalist) state as a condition for the possibility of classifying and hierarchizing people. The left, more empirical and rationalist, neglects the elaboration of a general representation in the form of the state. In its empiricism, it limits itself to denouncing the spurious generic nature of the capitalist state. In its rationalism, it rejects any transcendental referent as avoidable alienation. However, it cannot fail to refer to the generic. It then resorts to the concept of reason, history, progress, or a party as a bad substitute for the idea of the state. Only in the theory of hegemony does the left manage to incorporate the construction of good order into the construction of the state. Gramsci picks up the Aristotelian-Hegelian perspective that sees the essence of the state in ethical life, an ethical life that consists of the unification (not identity) of the universal and the subjective will.

---

21   Thomas Hobbes, *Leviathan: or the Matter, Form and Power of a Commonwealth Ecclesiastical and Civil* (London: McMaster University Archive of the History of Economic Thought, 1651), 106. [–Ed.]

The Inner Courtyards of Democracy

Subjectivity and Politics

First Published in Santiago, Fondo de Cultura Económica, 1990
Translated for this volume by Mariana Ortega-Breña, 2023

To Paulina,
More than ever

Foreword

From the number of imaginable cities we must exclude those
whose elements are assembled without a connecting thread,
an inner rule, a perspective, a discourse. With cities, it is as
with dreams: everything imaginable can be dreamed, but even
the most unexpected dream is a rebus that conceals a desire
or, its reverse, a fear. Cities, like dreams, are made of desires
and fears, even if the thread of their discourse is secret, their
rules are absurd, their perspectives deceitful, and everything
conceals something else.

ITALO CALVINO, *Invisible Cities*[1]

The texts here gathered were written between 1984 and 1987 for several
reasons and yet obey the same intent: to explore the subjective dimension of politics.

Why, you might wonder, should one opt for such an elusive approach,
already aware of the opaque nature of subjectivity as each mask refers
to another in an endless sequence of Russian dolls? My basic premise is
expounded in the above quote from Italo Calvino.

I assume that politics, like cities, is comprised of desires and fears.
It is not the exclusive work of the mind or simple chance and, therefore,
only by interrogating ourselves regarding the concomitant feelings can
we reflect on what a reasonable policy is. Moreover, when we speak of

---

1   Italo Calvino, *Invisible Cities* (San Diego: Harcourt Brace & Company, 1974),
     43–44.

our time as a time of crisis, we are referring precisely to a subjective experience: we perceive structural problems have reached an unavoidable moment of choice. How, then, are we to understand the crisis without taking a political look at the fears and longings caused by the present state of affairs?

What I do is no more than that. My reflection on the topic of certainty, for example, arose from a request to confront Marx and Tocqueville. For months, I reflected on this topic without hitting upon an "entrance," until I became aware of the factor of uncertainty and, taking my cue from that, tried to investigate, with the help of the "classics," its political dimension. That is to say that I am not interested in politics "in itself," but in the political meaning of those feelings of fear and helplessness, of disenchantment I discover in us. I write about what hurts me. Wounds must perforce close lest we bleed to death. We survive. To live, however, we must not forget the scars, the places where the skin lost its sensitivity. We cannot recover what was lost, but we can remember it. These writings are an exercise in memory: political memory.

I freely confess to my misgivings regarding the implacable nature of rigorous logic; it is no coincidence that my first article in 1970 (a study of the social sciences in Latin America) included a quote from Kafka: "The logic cannot be refuted, but someone who wants to live will not resist it."[2] I admire analytical discourse and can envy an author's lucidity, but after a while I fall into an indifferent drowsiness and start weaving my own dreams. These are long roll films I can never develop; they lack a plot and are without an ending. I suffer when I write, and not merely because of the effort it takes me to name those fuzzy images and pin down their profile. I find it even harder to thread them into an intelligible narrative. That is why my texts do not usually lead to any conclusions; like dreams, they are simply interrupted.

Fundamentally, they are merely a script that articulates an association of assorted images.

Each sentence confronts me with a crossroads, and the argument ends up taking an arbitrary path. Any ordering is ultimately illusory and,

---

2   Franz Kafka, *The Trial* (Franklin Center, PA.: Franklin Library, 1978), 271. [–Ed.]

nevertheless, it is only through the construction of such a context that each of the images acquires meaning. This tension has been addressed from a different perspective by filmmaker Wim Wenders when he states:

> I completely reject stories because, for me, they produce lies, nothing but lies, and the biggest lie is how they craft a connection where there was none. On the other hand, we need these lies insofar as it makes no sense to organize a series of images without them, without the lie of a story. Stories are impossible, but it would be impossible for us to live without them.[3]

Not only is a story made up of an assortment of images that are both fragmentary and mysteriously linked; reality itself is comprised of an infinity of fragments whose complex interconnection goes beyond any attempt at ordering. What we call order is ultimately nothing more than a proposal—an attempt to share. And we can only share what we elaborate intersubjectively, for only then is it our world, our time. Seen this way, political thought, like art or morality, means making the collective visible, reconstructing contexts, relating beliefs and institutions, linking images and calculations, symbolic expression and instrumental action. These are, of course, artificial constructions and partial connections that fail to account for the multiple threads that make up the social fabric. Which is why I am not overly worried when some friends point out the contradictions in my work. After all, no story is the "true" one and, yet, only to the extent that we can (tendentially) recognize ourselves in each tale does this tangle of phenomena acquire meaning. That is why we desire order above all else and always dream of a better one. This is what this book is about: the need for order, the possibility of a democratic order and, in short, what order we desire.

Here I return to the question of order already raised in *The Conflictive and Unending Construction of Desired Order.*[4] The Chilean situation

3   W. Wenders, "El estado de las cosas," *Medios Revueltos* (Madrid) (Spring 1988): 31.

4   N. Lechner, *La conflictiva y nunca acabada construcción del orden deseado* (Santiago: Ediciones Ainavillo, 1984); republished by Centro de Investigaciones

or the processes in Argentina, Brazil, or Peru during these past years have shown us that it is not enough to invoke democracy. Instead of taking it for granted, democracy should be understood as a problematic future. That is what my question regarding order is about. I conceive of order not as the perpetuation of what already exists, but as its transformation. I am not talking just about any change, of course. When we speak of order we always denote, at least tacitly, a utopia of good order. The notion has been misused, and yet we cannot do without it. The utopia of democracy is the self-determination of a people over their conditions and ways of life. It is from this perspective that I pose the question of order as it relates democracy and social transformation.

My interest in democracy, social transformation, and utopia is faithful to the socialist ideas of my first political experience: the 1968 movement and the Allende government. How valid, how thoughtless were our desires? We assumed, generously but erroneously, that we all shared the same dream. We pointed to a real problem—the construction of a collective order—while ignoring the conditions of a modern, secularized society. This does not obey a single rationale, nor can it be synthesized into a single vision. Democracy itself not only reflects a plurality of interests and opinions but is subject to very different interpretations. My concern for the political imaginary arose from trying to explain this diversity. By which I mean the images we construct of society as the collective-conflictive production of an order. There is no pre-established historical purpose, and each era, each group defines a sense of order based on its experience. In this context, I understand politics as a struggle for order where the imaginary plays a decisive role, particularly in unsettled cultures such as those in which we live.

I feel that our political imagination is becoming extinguished. The intentionality of political action has diluted, and we are arrested in a perpetual present. Of course, every policy (whether it admits so or not) institutes, ratifies, or modifies certain orientations of social activity. Today, however, such orientations are weak and contradictory, and our future slips out of our hands. In fact, scientific development and

Sociológicas y Siglo XXI Editores, Madrid, 1986. [Also included in *Works II*, 267–421.]

new technologies, changes in economic-financial processes, and social innovations seem to create seemingly inescapable imperatives that politics (any politics) can only obey. What Castoriadis observes across the whole of contemporary civilization also applies to politics: "the opposition [...] between an ever wider unfolding of production—in the sense of the (strict or ample) repetition of manufacture, use, elaboration, the amplified deduction of consequences—and the involution of creation, the exhaustion of potential new and wide-ranging representative and imaginary schemes."[5] The power of the necessary is constantly increasing, while our political-cultural capacity to redefine the possible and, even more so, the desirable, has been weakened. It is not that there are fewer possibilities or fewer desires; these grow as do needs, but they fail to find an interpretive framework. After having denounced the advance of the great global ideologies and plans, today and on the contrary, we regret the absence of any kind of project.

Latin America (and not just this region) is undergoing a project crisis. This may entail an abdication of our responsibility regarding the future, but it can also express a new conception of it. We intuit that tomorrow is a thousand possibilities no less contradictory than today with all its options. It is just as irreducible to a coherent and harmonious design. We intuit that dreams will also necessarily remain unfinished, always reformulated. In short, we envision an open future that is incompatible with the usual notion of a project. Therefore, more than an alternative project, we need a different way of facing the future.

"Thinking about defeat" does not merely entail revising a struggle strategy. It entails questioning the struggle itself and, therefore, redefining the meaning of politics. Seen in this light, political reflection in our countries still seems to me to be too cautious, as if we were afraid of identifying ourselves as vulnerable. It is these fears, unassumed or poorly integrated into life, that cause discouragement and unease. In such a context, I find that a certain "postmodern environment," with its disenchantment regarding illusions of fullness and harmony, a healthy aspect. Fantasies of omnipotence evaporate, and we discover ourselves fragile.

---

5   C. Castoriadis, "Transformación social y creación cultural," *Punto de Vista* (Buenos Aires) 32 (April–June 1988).

Could disenchantment (in this sense) not provide fertile soil for democracy?

To carry out political reforms, we need, first and foremost, a reform of politics. This entails looking beyond (institutional) politics. Only now and in retrospect do I perceive in these texts a hesitant exploration of the extra-institutional realm of "the political." After sketching the historical background of the political-intellectual debate in South America, from revolution to democracy, my inquiry turns to some intangible and usually neglected aspects of democracy. Institutional dynamics, stakeholder strategies, and economic constraints are often analyzed without due consideration of people's daily experience, fears, and desires. The alleys of everyday life might often prove dead ends, but sometimes they allow for a glimpse of what is hidden on the side of great avenues. Democracy, so dependent on the public light for its development, also comprises lonely backyards—some are sordid, others have simply been forgotten. The interest of this book, in my opinion, is exploring such corners (the cognitive-affective substrate of democracy) to attain a different viewpoint on politics. This is not a systematic re-examination, but an exploration that becomes all the riskier the more misleading the street signage gets. Its significance is appreciated only in context, however tentative this might be. I have gathered these fragments in a book for the same reason that we design the map of an unknown city: to establish some references, to trace possible relationships, and thus get some perspective regarding a path.

I

From Revolution to Democracy

1. A Change of Perspective

In the 1960s, the central subject of the political-intellectual debate in South America was revolution. The situation in the region, characterized by economic stagnation within the framework of a traditional social structure on the one hand and, on the other, by growing popular mobilization, was interpreted as a pre-revolutionary state. By contrasting the rapid and radical changes brought about by the Cuban Revolution with the obstacles encountered by developmentalist modernization, the unviability of the capitalist model of development in Latin America was confirmed alongside the consequent "historical necessity" of a revolutionary rupture. This idea became so powerful that even a centrist party like the Christian Democrats proposed a "revolution in freedom"[6] in Chile. Revolution appeared not only as a necessary strategy in the face of the dramatic "development of underdevelopment,"[7] but also as a response supported by social theory.[8] The intellectual debate revolved around "situations of dependence," either as part of historical-structural interpretations of imperialism and sociopolitical constellations in the several countries,[9] or in a more doctrinaire version that proposed

---

6   See *Obras I*, 183, note a. [–Ed.]

7   A. G. Frank, *Capitalism and Underdevelopment in Latin America* (New York: Monthly Review Press, 1967).

8   F. H. Cardoso and F. Weffort, eds., *América Latina: ensayos de interpretación sociológico-política* (Santiago: University Press, 1970).

9   F. H. Cardoso and E. Faletto, *Dependencia y desarrollo en América Latina* (Mexico: Siglo XXI Editores, 1969).

"socialism or fascism"[10] were the only two alternatives for Latin American societies. If revolution was the focus of Latin American discussions during the 1960s, democracy has been the central theme of the 1980s. As in the previous period, political mobilization is strongly nourished by intellectual debate. Its beginning, on a regional level, dates back to the 1978 conference on the "Social Conditions of Democracy" organized by the Latin American Council of Social Sciences (CLACSO) in Costa Rica:[11] Gino Germani's last speech and Raul Alfonsín's first international outing.[12] Since then, all attention has been focused on the processes of gradual (Brazil, Uruguay), accelerated (Argentina), or stagnant (Chile) transition—one that is supposedly leading to the establishment of democratic institutions while relegating the obstacles to democratic consolidation (Peru, Bolivia) to the background. After the authoritarian experience, democracy appears more as a hope than as a problem. It is therefore worth asking whether the current winds of democratization are mere conjunctural "weather conditions" or if, in fact, they are initiating a social transformation.

Before reviewing the development of the intellectual debate in recent years, I would like to highlight the difficulties inherent to this attempt. Regardless of an author's inevitable personal and national bias, it is hard to reconstruct a Latin American debate as such. The structural heterogeneity or, so to speak, the sui generis nature of the region, requires and, at the same time, refutes the concepts elaborated in developed capitalist societies. Alongside structural difficulties that complicate conceptualization, there are historical difficulties inherent to generalization; the same phenomenon (e.g., democratization) has a different meaning in Venezuela, Peru, or Uruguay. Both the diversity and instability of social processes as well as dissimilar historical experiences impact intellectual production, which tends toward dispersion and volatility. If we also consider the absence of social theory journals with regional circulation,

---

10   T. Dos Santos, *Socialismo o fascismo, dilema latinoamericano* (Santiago: Ediciones Prensa Latinoamericana, 1969).

11   See *Obras II*, 423, note a. [—Ed.]

12   The materials were published in *Crítica & Utopía* 1, 2, and 4.

it is surprising we can speak of a Latin American discussion at all, such as the ongoing debate in Brazil and the Southern Cone regarding processes of democratization (a regional topic because of its incidence on other countries).[13]

2. The Experience of the New Authoritarianism

Our perspective of democracy was born from the authoritarian experience of the 1970s. The military coup of 1973 in Chile, the previous coups in Brazil (1964), Peru (1968), and the subsequent ones in Uruguay (1973) and Argentina (1976) acquired a joint significance. Without bypassing the specific features in each country, particularly in Peru under Velasco Alvarado,[14] this new authoritarianism was constituted as a shared experience: an experience of systematic violence—of a programmatically authoritarian and exclusionary order.

The purpose of a coup is not so much the overthrow of a certain government as the foundation of a new order. However, to impose a new normativity and normality, procedures specific to a "rationale of war" are employed: the annihilation of the adversary and the abolition of difference. Hence an initial feature of the post-1973 intellectual discussion: the denunciation of authoritarianism in the name of human rights. Intellectuals did not fight in defense of a project, but for everyone's right to life. It was around human rights that international solidarity was organized, projecting intellectuals beyond their borders.

Intellectual criticism no longer invokes the future (revolution) versus the past (underdevelopment). On the contrary, it now defends a tradition of opposing violent rupture. Alongside this disapproval comes self-criticism regarding previous leading revolutionary stances (of which Régis Debray was the best-known incarnation). There was a clear

---

13 I limit my reflections to South America; to account for the intellectual debate in Mexico, Central America, and the Caribbean, other considerations should be addressed.

14 H. Pease, *El ocaso del poder oligárquico* (Lima: Desco, 1977).

break with the guerrilla strategy[15] and the great lesson of military coups was that socialism cannot (must not) be a coup.[16]

However, the main concern of intellectual debate during those years was to analyze the origins and nature of the new authoritarian regime. Very early on, it was made clear that this was not fascism, a notion relegated to partisan agitation work. Based on Guillermo O'Donnell's seminal text on the authoritarian bureaucratic state,[17] the state became the unifying axis of social research throughout the region. Both the *Revista Mexicana de Sociología*[18] and some anthologies[19] offer an overview of this extensive production, some of which is excellent.

Why was the study of the state interrupted around 1981? There is no critical balance of the debate, which illustrates the scarcity of intellectual self-reflection and, therefore, the difficulties in shaping an intellectual tradition. The discussion on the state perhaps exhausted itself insofar as it was nothing but a kind of "vogue" (much as dependency theory before). The authoritarian bureaucratic state was a "novelty" that had to be accounted for, but once it appeared consolidated and acquiring long-term viability, the search for innovation (that is, the transformation of the existing state of affairs) was relocated outside of it. This suggests a deeper reason for the sudden shift in the debate: criticism of the authoritarian state leads to criticism of the statist conception of politics, which had been in force until then. Indeed, concern regarding development tended to go hand in hand with an emphasis on the state as its main agent. Faced with the insufficiency or outright spuriousness

---

15   T. Petkoff, *Proceso a la izquierda* (Barcelona: Planeta, 1976).

16   F. Weffort, *¿Por qué democracia?* (São Paulo: Editora Brasiliense, 1984).

17   G. O'Donnell, *Reflexiones sobre las tendencias de cambio en el Estado Burocrático-Autoritario* (Buenos Aires: Documento CEDES, 1976); also in *Revista Mexicana de Sociología* 1 (1977).

18   *Revista Mexicana de Sociología* 1 and 2 (1977), and 3 and 4 (1978).

19   J. Malloy, ed., *Authoritarianism and Corporatism in Latin America* (Pittsburgh: Pittsburgh University Press, 1977); D. Collier, ed., *The New Authoritarianism in Latin America* (Princeton: Princeton University Press, 1979); N. Lechner, ed., *Estado y política en América Latina* (Mexico: Siglo XXI Editores, 1981).

of a "bourgeois democracy," the state was assigned the responsibility of solving social problems. Particularly on the left, the Hegelian idea of the advance of the state as an unfolding of freedom predominated: by expanding state intervention, people would emancipate themselves from the conditions of misery that had so far alienated them. This collective imaginary, however, was thrown into question by the omnipotence and omnipresence of the military dictatorships. In Latin America, it is the authoritarian state (not a Keynesian welfare state) that becomes the Leviathan against which the strengthening of civil society must be invoked. In this way, it is precisely the development of the (authoritarian) state that forces us to rethink our ways of doing politics.

The reflection on authoritarianism continues, at least partially, in studies on neoliberal thought. We should, however, highlight that, despite the strong influence of neoliberalism and neoconservatism on authoritarian governments (especially in their "economic model"), this is not a Latin American school of thought. These are translations of Hayek, Huntington, or the school of public choice. This refers to a more general phenomenon: despite the power of the (traditional or "neo-capitalist") right in the social and political development of the region, there is no right-wing intelligentsia. There are some isolated figures, but they do not present a strong brand political thought that can polemicize with the left—help it elaborate its own stance (e.g., the polemic of Gramsci with Croce or Habermas with Luhmann).[20] Unable to confront a liberal-conservative interpretation of Latin American reality, the leftist intelligentsia tends to elaborate its critique via European or North American sources, which can distort its efforts to theorize regional social practice. Above all, it obscures the struggle to define the meaning of democracy.

---

20   A. Gramsci, *El materialismo histórico y la filosofía de Benedetto Croce* (Mexico: Juan Pablos, 1975); J. Habermas and N. Luhmann, *Theorie der Gesellschaft oder Sozialtechnologie Was leistet die Systemforschung?* (Frankfurt: Suhrkamp, 1971). [—Ed.]

3. The New Intellectual Environment

We already know about the "institutionalized violence" that destroyed college life and repressed cultural activity. Many intellectuals had to flee into exile, while others managed to stay in their countries and created "informal work centers." Both "survival solutions" modified intellectual production. I will now highlight four aspects that affect our revaluation of democracy.

1. The coups entailed a dramatic disruption of daily life. Although not very visible, this fact greatly impacted the rather elitist and book-ish tradition of the intelligentsia. For many intellectuals, the loss of material security and the erosion of normalcy criteria caused a state of uncertainty (both cognitive and emotional) that favored not only a biographical review, but also reflection on problems that went usually unconsidered—such as, for example, daily life itself. Uncertainty, how-ever, also has another consequence I find crucial: it fosters a different appreciation of formal-democratic procedures. Many intellectuals had experienced "bourgeois democracy" as an illusion or manipulation incapable of undertaking the imperatives of development; dictatorships taught them the political character of supposedly technical issues.

If there is no established "truth" or habits recognized by all, then it is essential we establish some "rules of the game" that allow for the defense of "vital interests" and negotiate an agreement regarding opposing opinions. The reevaluation of the previously criticized "for-mal democracy" thus starts from individual experience rather than theoretical reflection. And despite its primarily defensive character, it is likely that this experience had an impact on the left's affective roots for democratization.

2. Exile but also work in national private centers entailed an unprec-edented international circulation of intellectuals. Santiago de Chile until 1973 and later Mexico City[21] became centers for a Latin Ameri-

---

21   Mexico City hosted most of South America's exiles during the military dic-tatorship period. In particular, the PRI's policy of receiving and supporting

can debate. This is not only a question of "Latin Americanization" via enforced exile. In the mid-1970s, regional seminars began to multiply and, following CLACSO's initiative, regional working groups formed a kind of itinerant university system that replaced the previously guarded cloisters. This transnationalization diminished provincialism (which often went hand in hand with an uncritical "Europeanism") and facilitated the renewal of a kind of political thought that was relatively autonomous from extant party structures in each country. By acquiring greater autonomy from political organizations, intellectual discussion (especially on the left) managed to develop a more universalist (that is, less instrumental) approach to politics.

3. Another aspect that was particularly relevant to left-wing intellectuals was intellectual openness. Military coups demystified revolutionary faith and did away with dogmatic Marxism (e.g., the influence of Althusser and Poulantzas in the 1960s). In a cruel and oft traumatic way, a "paradigm crisis" took place with ultimate beneficial effects: the broadening of the cultural horizon and the confrontation with work that had been

---

academics (as with the Spanish exiles of the Civil War) allowed for the creation and consolidation of spaces for social science discussion such as FLACSO, Sede México (1975) and the Centro de Investigación y Docencia Económicas (1974), among others. See C. Véjar Pérez-Rubio, *El exilio latinoamericano en México* (Mexico: Centro de Investigaciones Interdisciplinarias en Ciencias y Humanidades, UNAM, 2008). Likewise, the General Secretariat of CLACSO (in conjunction with other organizations) carried out educational programs aimed at favoring students, professors, and researchers at the university level in order to transfer academics from countries under dictatorships to others where they could continue their work in addition to contributing to the host country. For example, "the [...] Escolatina program, for graduates in economic sciences, which was already well consolidated, was transferred to the graduate division of the National Autonomous University of Mexico, along with most of the Latin American students and professors that composed it. Also, the measures implemented toward the end of 1973 and later gradually turned FLACSO, a graduate school for social sciences in Latin America, into a regional intergovernmental postgraduate, and research university." E. Oteiza, "Examen retrospectivo de una experiencia latinoamericana de educación para refugiados" (Buenos Aires: CLACSO, 1985).

previously scorned or ignored. A socialist publisher, for example, significantly translated the political writings of Weber and Carl Schmitt.[22] The massive response to Gramsci in the mid-1970s, Foucault afterward, and the current interest in Habermas point to some of the main interests. These were often "trends" that did not lead to a critical appropriation of the approaches. Today, a certain eclecticism prevails: elements of Max Weber, Agnes Heller, and Norberto Bobbio can be mixed, and I consider this a healthy phenomenon insofar as it resulted in the abandonment of exegesis or the "application" of a preconstituted theory, giving way to a need to account for a certain social reality.

It is in this context that the role of Marxism should be situated. Although it influenced economic ("structuralism") and sociological ("dependency") thought, it never took massive root in the region. In countries with a predominantly agrarian structure, marked by the world of finance, a long history of *caudillismo* and coups d'état alongside the perennially updated experience of imperialism, it frankly makes more sense to take a Leninist approach. And yet, this is still a traditional approach insofar as it refers to a hidden truth to be unveiled and realized by revolution. Today, the complex social differentiation in South America no longer allows us to conceive the struggle for freedom and equality in essentialist terms. Of course, Marta Harnecker's manual is still getting published[23] but, in general, Marx has lost his quasi-religious connotation. In the case of South America (unlike Mexico and Central America), it is perhaps more accurate to speak of post-Marxism, at least in intellectual debate. The writings of Ernesto Laclau and José Nun[24] against reductionism or historical analyses of the so-called dis-

---

22   The two main translations of the publisher Folios (Buenos Aires and Mexico) in which José Aricó played a fundamental role were C. Schmitt, *El concepto de lo político* (Mexico: Folios, 1984), and M. Weber, *Escritos políticos* (Mexico: Folios, 1981). [—Ed.]

23   M. Harnecker, *Los conceptos elementales del materialismo histórico* (Mexico: Siglo XXI Editores, 1969).

24   E. Laclau, *Política e ideología en la teoría marxista* (Madrid: Siglo XXI, 1978); J. Nun, "El otro reduccionismo," *Zona Abierta* (Madrid) 28 (1983).

agreement between Latin America and Marx[25] as well as the vicissitudes of "Latin American Marxism"[26] are a kind of settling of accounts with "Marxisms" and, simultaneously, attempts to update that tradition so it can serve as starting point to address the democratic transformation of society. So far, these renewal efforts have been reduced to the intellectual realm, finding little echo in left-wing parties.

4. A fourth point is the growing academic professionalization of intellectuals, either through the expansion and modernization of the university system (Brazil), or precisely the other way around, due to their displacement to a highly competitive informal market (private centers). These accelerated processes of specialization erase the traditional image of the intellectual as creator and transmitter of the meaning of social life. The critic again prevails over the prophet, and political vocation is no longer based on our commitment to partisan militancy.

To summarize the transformation in the intellectual environment, I want to emphasize the new density of ongoing debate, the consequence of greater intraregional contact (especially in the Southern Cone), greater academic discipline, and greater political responsibility. Despite the oft-erratic nature of the research, knowledge of the different national realities is today much deeper and more extensive. Although it sounds paradoxical, even in circumstances as adverse as those in Chile, the social sciences have had their greatest development during this past decade in terms of thematic diversity, richness of analysis, as well as productivity.[27]

---

25 J. Aricó, *Marx y América Latina* (Lima: CEDEP, 1980).

26 J. Aricó, ed., *Mariátegui y los orígenes del marxismo latinoamericano* (Mexico: Siglo XXI Editores, 1978); J. C. Portantiero, "Socialismo y política en América Latina," in N. Lechner, ed., *¿Qué significa hacer política?* (Lima: Desco, 1982); T. Moulian, *Democracia y socialismo en Chile* (Santiago: FLACSO, 1983), and the journal *Socialismo y Participación*.

27 A. Portes, "From Dependency to Redemocratization: New Themes in Latin American Sociology," *Contemporary Sociology* (September 1984).

4. Thinking about the Alternative

Since 1980, and especially since the economic crisis worsened in 1982, attention shifted from authoritarianism to democratization. As far as the debate on the democratic alternative is concerned, I perceive two standout factors that prepare a renewal of Latin American political thought.

On the one hand, there is a revaluation of politics. The left, confronted with the national security doctrine[28] and the offensive of neoliberals and neoconservatives,[29] has discovered that politics does not have a single and univocal significance. A fundamental element of the political struggle is precisely the struggle to define what it means to do politics.[30] With the critique of military doctrine and neoliberal thought, the intellectual debate now elaborates a resignification of politics, of which I will mention three characteristics.

1. The contraposition of a "political rationale" to the "rationale of war." Social relations are conflictive in every class[-based] society, and conflicts turn into wars when the life of one subject—their raison d'être— is dependent on the death of another. Interpreting social divisions as exclusionary antagonisms (socialism or fascism, freedom or communism), relations are reduced to a single classificatory limit: friend or foe. The rationale of politics does not aim to annihilate the adversary but, on the contrary, to establish reciprocal recognition of subjects among themselves.

2. A democratic politics cannot be conceived based on "national unity" or some pre-social identity, but on the basis of difference. It is, in the words of Hannah Arendt, the human condition of plurality; plurality is,

---

28   G. Arriagada and M. A. Garretón, "Doctrina de Seguridad Nacional y régimen militar," *Estudios Sociales Centroamericanos* (San José, Costa Rica) 20 and 21 (1978).

29   *Revista Mexicana de Sociología*, special issue (1981).

30   N. Lechner, ed., *¿Qué significa hacer política?* (Lima: Desco, 1982).

specifically, the condition of all political life.[31] This point, like the previous one, entails self-criticism regarding the traditional approach of the left: the class struggle cannot be conceived either as a war of life and death or as a struggle between preconstituted subjects. Only by abandoning the idea of an economic predetermination of political-ideological positions does it become possible to think about the political.[32] And one of the specific features of the construction of a democratic order is, precisely, the production of a plurality of subjects.

3. A self-critical review of the left also follows from a third objection to authoritarian-neoliberal conceptions: the instrumentalist significance of politics. The Marxist tradition, military doctrine, and neoliberal thought share the same interpretative scheme under different signs: the present as a "transition" toward the realization of utopia. Whether the future is imagined as the market or as a classless society, it is seen in terms of a post-political order. And by conceiving the "abolition of politics" as a feasible goal, present political action takes an exclusively instrumental character. To overcome this approach, a reconceptualization of utopia has been proposed: an image of impossible plenitude, but indispensable in terms of discovering what is possible.[33]

On the other hand, there is a revaluation of civil society. In some countries, such as Brazil, this reflects a drastic and successful modernization process.[34] In other countries, such as Bolivia and Peru, but also in relatively developed societies such as Argentina, Chile, and Uruguay, there is, on the contrary, a deep concern about the serious deterioration of living conditions. In both cases, the interest in civil society has a clear political connotation: the social conditions of democracy. In this way, it

---

31   H. Arendt, *La condición humana* (Barcelona: Paidós, 1978).

32   E. Laclau, *Política e ideología en la teoría marxista* (Madrid: Siglo XXI, 1978).

33   F. Hinkelammert, *Crítica de la razón utópica* (San José [Costa Rica]: DEI, 1984).

34   M. H. T. de Almeida and B. Sorj, *Sociedade e política no Brasil pós-64* (São Paulo: Editora Brasiliense, 1983).

becomes possible to "politicize" the preference for foreign foundations of empirical analyses (demography, basic needs, the situation of women and the youth) without falling into unacceptable interventions, such as the famous Camelot Project of the CIA in the 1960s.[35] Whether we are dealing with classic themes of Latin American sociology (social structure, agrarian development, trade unionism) or new ones (social and regional movements, urban violence, popular culture), approaches tend to emphasize the previously unconsidered political aspects of the social process. In this regard, nothing is more relevant than the effort of some of our main sociological research centers to publish sociopolitical journals for a broad audience:[36] for example, in Lima, *Quehacer* and *Social-*

35   Project Camelot was a social science research program conceived by the Office of Special Operations Research at the University of Washington, which was run by the Pentagon and had a group of more than one hundred sociologists and anthropologists. The project was developed in 1964 and was intended to study the ethnic and motivational factors involved in the management and generation of local wars (this was within the nascent field of area studies). It sought to understand what conditions generated instabilities and what attitude governments should take when engaging in counterinsurgency and destabilizing activities. Implementation was initially attempted in Chile with the collaboration of anthropologist Hugo Nutini, but after several denunciations in which he highlighted the roles of Johan Galtum, the General Secretariat of the University of Chile, and the students, it was officially canceled in 1965. See F. Manno and R. Bednarcik, "El proyecto Camelot," *Foro Internacional* 9, no. 32 (October–December 1968); I. Horowitz, *The Rise and Fall of Project Camelot: Studies in the Relationship Between Social Science and Practical Politics* (Cambridge: MIT Press, 1967). [–Ed.]

36   The Peruvian journals *Socialismo y Participación* and *Quehacer* were created in 1976 and 1979, respectively. The first as a forum for political debate issued by the Center for Studies for Development and Participation (Centro de Estudios para el Desarrollo y la Participación, CEDEP), and the second as a publication of the Center for Development Studies and Promotion (Centro de Estudios y Promoción del Desarrollo, DESCO), on a bimonthly basis. In Argentina, *Punto de Vista*, a magazine of cultural criticism that appeared in 1978 as a space for the opposition to the dictatorship, was managed for thirty years by Beatriz Sarlo. *La ciudad futura*, founded in Buenos Aires in 1986 by José Aricó, was the publication and debate organ of the Club de Cultura Socialista; its directors were Juan Carlos Portantiero and Jorge Tula. In Brazil,

ismo y Participación by DESCO and CEDEP, respectively; in São Paulo, *Novos Estudos* and *Lua Nova* by CEBRAP and CEDEC; in Buenos Aires, *Punto de Vista* and *La ciudad futura* by Club Socialista.

This attempt to socialize intellectual debate is still precarious (and a market restricted by the economic crisis itself); however, it demonstrates the interest of intellectuals in rooting democratization in the concrete problems of ordinary people. The concern for the reconstruction of the social fabric responds, of course, to a legacy of devastating dictatorships, but is influenced, at the same time, by neoliberal approaches. By collecting anti-statist objections, it is preparing to overcome the Bourbon (and Napoleonic) tradition of the state that prevailed in the region, although often at the price of a naive liberalism. Considering the strong roots of authoritarianism and statism in Latin American societies, this might be an inevitable reaction that enables us to approach the issue of the state from a democratic perspective.

5. The Theoretical Debate on Democracy

A distinction should be made between transition processes and democratic consolidation processes, as they face different priorities. In the first case (Chile), the discussion on democracy tends to be more paradigmatic, seeking to determine and legitimize an alternative order to the authoritarian one. The difficulty of theoretical reflection lies in the fact that there is no radical and integral rupture between dictatorships and democracy, but rather, "situations of encounter."[37] Once demo-

---

Novos Estudos, from the Brazilian Center for Analysis and Planning (Centro Brasileiro de Análise e Planejamento, founded by Fernando Henrique Cardoso), has published quarterly issues since 1981 and covers the humanities and social sciences. *Lua Nova*, from the Center for Contemporary Culture Studies (Centro de Estudos de Cultura Contemporánea, CEDEC), was founded in 1984. [–Ed.]

37   F. Delich, "Teoría y práctica política en situaciones de dictadura," *Crítica & Utopía* (Buenos Aires) 8 (1982).

cratic institutions have been established, attention is focused on specific problems, structuring the debate around sectoral issues (inflation and unemployment, urban marginalization, restructuring of the university system, etc.).

Restricting myself to the theoretical revision of the issue of democracy by the political left, I will highlight, aside from the points in the previous paragraph, the pact regarding the "rules of the game."

The bulk of the intellectual political debate can be located within a "neo-contractualist" scope. In convulsed societies whose political history is characterized by situations of catastrophic stalemate and reciprocal vetoes (Argentina, Bolivia), by a strong ideological polarization (Chile, Peru) or by traditional mechanisms of domination (Brazil, Colombia, Ecuador), the idea of a pact and strategies of *concertación* (the establishing of covenants) are important innovations. These answer, after the experience of disorder under authoritarian governments, to a generalized aspiration for stable and participatory institutionality. Let us remember the plebiscite of 1980 in Uruguay, the mass mobilizations of 1983 in Argentina, and 1984 in Brazil. Bolstered by such massive support, the notion of a pact expresses a search for a complex and confusing agreement in which the restoration of the fundamental "rules of the game," the negotiation of a minimum itinerary and agenda for the transition, as well as the establishment of mechanisms for socioeconomic consultation get superimposed. Although we can analytically distinguish between a constitutional pact (and the corresponding debate on the validity of a kind of "social contract" nowadays), a political pact for the transition (such as the Multipartidarias in Argentina and Uruguay or the Democratic Alliance in Brazil) and a social pact *strictu sensu* (an employer-union-state agreement), these three levels are necessarily intertwined in situations of transition.

Another difficulty facing the debate around the pact lies in the tension between the reconstruction of the political system and the demands of governability. Alfonsín's example dramatically illustrates how the purpose of arranging a political system is interfered with and even contradicted by the urgency of governing. The issue of political decision in turn refers to a classic problem of democratic theory: the relationship between plurality and collective will. From this point of view, the

Latin American situation highlights some questions of democracy with greater impact than does the European debate.[38]

In Latin America, the current revaluation of the formal procedures and institutions of democracy cannot be based on established habits and norms recognized by all. It is not a question of restoring regulative norms, but of creating those that are constitutive of political activity: the transition requires the elaboration of a new "grammar."[39] That is to say, the beginning of the democratic game and the agreement on the rules of said game are two (simultaneous) sides of the same process.

This gives rise to three types of problems. A first point of the discussion refers to the articulation between institutional forms and political content or, to use an expression employed by Ángel Flisfisch, between pact and project. Faced with the seriousness of the economic crisis (unemployment, inflation, foreign debt), the left tends to prioritize the design of a development project, one capable of satisfying social demands as widely and quickly as possible. To presume that "basic needs" are objective data that can be solved by means of technical solutions will repeat the technocratic approach of military governments. The resolution of the crisis must be approached as a political decision. And this implies institutional mechanisms for the elaboration of options and decision-making. That is to say: there is no project without a pact. The resolution of the economic crisis and the construction of the democratic system must be approached as simultaneous processes.

In second place, we have the issue of the binding force of formal procedures. The validity of a "contract" refers to a normativity that is external to it. And, in these countries, there is no fundamental norm or a basic social consensus on which to base a general recognition of institutional procedures. It is therefore necessary to draw up, alongside the rules of the game, the normative basis by means of which they acquire meaning.

---

38   N. Bobbio et al., *Crisis della democrazia e neo contrattualismo* (Rome: [Editori riuniti; Centro Mario Rossi per gli studi filosofici], 1984); N. Bobbio, *El futuro de la democracia* (Mexico: Fondo de Cultura Económica, 1986); S. Veca, "Identitá e azione collectiva," *Materiali Filosofici* 6 (1981).

39   E. de Ipola and J. C. Portantiero, "Crisis social y pacto democrático," *Punto de Vista* (Buenos Aires) 21 (1984).

In other words, in the absence of a common agreement on the significance of democratic politics, there is no horizon of possibilities that—shared by all—channels the strategic calculation of each participant. We must redefine the possible, not as the unilateral perspective of each actor, but as a collective work.[40] It is by means of such a collective framework of possibilities that a society delimits which strategies are rational and which decisions are legitimate.

Now, how can the collective be instituted in societies characterized by profound structural heterogeneity? This brings us to the third problem. The agreement on the "rules of the game" cannot be conceived as a pact between subjects constituted ex ante. Unlike what happens in Europe, where political processes are much more institutionalized, in Latin America there is a more visible and permanent decomposition and rearrangement of political identities. Here too, historical inertia operates. However, it is precisely in situations of crisis that the productivity of politics as a constituent of collective subjects emerges. The pact would not be something external and subsequent to the subjects, but the institutionality through which and together with which collective identities are constituted. I therefore find the liberal idea of democracy as a "political market" inadequate. Nor should we restrict it to extant corporations. An outstanding feature of the processes of democratic transition would seem to be precisely this: order and subjects are formed together, in the same movement.[41]

The difficulties of democratization in Latin America are therefore evident: Is it possible to find the kind of reciprocal recognition through which political identities are constituted under conditions of strong social inequality? In Latin American societies, particularly in the Andes, social differences (economic, cultural, ethnic, or regional)

---

40   Á. Flisfisch, *Hacia un realismo político distinto*, working document (Santiago: FLACSO, 1984); O. Landi, *El discurso sobre lo posible* (Buenos Aires: Estudios Cedes, 1985). [Both texts have also been published in N. Lechner, comp., *¿Qué es el 'realismo' en política?* (Buenos Aires: Catálogo Editora, 1987.]

41   R. de Castro Andrade, "Sociedad, política, sujeto: variaciones sobre un viejo tema," *Crítica & Utopía* (Buenos Aires) 8, (1982); O. Landi, *Crisis y idiomas políticos* (Buenos Aires: Estudios Cedes, 1982).

either crystallize into relations of inequality or are not even integrated, leaving a juxtaposition of "islands" scattered across an archipelago. In neither case is this an issue of a difference that constitutes plurality. Consequently, conflicts tend to be closer to those involving war relations than competitive distinction. The "national question"[42] and, more specifically, the delimitation of a political space, remains pending.[43] In these situations, how valid can the idea of a "community of free and equal people" as a representation of "the collective" be? By what instance can these societies recognize and affirm themselves as collectivity? The "classical" instance is the form of the state, and yet the collapse of the authoritarian state puts this into question. On the other hand, we do not have a re-creation of the state as a democratic state, and this seems to me to be the main gap in the debate on democratization.

The problems here outlined could be summarized in a refrain that—while incipient—helps the current discussion coalesce: the secularization of politics. In a region so permeated by the Catholic Church and popular religiosity, it is not easy to renounce the pretense of seeking to save souls through politics. While this explains many features of political practice in Latin America, we must not fall into the opposite extreme: a kind of hypersecularization that identifies rationality with formal rationality. What a secularized conception seems to require is that we renounce utopia as a presumably feasible goal without abandoning utopia as the referent through which we conceive the real and determine what is possible. Thus, a central task of democratization entails a change in the political culture. Its possibilities and tendencies are conditioned by the criteria of normality and naturalness that ordinary people develop in their daily lives. It will be concrete experiences of violence and fear, of misery and solidarity, that give sense to democratization and socialism.

---

42 J. Cotler, Clases, *Estado y nación en el Perú* (Lima: Instituto de Estudios Peruanos, 1978).

43 F. Calderón, *La política en las calles* (Cochabamba: Ceres, 1982).

6. The Socialist Debate

In the end, what became of the driving idea of the revolution, socialism? In South America, too, the left is suffering a project crisis. What transformations do they advocate? What is the possible and desired order? I do not think it is overstated to speak of an identity crisis. What does socialism mean today in these societies? The idea of a socialist society seems to have lost its relevance. In some countries, the reference to socialism appears as a nostalgic dream or simply démodé. In others, where it had greater historical roots, the traditional referents have been emptied out, giving rise to organizational fragmentation. In this context of disintegration and thinking from a position of defeat, we should credit left-wing intellectuals for having raised democracy as the central task of society. The construction of social order is conceived as a democratic transformation of society.

The shift of intellectual discussion toward the democratic question is an important innovation among a left traditionally more interested in socioeconomic changes.[44] A process of renewal is underway, but its results are not yet foreseeable. By its very intellectual character, more given to criticism and doubt than to slogans, the debate has managed to question consecrated affirmations, but without elaborating a new conception. How are democracy and socialism articulated? Two examples illustrate the difficult trajectory of a discussion halfway between orthodoxy and renewal. A significant case is the privileged place traditionally occupied by class struggle. Criticizing the connotations of a Leninist interpretation (irreconcilable antagonism, the working class as a preconstituted subject, the party as the vanguard, revolutionary war), renewal thought abandons the concept of "class struggle" without specifying an alternative approach. And primarily concerned with the conclusion of a viable and stable order, it also tends to avoid conflict itself. The emphasis on compromise—a legitimate approach in the light of historical experience—runs the risk of promoting a depoliticized

---

44   Two magazines have recently devoted a special issue to the left and the socialist debate in the region: *Amérique Latine* (Paris) 21 (1985), and *Plural* (Rotterdam) 3 (1984).

"neutralization" of social conflicts, forging a harmonious and, therefore, mistaken vision of democracy.

A second example is the very notion of socialism. This is invoked mainly by the orthodox sectors, which continue to pose it as a "historical necessity," a consequence of the crisis and collapse of capitalism. The renewal currents, on the other hand, privilege political democracy but forgo similar creativity when it comes to rethinking socialism. At most, we are met with the idea of socialism as a deepening of democracy.[45] Such perspective eliminates the teleological and objectivist connotations of the orthodox approach, but raises another question: How to reconcile the priority given to formal procedures with the defense of certain contents that are historically related to overcoming economic exploitation and social inequality? In this regard, the absence of detailed studies on the current state of capitalism in Latin America (of a "critique of the political economy") is duly noted. This could explain, at least partially, the bewilderment of socialist groups in the face of seemingly inexorable constraints (Is there a socialist policy of economic austerity within the framework of a democracy?). Basically, it is a question of redefining the social referent for a socialist majority or, in other words, of rethinking a project of social transformation with which the broad majority can identify. Advances have been minimal in this field and not even in countries with a strong leftist presence (Peru, Chile) can we sincerely speak of a socialist project.

We can only presume that the theme of socialism will resurface from this same democratization. Its topicality, however, would no longer lie in the revolutionary creation of a "new man" (Che Guevara),[46] but in the dynamics of a process of subjectivation, a perpetual tension between the utopia of full subjectivity and the possibilities of institutional reform.

---

45 T. Moulian, op. cit., and F. Weffort, op. cit.

46 E. Guevara, *El socialismo y el hombre nuevo* (Mexico: Siglo XXI Editores, 1979). [–Ed.]

II

The Study of Everyday Life

1. The Historical-Social Context

Why the growing interest in everyday life? Is it not a new vogue, like previous ones that, in successive waves, focused research on issues such as marginality, dependency, or the state? Although this was indeed a fashionable interest, the subject was not innocently selected. Assigning practical and theoretical relevance to everyday life is a fact worthy of reflection.[47]

It is best to begin with a historical retrospective, since this will help us glimpse the context in which the current concern for the topic arose. Alvin Gouldner, in his thought-provoking reflection on "Sociology and the Everyday Life,"[48] mentions three constellations I will now briefly summarize.

In classical Greek thought, everyday life as the domestic-private sphere represented an inferior existence with regard to the public world, the polis. Only by overcoming the world of needs and, thus, domination and inequality, could Greek men realize themselves as free and equal

---

47 This article, written in July 1984, readdresses and extends some reflections that inspired my *Notas sobre la vida cotidiana*: a) "La experiencia escolar" (*Material de Discusión* 38); b) "Habitar, trabajar, consumir" (*Material de Discusión* 53 and 54); c) "Agonía y protesta de la sociabilidad" (*Material de Discusión* 50), and d) "El disciplinamiento de la mujer" (*Material de Discusión* 57), published by FLACSO-Santiago. [These texts are also published in *Obras* II, 463 ff.] I would also like to mention the work of Humberto Giannini, *La "reflexión" cotidiana. Hacia una arqueología de la experiencia* (Santiago: Editorial Universitaria, 1987).

48 A. Gouldner, "Sociology and the Everyday Life," in *The Idea of Social Structure*, ed. L. Coser (New York: Free Press, 1975).

individuals. To access politics and live "the good life," a man would have to leave everyday life behind—a vain existence insofar as it was not reflective. However, in Greek antiquity this was being revaluated already, and we can see it in the preeminence of the choir in Euripides's tragedies—an unindividualized mass of women and youths, the elderly, and slaves. They take a critical stance toward the hero, his competitiveness, and insatiable aspiration for individual superiority, his desire for glory and immortality, his world of beautiful speeches and cruel wars. Against the heroic life, the vanity of great gestures, and empty words, stands the rebellion of the choir. Vindicating the needs of "ordinary people" vindicates the value of everyday life.

A second and equally ambivalent constellation is that proffered by Christianity. On the one hand, everyday life represents the carnal-materialistic existence of humanity—that is, the realm of sin. It is the worldly life opposed to the *Civitas Dei* or, rather, the valley of tears that only acquires meaning via the existence of what lies beyond, of transcendence. On the other hand, however, daily life is also that environment in which people bear witness to their own virtue, perform good works, and prove themselves worthy of divine love. Daily life thus represents both the dangers of perdition and the path toward the salvation of the soul. The Reformation extolled the role of everyday life by polarizing the tension between the sacred and the profane. The "spirit of capitalism," with its internalized religiosity, promotes an ascetic way of life that transforms daily life, insofar as it exists as a sphere of gratification, into a monument to God's glory and grace.

The meaning of daily life, which for the Christian world was derived from a tale of human redemption, is later determined in exclusively social terms. In a critique of religious obscurantism, on the one hand, and the elitism of the absolutist state and the luxury of court life on the other, the bourgeoisie reinterpreted everyday life as the sphere of individual self-realization: daily life embraced the realm of needs, production, and commodity exchange in which individuals experienced freedom and equality; this became true life and not just its anteroom. However, the right to happiness promised to all by the French Revolution had little to do with the sad realities of the Industrial Revolution, which in turn led to a Romantic reaction: life had to be more than the misery of everyday life. To counter the gray banality of the everyday,

THE INNER COURTYARDS OF DEMOCRACY 97

stripped of all forms of transcendence, Romanticism proposed the cult of genius, mystery, refined taste. Extolling the sublime and heartrending nature of extraordinary experiences, it relegated normal existence and its massive, routine nature to a lower level. Everyday life was identified with nature and technique and separated from the world of culture.

Our current situation must be addressed as a fourth constellation. Current, massive interest in everyday life in Europe and the United States seems to stem from two processes. On the one hand, the development of the Keynesian welfare state: multiple aspects that were previously considered part of the private world have now become subject to state regulation. Not only the conditions of work and accumulation, but also divorce and abortion, our diet and the harms of tobacco, the promotion of sports and what a "good home" entails have become public issues incorporated into the political debate and the circuits of mass media. As it comes out into the open, everyday life acquires a new meaning: it represents the concrete area in which a way of life is defined. The conflict shifts from the sphere of production to the sphere of consumption, and a revaluation of the present time and, specifically, of free time contributes to this. As the idea of progress and the advent of a harmonious order fades away, there is growing concern for our current quality of life.[49] And "lifestyle" quality is measured by everyday well-being.

What good can this retrospective do for our Latin American societies, barely shaped by the Enlightenment, Romanticism, or the welfare state? It helps us to see everyday life as a field of struggle as well as an instrument of struggle. The conflict to define what and how daily life is has yet to be determined in the ordering of society. We could undertake a historical reconstruction of daily life in Latin America from this perspective, starting with the chroniclers of the conquests to the stories of travelers in the early nineteenth century, from the debates on the "social question" and the "Indigenous question" to recent studies on "popular culture." And yet, that is not the topic that concerns us, and we will modestly limit ourselves to accounting for the current interest in the everyday.

---

49 T. Evers, "De costas para o Estado, longe do Parlamento," *Novos Estudos* (São Paulo: CEBRAP, April 1983).

I presume that the interest in everyday life is due to discontent with it. In this regard, I would like to draw attention to two triggers. First, it seems to me that daily life is now visible because of the ruptures suffered by Latin American societies as a result of authoritarianism. The rise of military regimes caused a drastic change in the daily life of all social groups and, especially, intellectuals. It is the breakdown of habits and familiar expectations that inspires our sensitivity to everyday life. Things that did not attract our attention before precisely because of their everyday nature now become problematic. Although this is a generalized process, I insist on the role of intellectuals and, specifically, that of social scientists. Persecution and expulsion from universities, the repression of critical thought, the censoring of creativity, relegation to internal or foreign exile were all new experiences that marked their horizon of reflection. The disruption of what had been the "intellectual life" in Buenos Aires, São Paulo, or Santiago led to an awareness of the everyday environment and, consequently, social scientists began to worry about this quotidian microworld. I highlight this apparently anecdotal phenomenon because it points us to an important methodological aspect: the presence of the intellectual's day-to-day existence in social research. I will return to this point later. For now, let us look at the "translation" of personal experience into a research program.

Everyday life is thematized as an object of analysis to the extent that the concrete experience of authoritarianism fails to recognize itself in interpretative "models" of reality. The study of the authoritarian state does not account for the fears and aggressiveness of common individuals; the analysis of the neoliberal market economy tells us nothing about the meaning of consumption and unemployment; a description of changes in the educational system remains silent about effective learning processes. There is a gap between the schemes with which we try to account for the new social structures and their experience that, at a certain point, comes to be perceived as a social problem. Epistemologically speaking, the problem would be the distance between knowledge and consciousness, between science and common sense. What is new is that intellectuals now abandon their usual ways of reflecting on social conditioning (the sociology of knowledge or the philosophy of science) and, returning to the phenomenological tradition of Husserl and Schutz, reverse their approach and understand the subjective experience of structural conditions as a way of reflecting on society.

Second, interest in everyday life can be linked to a more general discontent: discontent with habitual ways of doing politics. The authoritarian situation can be considered an extreme experience of a widespread phenomenon: the crisis of democracy. Those who are most committed to a democratic ordering of society can only worry about the growing distance between political institutions and citizens. As more social activities are subjected to political-legal regulation, the people on the street lose more and more control over their social context. This is not an excess of politicization (as old and new conservatives believe) but, on the contrary, a regression and deterioration of political practice incapable of producing and reproducing the "sense of order" in reference to which people manage to contextualize the various aspects of their lives. Even if old party loyalties survived military rule, ordinary people find it difficult to objectify feelings of social rootedness and collective partisan belonging. To the extent that political organizations are increasingly specialized (bureaucratized) and separated from the daily work of "the people as one," they no longer create or secure collective identities; in fact, they tend to recompose themselves on the margins and even in opposition to institutions. However, there were also areas of informal sociability (such as the neighborhood, the football club, or the university itself) in which emotions and passions, memories and dreams were shared and, in short, constituted collective references. What "beacons" can help illuminate the world of individual lives? Around what is collective life now created? Both sociological thought (Habermas, Touraine) and Marxist analysis (Heller) begin to question the constitution of subjects and this, I think, is the leitmotif behind the exploration of everyday life as a reflection on the existing social situation.

2. The Problems of Conceptualization

There is already a risk that our approach to everyday life will be transformed into an "imperialist" research strategy. Any problematization of a previously unconsidered social phenomenon leads to a revision of all social theories, a revision that tends to subsume the most diverse social processes under the new topic. We know how many aspects of society were absorbed (at least temporarily) under the viewpoint of dependency or state studies. Similarly, the "sociology of daily life" could become the framework of all sociology. Conceptualization is required to avoid the indiscriminate use and undue extension of the notion, and this is precisely what we are missing: we do not have a concept of everyday life.

It is not idle to presume that the interest in everyday life is in large part due to vague and equivocal meanings of the term. For this reason, such a term is apt to designate a scattered and heterogeneous universe of phenomena whose delimitation and reciprocal relations would be precisely the task of the study of everyday life.

What is meant by daily life? This is a multifaceted notion, loaded with often controversial but unexplicit connotations. And this question usually leads us to another: What would be non-daily life? Although everything suggests that everyday life is usually resorted to as a critical reaction against certain processes and/or social theories, the opposition tends to remain shadowy. A selective list of European literature provided by Norbert Elias[50] shows the total lack of homogeneity regarding the use of the term as well as its respective implicit referents.

1. Daily life	Party
2. Repetitive routines	Extraordinary actions
3. Working life/"bourgeois" life	(Not dependent on work), leisure
4. The life of the masses	The life of dominant groups
5. Daily events	Historical events
6. Private-family life	Public-professional life
7. The sphere of natural, reflexive-spontaneous experiences, instrumental actions	The sphere of experience
8. Ideological perception, false awareness of reality	Scientific knowledge, true awareness

---

50   N. Elias, "Zum Begriff des Alltags," *Kölner Zeitschrift für Soziologie und Sozialpsychologie* 20 (1978).

By failing to assign an explicit meaning to the notion, this becomes loaded with prejudice and is not empirically controllable. The meanings listed in points 7 and 8 are illustrative. In the first case, we have a romantic view of everyday life that comes to replace the old category of "community" as opposed to a "society" oriented by formal rationality. The notion is imbued with positive connotations of harmonious coexistence untouched by modernization. In the second case and on the contrary, everyday life is identified with "traditional society," full of superstitions and atavistic beliefs that stand in opposition to the rationality of "modern society." In both cases, the study of everyday life can be more easily identified as the illustration of a worldview rather than a sociological analysis of a social phenomenon.

It is a fact, then, that interest in daily life exists in the absence of theoretical reflection, which fully justifies a denunciation of the use and abuse of the notion. Elias's warning, however, overstates historical perspective. In his great work on the passage from a feudal-warrior society to an absolutist-courtly society, Elias[51] satisfactorily shows how transformations of political structures are intertwined with changes in social habits and emotional attitudes. His analysis of the changes in criteria regarding "good conduct," table etiquette and bedtime routines, in the barriers involving aggressiveness and shame, his description of progressive affective self-control, and the formalization of social interaction (in short, the development of "courtesy" and its influence on forms of political struggle) are an excellent reconstruction of the conformation of daily life in a certain historical-social process. In the same vein, works such as Ariès's on childhood and the attitude toward death,[52] Shorter's on the family,[53] or Sennett's on the public sphere[54] are

---

51   N. Elias, *Über den Prozess der Zivilisation*, 2 vols. (Frankfurt: Suhrkamp, 1979); *El proceso de la civilización: investigaciones sociogenéticas y psicogenéticas*, 3rd ed. (Mexico: Fondo de Cultura Económica, 2009).

52   P. Ariès, *Centuries of Childhood* (New York: Vintage, 1962); *L'homme devant la mort* (Paris: Seuil, 1977).

53   E. Shorter, *The Making of the Modern Family* (New York: Basic Books, 1975).

54   R. Sennett, *El declive del hombre público* (Barcelona: Península, 1978).

valuable contributions to delimit the everyday in each era. These studies are so fruitful because the historical approach is suited to a characteristic feature of everyday life: the sedimentation of a set of activities and attitudes as routines and habits that remain consistent for a prolonged period. What varies from day to day, from year to year (that is, novelty) does not comprise the everyday. It can even be said that, in the end, one only becomes aware of everyday life as the past, since it is mainly a break with daily repetition that allows us to discover, via the new, the interrupted continuity. It is through temporal distance that we perceive everyday banality as something meaningful. Does this mean that only a historical approach can account for everyday life? No: common sense perceives daily life here and now, and social analysis must account for this phenomenon.

Unlike Elias and as per Gouldner, I believe it is possible to analyze everyday life as a contemporary phenomenon[55] and that this is fundamentally an enterprise of critical reflection. This is not (yet?) a critical concept, but a critique in two senses. Above all, it is a critique of everyday life itself. It has already been highlighted that there is no recognized conceptualization of what everyday life is. We can tentatively circumscribe it to the banal and routine existence that is barely perceived precisely because of its common and repetitive nature. As Gouldner beautifully and succinctly states, "Everyday-Life is the seen-but-unnoticed life."[56] It is that sum of routines that is always present, but never recorded because it is taken for granted. Or, to highlight one of the most important aspects: everyday life is the realm of the normal and the natural.

By taking a part of our life as normal and natural, we are elaborating a certain scheme of interpretation to conceive the other aspects of our living. By defining a set of activities as everyday, we are defining

---

55   Analyzing daily life here and now certainly posits greater difficulties because the researcher is part of his field of research. Without the distance created by historical perspective, the researcher must: a) distinguish what sedimented past is natural and normal in a present lived as a conjuncture, and b) problematize what are routine experiences and, therefore, unproblematic even for this same researcher.

56   A. Gouldner, op. cit., 422.

criteria of normality with which we perceive and evaluate the abnormal—that is, what is new and extraordinary, the problematic. Perhaps the most relevant aspect of everyday life is the production and reproduction of those basic certainties without which we would not know how to discern new situations or decide what to do. For an animal of polyvalent instincts, such as the human being, creating this basis of stability and certainty is an indispensable requirement; we need a secure environment to face the risks of a non-predetermined life. Faced with an open future, we resort to a familiar world where we can find the reasons "why," which in turn allow us to determine the reasons "for."[57] The question becomes, what criteria of normality are elaborated by what social groups in a given historical period. By focusing on everyday life, we allude to the experiences that make the social construction of the patterns of social coexistence appear as a natural order. The study of everyday life thus largely points to a critique of the production and use of those basic certainties we term "common sense."

Here, I must at least mention the issue of the relationship between science and common sense. Not knowing how to address such a difficult epistemological problem, perhaps it is enough for now to state two things. On the one hand, today it would be foolhardy to presume a fundamental identity shared by science and common sense that would in turn lead (as Gramsci appears to suppose)[58] to a progressive purification of common sense, to the point that everyone would eventually share the same scientific (i.e., objective) vision of the world. Faced with this type

---

57 A. Schutz, *El problema de la realidad social* (Buenos Aires: Amorrortu, 1974), 86 ff.

58 For Gramsci, the aim of philosophy must be the progressive, critical reflection of common sense. "To criticise one's own conception of the world means therefore to make it a coherent unit and to raise it to the level reached by the most advanced thought in the world. It therefore also means criticism of all previous philosophy, in so far as this has left stratified deposits in popular philosophy. The starting point of critical elaboration is the consciousness of what one really is, and is 'knowing thyself' as a product of the historical process to date which has deposited in you an infinity of traces, without leaving an inventory," Antonio Gramsci, *Selections from the Prison Notebooks of Antonio Gramsci* (New York: International Publishers, 1973), 627–28. [–Ed.]

of reductionism,[59] we must insist, following non-Cartesian principle, on the difference between knowledge and awareness. On the other hand, there is no scientific rationality detached from common sense, if only because they share the same language where the different meanings cannot be isolated. Even where scientific criticism reveals perceptions of common sense as appearance, such an appearance is still a moment of reality.[60]

In this context, I wish to return to the daily life of the researcher as part of scientific research. Social scientists also address and interpret the events that catch their attention and consider significant based on those categories and common places of daily life they share with others and which usually go unregistered. The analysis of social reality is not an aseptic task; it is permeated by everyday life and its presumptions of normality. Hence, Gouldner, in the aforementioned article, states that a "reflexive sociology" should exhibit the way in which theory is based on everyday life: "sociology's distinct function is to liberate everyday life from the neglect that is the fate of the commonplace. Which is to say, its task is to focalize the seen-but-not-unnoticed. Sociology's task, then, is to transform the common perspective on the common and, as a special case, to heighten the stable accessibility of the common: to make it visible. Sociology's task is thus to liberate subjugated reality, to emancipate the underprivileged reality."[61] Seen in this manner, sociological work does not lie so much in "discovering" the new as in "rescuing" what is already known. Gouldner draws a second conclusion from the fact that a social scientist and society both share an everyday life. The researcher is similar (though not identical) to the "object of study" and, therefore, cannot "explain" the latter because the explanation implies: 1) the judgment of an external witness directed toward another external witnesses, and 2) being impervious to judgments from the "inside." The

---

59   J. Nun, "El otro reduccionismo," in various authors, *América Latina: ideología y cultura* (San José, Costa Rica: FLACSO, 1982).

60   M. Beltrán, "La realidad social como realidad y apariencia," *Revista Española de Investigaciones Sociológicas* (Madrid) 19 (1982).

61   A. Gouldner, op. cit., 425.

social scientist's analysis will always be an interpretation whose validity depends not only on the conventions within his scientific community, but also on the intersubjective recognition of those being studied. In other words, society is not just the "material" but, simultaneously, the "interpreter" of said material. An approach that does not consider people's self-interpretation of their life and turns them into simple "objects" of study does not analyze social reality but changes it politically. I quote Gouldner: "To the extent that we treat men as things, and reward them for compliant thingification, we are not simply studying them in their 'natural' state but, rather, reinforcing and creating in them—rather than 'discovering'—the very thingified condition we have defined as 'natural.' [...] We are thus creating the very condition we will later claim to discover."[62] This is not the framework for deepening the epistemological debate, but the framework for recalling the impact of everyday life on the reflections in our scientific work.

The analysis of everyday life is also important in a second sense: a critique of non-everyday life. To opt for a study of everyday life is to opt for "the rebellion of the choir"[63] against a heroic conception of the world, of a social life restricted to the public-political space, of a way of life with its back to the means of living. It is, to again quote Gouldner, a critique of "heroic, achieving, performance-centered existence."[64]

We can direct this criticism in two directions. On the one hand, it is a critical reaction against a policy assumed as heroic act and redemptive sacrifice, conceived as the epic deeds of great men and the historical struggle of mass movements. In approaching everyday life, we approach a pre-political sphere in the sense of actions not directly related to the formation of the social order. Still, this does not mean that we should decouple everyday life from politics. On the contrary, if everyday life involves the production and reproduction of those basic certainties with which we evaluate the novel and problematic, we also deduce a good part of the criteria with which we face political decisions from

---

62   Ibid., 426.

63   J. Nun, "La rebelión del coro," *Nexos* (Mexico) 46 (1981).

64   A. Gouldner, op. cit., 421.

our daily experience. For me, it is precisely this relationship between pre-political experiences and political actions that is one of the main reasons for the relevance of everyday life studies.

On the other hand, these studies entail a critique of social transformations conceived exclusively as radical, rapid, and profound changes. It is not a question of ignoring revolutionary ruptures, but we learned from the convulsions of recent decades that structural changes are only such (i.e., relatively "irreversible") if they are accompanied by changes in everyday life. Therefore, the study of "social change" requires research on those almost imperceptible molecular modifications that are changing precisely the notions of what is normal and natural and helps us judge rupture as such. These small changes in the daily lives of different social groups are our indicators regarding the depth of social development.

An aside meant to avoid misunderstandings: I do not propose that we take everyday life for a kind of primary existence with respect to historical events, or for the "proper" form of life from which the various forms of economic and political organization would arise. That daily life manifests as relative permanence in time does not imply it exists outside the regulative principles of the social order. Also, that which is durable, apparently inert, is socially organized and must be reproduced day by day. Paraphrasing Marx, I would say that it is not enough to note that men always work, sleep, eat, and fight, but that one must determine how they do it.

3. The Field of Analysis

To avoid the aforementioned "inflation" of everyday life, the extension of the term toward a set of immeasurable phenomena, we should ask ourselves two questions.[65] First, is it a universal category? The question is whether what we understand as everyday life would be a characteristic

---

65   See N. Elias, "Zum Begriff des Alltags," op. cit., 28, and Ch. Lalive d'Épinay, "La vie quotidienne," *Cahiers Internationaux de Sociologie* LXXIV (January–June 1983).

of every society, across the world and throughout time. Can the notion be applied to the study of the English working class and the Vietnamese peasantry, Sor Juana Inés de la Cruz and the marginalized populations of Mexico City? Does it make sense to talk about daily life in colonial Peru?[66] One strategy would be to insert everyday life into the opposition between the private and public spheres and situate this in the differences that are peculiar to capitalism. Similarly, we could restrict the notion to the set of situations and practices almost completely devoid of symbolization as an aspect of the "process of disenchantment" (Weber) in the modern world. Or presume that every social order distinguishes and hierarchizes the times, establishing a limit between the everyday/banal/insignificant and the extraordinary/unique/significant. In this case, the question is not whether one can speak of a daily life in different societies and at different times, but of reconstructing the pillars of symbolic classification that a certain society elaborates to structure social life. If we accept period specificity, such as that employed by Alvin Gouldner regarding the varying meaning of "everyday life," then the precision of what is meant in an explicit historical-social context seems, to me, a legitimate undertaking.

The question, however, implicitly points to another fundamental observation: there is no daily life. The social differentiation among our nations leads to different structures and very different living situations; it consequently conditions different ways of life. We cannot study daily life, only a certain kind of daily life. How do we determine it? The delimitation of the everyday in reference to the non-everyday has already been pointed out, but I want to add two notes to clarify this construction of limits: 1) Although the concrete meaning of daily life is a singular definition (the experience of a particular individual), it always participates in a collective act of significance. Establishing the collective elaboration carried out by each social group of the respective meaning of daily life is precisely the task at hand. That said, 2) such a study cannot be restricted to an isolated group. Each social group conceives its daily life in reference (whether tacit or explicit) to other groups, assimilating or

---

66   J. Descola, *La vida cotidiana en el Perú en los tiempos de los españoles, 1710–1820* (Buenos Aires: Hachette, 1962).

modifying, aspiring or rejecting what it understands by the daily life of the former. We thus find many different daily lives determined by the context in which the different groups develop.

A second question now arises: Does everyday life exist as a specific area with its own structure? That is, does it represent a relatively autonomous field of analysis, with specific regularities that could be analytically isolated, or is it a false abstraction, so to speak—an empty notion that would be better replaced by the known categories of the private sphere, free time, family interaction, etc.? Indeed, when we try to empirically investigate everyday life and "operationalize" the notion, we resort to aspects usually considered by the sociologies of work, family, sexuality, deviant behavior, etc. And yet, talking about everyday life is not merely giving a fashionable name to classic lines of sociological research. There is a plus here, something more than "new wine in old wineskins." To focus on everyday life is to focus on an articulation that cannot be reduced to a series of juxtaposed phenomena. Family life + school experience + work environment + neighborhood interaction + sexual habits + ... *n* does *not* equal daily life. For example, school is meaningful to the child as a student, but also as a son or daughter, and member of a neighborhood gang. Children not only develop different temporal expectations (the school year, family life, play time) and spaces with different qualities (the classroom, the home, the street); they also modify the meaning of the same situation (say, obedience to the teacher) depending on whether they are at school, in front of their father, sister, or friends. It is the conjunction of an accumulation of situations and activities and the significance that each of them acquires in relation to the others that makes everyday life a limited scope. And though a limited area, it is not susceptible to a single approach: the example given could not be analyzed in exclusively sociological (role play, organizational rationality) or psychological (authority, socialization patterns) terms. Hence, I conceive everyday life as a hinge space of the social sciences, one requiring a multidisciplinary analysis.

From this perspective, everyday life is not an "autonomous" field with clear and precise limits, a preconstituted object of analysis. I reiterate that the very limits of everyday life are the subject of research. We cannot analyze everyday life without analyzing its delimitation with regard to the non-daily, and analyzing the layout and displacement of

such limits forces us to situate the daily within the set of social structures. Daily life is a limited but not isolated area. Only in relation to a
social totality and, specifically, to a structure of domination, can the significance of daily life as the "hidden face" of social life be apprehended.
Such a statement is valid for any social phenomenon. I highlight this
given the importance of ethnomethodological studies and their deficiencies in this regard. Despite the masterful subtlety of a Goffman[67]
interpreting face-to-face situations typical in daily relationships, the
lack of reflection on the historical-structural context leaves the analysis
of such microsocial interactions lacking reference. In other words: such
an approach only describes what the actors understand as normal and
natural but is unable to criticize what their behaviors merely reproduce
of the inversion of subject and object (of living labor and dead labor,
in Marx's terms).[68] By assuming extant capitalist structures as a given
external to the analysis, the analysis itself ends up reproducing the rei-
fication of social relations.

Without ignoring the contributions of Goffman or Garfinkel, I
want to recall Agnes Heller's definition. She understands "'everyday
life'" as the aggregate of those individual reproduction factors which,
pari passu, make social reproduction possible."[69] She thus emphasizes
the mediating character that relates singular practices to the production
and reproduction of the social order while accounting for the structural determination of subjective experiences. We can conclude, alongside Norbert Elias, that there is no good reason why research on the
structures of social coexistence (which, carried out unilaterally, may
well be called "objectivist") and research of the meaning with which the

---

67   E. Goffman, *La presentación de la persona en la vida cotidiana* (Buenos Aires:
     Amorrortu, 1971). [–Ed.]

68   The distinction between living work and dead work is developed by Marx in
     Grundisse (1857–58). Living labor is unobjectified labor, the labor of the living
     subject that exists as a transforming capacity; dead labor exists in its objecti-
     fied condition in space and time as already done by living labor. See K. Marx,
     Elementos fundamentales para la crítica de la economía política 1857–1858
     (Buenos Aires: Siglo XXI, 1971). [–Ed.]

69   Agnes Heller, *Everyday Life* (London: Routledge & Kegan Paul, 1984), 3.

participants themselves live the different aspects of their coexistence (which analyzed unilaterally, may well be called "subjectivist") should be incompatible. Especially if we consider the process of social change, the study of experience (i.e., how people relate to their experience of social structures and contribute to their reproduction and transformation) is as indispensable as the study of the long-term, unplanned, and blind mechanisms of linkage present in structural change.[70]

Summarizing the above, I propose placing everyday life at the crossroads of two relationships. On the one hand, the relationship between macro and microsocial processes. Instead of reducing microsocial processes to the level of the individual (as opposed to society), everyday life should be seen as a crystallization of social contradictions that allow us to explore the "cellular texture" of society for some constitutive elements of macrosocial processes. From this point of view, everyday life becomes the field of analysis of those contexts in which diverse, specific experiences are recognized as part of collective identities. This refers, on the other hand, to the relationship between the concrete practices of people and their objectification under certain life conditions. Instead of reducing daily life to the reproductive habits of social inequality (Bourdieu),[71] we should also be noted how, given the subjective experience of said structural inequality, everyday practices produce (and transform) objective living conditions. Seen in this manner, everyday life proffers itself as a privileged place to study what, using Sartre's propitious expression, man does with what has been made of him.

---

70   N. Elias, "Zum Begriff des Alltags," op. cit., 23.

71   See P. Bourdieu, *The Distinction: Criteria and Social Bases of Taste* (Madrid: Taurus, 1988). [–Ed.]

III

Political Realism:
A Matter of Time

1. Realism as a Matter of Time

Everyone invokes realism as a fundamental condition for democracy—
for its establishment and development. What does it mean, however, to be
realistic? It is a call to determine, in theoretical and practical terms, what
might be? It is not about what is or what should be, but about what is possible?[72] I understand political realism as a critical category referring to the
construction of a new order. Social transformation demands a critique of
historical givens, but also of the possible future. Machiavelli already analyzed the power struggle from this point of view: the conquest of power is
part of the order to be built and, therefore, we must choose between the
multiple possibilities each situation opens so that the changes undertaken
can give rise to a stable order. Here is the topicality of Machiavellian realism for our countries: linking innovation to duration.

    The social order is not a fact of nature, nor does it respond to historical
necessity. It is a human creation. Hence, the ordering of society is an artificial and precarious construction. Here, it is worth noting the artificiality
and precariousness of all orders meant to take account of time.[73] In our soci-

---

72   See the analysis F. Hinkelammert, "El realismo en política como arte de lo
    posible," in ¿Qué es 'realismo' en política?, ed. N. Lechner (Buenos Aires: Edi-
    torial Catálogos, 1987).

73   I have long been preoccupied with time, though I always felt overwhelmed
    by the subject. For this reason, I undertake this essay without further bib-
    liographic support. I rely mainly on N. Luhmann, Vertrauen. Ein Mechanis-
    mus der Reduktion sozialer Komplexität (Stuttgart: Enke Verlag, 1973) (English

eties, convulsed by a dizzying sequence of events, it may be appropriate to emphasize the importance of duration. It is not that ruptures and changes are irrelevant, but they will be futile if they do not contribute toward developing a lasting order. Only in time does human activity take shape.

A fantasy can be thus described: "not that love and death did not happen there, but there was no time in which they could have a meaning."[74] But social practice takes time in order to make sense. We must have time; that is, we need to structure time so that it does not get diluted into a series of aimless instants. Time always runs, spelling finitude and putting an end to life. The desire for immortality arises against the course of time; it is the wish to suspend time and overcome the limits of individual existence. If there is no eternity, at least there is always a search for continuity.

Creating order is a way to create continuity. It is about articulating countless changes (no one knows whether these are great or ephemeral) so they can be experienced as a process: past, present, future. Time is constituted in the tension between an event and its duration. I cannot address a topic as difficult and unknown as a theory of time. I can only presume time is an external variable or precondition of any political action as well as an object of political decision. Doing politics involves structuring time.

Whoever wants to do something needs time. Every possible action takes time. Anyone knows that the fruits of an agricultural plan or an industrial investment, a research project or commercial expansion require a time of maturation, and proposed goals depend on the amount of time available. Having time is a most precious good, and all the drama of politics is revealed in one little phrase: "but time was not allowed to the Commune."[75] Considering time's value, we must decide how to use it. This is an important decision because time can be wasted by not acting in a timely manner, by spending too much time on something, or by

---

translation, *Trust and Power*, New York: John Wiley, 1979), and K. Heinemann and P. Ludes, "Zeitbewusstsein und Kontrolle der Zeit," *Kölner Zeitschrift für Soziologie* 20 (1978). Interesting contributions on the "economy of time" are found in the debate "On Time," *Quarterly Journal of Economics* 4 (1973).

74   D. M. Thomas, *The White Hotel* (London: Penguin Books, 1981), 14–15.

75   Karl Marx, *The Civil War in France* (Chicago: Charles H. Kerr & Company, 1934), 58.

proposing that too much be done in the time available. It is a problem of proportions, a problem of realism: the elaboration of possible options and the selection of "the best possible one" is also a matter of time.

There is an objective time that allows us to measure and classify events temporally, but that tells us nothing about the subjective experience of it. What is urgent, slow, or medium-term varies according to our individual time consciousness, the value we assign to it, and our time horizon backward and forward. That is to say: social diversity implies different temporalities. There is no single time; there are times, social times.[76] A worker or an entrepreneur, a retiree or a student, an unemployed person or a civil servant, a woman or a man, all have different notions of time and, therefore, tend to use their time differently. At the same time, however, there is a simultaneous reality for all of them. A difficulty of politics is to link both dimensions (subjective urgency and objective deadlines) to create a contemporary order.

How can we synchronize the different temporalities? This question presents us with a decisive aspect in the construction of the social order and, specifically, of a political system.

2. The Loss of Familiarity

Realism is a matter of time in two ways: 1) as historical awareness of the effectiveness of the past in the present moment, and 2) as a choice of what to act for in an open future.

Both aspects are linked: the anticipation of the future usually resorts to the past.[77] Generally, our future projects (our "what for" reasons) are

---

76 Conceptions of time shape social reality and are structured by it. Generally, social representations of time have been related to economic and social activity, age, family structure, income level, and education. See D. Mercure, "L'étude des temporalités sociales," *Cahiers Internationaux de Sociologie* (Paris) LXVII (1979).

77 See A. Schutz, *El problema de la realidad social* (Buenos Aires: Amorrortu, 1974) (chapter 3, "La elección entre diversos proyectos de acción").

based on our past experiences (the reasons "why"). The past offers us a familiarity that does not require, in each specific case, a conscious explanation of the world and its reason for being. We are born and raised in a familiar world with a self-evident sense, and it is against this backdrop that we develop relatively secure expectations about what will come to pass. It is assumed that the familiar remains, that the proven is repeated, that the known is prolonged into the future. In this way, historical consciousness offers, day by day, the criteria for anticipating tomorrow.

This resource of history is only rational to the extent that there is a continuity with the past. Today, due to rapid and drastic social changes, we no longer have historical experiences that serve as a fixed reference. We find, in all modern societies, both capitalist and "socialist," an erosion of social continuity that causes a temporary constraint and contributes substantially to the "crisis of governance." In the words of Alvin Tofler, "Too many decisions, too fast, about too many strange and unfamiliar problems—not some imagined 'lack of leadership'—explain the gross incompetence of political and governmental decisions today."[78]

In our countries, the loss of the familiar world is much more traumatic because of the violence with which it occurred. What is more, we now must face the authoritarian mutilation of our past alongside the simultaneous construction of a new order. The difficulties inherent to this task are thus further aggravated. The structuring of social relations can no longer resort to the familiarity of the past as the realm of the normal and the natural. Political renewal must create its own time horizon. And this coincidence of the restructuring of society and the restructuring of time marks the specific characteristics of what it is to "be realistic" with regard to democratization.

Our problem, more concretely formulated, is to have to elaborate a time horizon in the conditions created by a dictatorship that is not only reluctant to attempt to structure the future by means of deadlines, but also, and through its own decomposition, locks us in an immediate present.

How can we conceive, within the narrow horizons of this crossroads, the perspective of the future required for solving the crisis?

---

78   Alvin Toffler, *The Third Wave* (London: Pan Books, 1981), 427.

3. Two Time Problems

The construction of a democratic order demands the synchronization of different temporalities and faces two major problems: time constraints and unpredictability.

First, time is a scarce commodity and, therefore, valuable. Capitalism coined the slogan of modern times: "time is money." There is never enough free time available; anticipating the future, setting goals, and selecting means are always limited by time pressures. Time moves on, does not stand still, and sometimes passes so quickly that it renders bills obsolete before they are even enacted. Awareness of ephemeral time increases even more when actions are no longer embedded in established routines and normative frameworks. The erosion of usual boundaries does not increase time availability; on the contrary, time gets wasted. So that time does not fly away as during a vacation day, it is necessary to distribute its uses and establish deadlines.

The scarcity of time entails a classification of demands according to a scale of priorities. On the one hand, the value of each activity depends on its temporal priority. On the other hand, what has a deadline has priority. Deadlines (whether external or self-imposed) indicate what needs to be done.

Setting deadlines is a matter of power: whoever sets a deadline conditions the use of the other person's time, and what activities can be finished in the allowed time span. That is, determining a time limit also determines the limits of what is possible. The multiple possibilities of the future are reduced to what is possible in a specific timeframe. Hence, the political struggle is also a conflict regarding available deadlines. It seeks to extend one's own deadlines (the extreme slogan being "goals and not deadlines") and shorten the deadlines of others (i.e., the ultimatum). Regarding the first goal: the longer the term, the greater the range of possibilities, the less weight each option has, and the greater the freedom of selection. Regarding the second goal: the shorter the deadline, the fewer available possibilities, the more rigid the alternative, and the more reduced freedom of decision. In both cases, the field of political action depends on temporal pressure. Everyone is trying to gain time—that is, ensure a greater range of possibilities within a given period and, therefore, a greater freedom of action. On the other hand, those who lack time lose autonomy, for a rush dictates their use of time.

Deadlines can be partially influenced (timing) to prevent them from coinciding. And yet, there can always be an accumulation of equivalent priorities which, in extreme cases, will lead to overload and, eventually, a paralysis of the selective and resolutive mechanisms. Not only is the anticipation of the future lost; control over ongoing events also gets mislaid and, looking back, even acquired continuity crumbles. From this point of view, being realistic requires a careful budget of time so as not to get caught during the wrong period, unable to react.

Of course, we understand that calculating time is not a mathematical equation. Sometimes events precipitate and multiply in such a way that time seems lacking; sometimes nothing happens, nothing new comes up, and time languishes, stagnates, and flies away. In both cases, realistic calculation acts on time. Being realistic entails taking the time not to be overrun by the urgency of events or even limiting time to crystallize emotional energies within a symbolically significant horizon.

The second difficulty lies in the radical unpredictability of the future. In principle, and having discarded the impossible (i.e., utopias), everything is possible. However, if everything were indeed possible, if we did not have certain expectations and certain evidence regarding the future, we would not dare get out of bed. Dread would paralyze us. In fact, not everything is possible. However, the question of what in fact *is* remains. We face an open future that contains many more possibilities than can be realized. Meaning that not every possible future becomes updated as the present. The question is: How do we reduce the complexity of the possible future to a real present?

To clarify the question, Luhmann distinguishes between the actual future and the present to come. Every present has its current future as a direct horizon of its possibilities. We are, so to speak, contemporaries of a future that will only partially be our present later. Moving toward the future, new presents and, simultaneously, new future horizons are produced via a selection of open possibilities. That is, the current future is permanently condensed into a coming present that, in turn, generates a new future. However, duration is produced to the extent that the actual and the coming present remain identical. Instead, there are events where discontinuities arise between the present future and the present to come. Uncertainty is born out of the awareness of this difference.

How do we reduce uncertainty—that is, the distance between the actual future and the present to come? This has been the theme of political realism since Machiavelli: "No government should ever believe that it is always possible to follow safe policies. Rather, it should be realized that all courses of action involve risks: for it is the nature of things that when one tries to avoid one danger another is always encountered. Still, prudence entails knowing how to assess the dangers, and to choose the least undesirable course of action as being the right one to follow."[79]

For Machiavelli fortune is an inescapable moment of politics, with a rank equivalent to necessity and virtue. Politics is a continuous confrontation with the unexpected, either defending the established order through dikes and channels that conduct the overflow of the normal riverbed, or by boldly attacking "irruptions." Subsequently, with the advance of formal rationality (calculation-means-end), politics will be charged with the task of foreseeing and mastering events. That is, it will be intended to reduce uncertainty by controlling time.

Modern politics is characterized by the attempt to reduce insecurity (what is possible?) to a set of causalities from which to select those options that produce the desired ends. Instead of waiting for the future, by letting it become the present, we seek to anticipate it, creating it as the projected result of present decisions. In other words, it is about ensuring the connection between the actual present and the present to come by planning for the future: planning as foresight. If we could calculate and thus master the possibilities of the future, we would effectively eliminate insecurity— if everything was under control, time would not be a problem.

Each reading of the newspaper confirms the narrow limits within which we can dominate the course of events; the optimism of technical reason lies behind us. The projection of long and complex causal chains does not diminish possibilities but increases them. Each variable considered multiplies possible correlations, and instead of a reduction in complexity there is an increase. That is, planning makes the possibilities we

---

79   Niccoló Machiavelli, *The Prince* (Cambridge: Cambridge University Press, 1988), 79.

are likely to face in the future explicit but says nothing about which of them will actually come to pass. This forces us to reconsider the usual idea of planning.

The meaning of the plan is not derived from the efficiency of a formal means-to-end rationality but, on the contrary, from its insufficiency. There is an irreducible unpredictability. Whether a decision (political or economic) is correct or not can only be checked ex post once it either succeeds or fails. Success and failure are judgments that follow action, but decision happens earlier. We need to compromise (take a "gamble") without knowing the outcome of the action. There is therefore a temporal distance that cannot be bridged by any kind of foresight.

While it is impossible to foresee future reality, it is possible to decide the desired goals ex ante. That is, establish the criteria by which to select among the open possibilities. Such a selection is a bet insofar as it anticipates an outcome that is unknown to all. We can define the political decision as a risky anticipation of the future (Luhmann). This is an inevitable risk that gets absorbed by specific roles. Unlike the civil servant, the politician (or the business manager) is judged according to the success or failure of their decisions and not according to compliance with formal rules.

One way to link the previous decision and the outcome of the action is the plan. This provides a temporal bridge that allows us to contrast the coming present with the desired future. It is not a forecast, but a bet: the commitment to a determined, but unpredictable, outcome. Whoever submits a plan shoulders responsibility regarding the proposed result. The meaning of the plan, however, goes further. Although for the politician and, of course, for the country it may be decisive whether the proposed goal is met or not, the validity of the plan does not depend on its success. Also, a plan that is not fulfilled serves as a reference against which we can evaluate possibilities and order events in terms of their significance. Without plans we would drown in a sea of arbitrary facts. The plan, then, serves as a structuring of time that allows us to articulate the coming events with the current future horizon.

4. The Freedom of the Other

Here we are interested in the problems of time in social relations, from which issues the fundamental criterion of realism: the freedom of the other. Other people are free to act, and how they will use their potential possibilities in the different available situations is not foreseeable. I cannot determine the future actions of others; I can only fix my own stances in relation to them.

Here I do not seek to address the dynamics of decision-making, but merely hint at the underlying problem: How to respect the freedom of others and, at the same time, reduce their unpredictability?

The question assumes that the demand for realism in politics is only addressed, 1) in a situation of uncertainty, and 2) that uncertainty cannot be eliminated, but limited.

A first reduction of (in principle) infinite possibility is enabled, as we said, by the presence of the past as a familiar world. Its permanence allows us to project self-evidence into the future. In this case, the temporal dimension solves the problem inherent to the social dimension: the exclusion of unexpected actions. However, to the extent that such familiarity is no longer accessible to everyday experience, the delimitation of unpredictability must be socially constructed.

The main social mechanism for reducing the unpredictability of the other is the development of expectations.[80] We form expectations about the future behavior of others based on our own personal experience, our knowledge of social regularities, the degree of validity of social norms, the existence of routines and habits as well as a "sense of the situation" in each specific case. That is, we reduce a limited set of possibilities to a framework of probabilities and act "as if" we know each other's future actions. The expectation imputes to others a certain pattern of behavior but does not force them to comply with it. Others retain their freedom of action and will not renounce possible innovations unless they receive relative security. That is, the efficiency of expectations requires some reciprocal adjustment.

---

80 Heinemann and Ludes offer a systematic view; see note 73.

As we go on, I will not deal with that reciprocity of expectations based on a legal order, even though that aspect is the most important. From the viewpoint of realism, the pre-juridical field is more interesting: that scattered space where the social and moral obligations that lead us to expect others' effective compliance with legal prescriptions (e.g., *pacta sunt servanda*) are created. Being realistic, we refer more to what others can (and not what they should or should not) do. What can or cannot be done depends on the time available and, above all, time expectations. Consequently, differences in objective availability as much as in subjective expectations of time become a basic aspect of realism.

The differences arise, on the one hand, from the very differentiation of society. Each social field creates specific time horizons that, in turn, structure the various social activities. The temporality of the rural world is different from that of the urban space, and the temporality of political life is also different from the temporality of family life. Additionally, there are different horizons within each activity, and it is not the same for a laborer or an entrepreneur, a minister, an opposition deputy, or a municipal councillor.

The differences in our societies can be of such magnitude that adjustment becomes quite difficult. The urgency of an unemployed laborer to obtain work, or of a resident to access housing is hardly compatible with the equally legitimate deadlines for the fiscal budget or economic productivity. Time has a different value. Are such differences measurable by means of a general equivalent? It seems that "time is not money." At least in Latin America, assessments of what is meant by "urgency" or the "medium-term" seem to be far too distant to be transformed into an "objective date" (e.g., within a month).

How can we synchronize our differing time expectations? Generally, time is structured in a cooperative way: no calls at night, appointments start on time, contractual expiration dates are honored, etc. This implies a similar awareness of time among the participants, the result of extensive cultural development.[81] In these cases, a tacit synchroni-

---

81   On the interaction between political changes and psychosocial mutations in a "long wave," see N. Elias's great text, *Über den Prozess der Zivilisation* (Frankfurt: Suhrkamp, 1979); *El proceso de la civilización: investigaciones*

zation takes place based on the internalization of natural needs (rest time), social norms (rules of courtesy), and legal norms (mandatory legal deadlines). These mechanisms, which we continually use in everyday life, seem insufficient in political life, especially if we consider the aforementioned lags in the conception of time. A discontemporaneous quality that questions the very notion of continuity is superimposed on the objective simultaneity of facts. How to build a political order when some demand the perpetuation of what exists, others claim for revolution now, and others postulate agreed ruptures?

5. To Be Realistic by Trusting

Democratization cannot wait for a cultural homogenization of time conceptions. On the other hand, however, the social roots of its institutions require a generalized notion of continuity. The viability of any political system, and of the democratic system in specific, entails it being seen as durable. When the continuity of order is not relatively assured, no one will risk investing their time and energy, well-being and hopes in an order sans perspective. Therefore, in our countries, the institutional construction of democracy must be accompanied by a synchronization of the different temporalities that make it possible to structure a shared horizon.

A first structuring is offered by the democratic institutions themselves through periodic elections. These make it possible to calculate in advance when social changes may occur, and this is linked to the alternation of the parties in government. However, even if we assume that the elections represent a shared time limit, the differences themselves are not resolved within each period.[82] Realism requires mechanisms of reciprocal adjustment of expectations to bridge the gap between the

---

sociogenéticas y psicogenéticas, 3rd ed. (Mexico: Fondo de Cultura Económica, 2009).

82   Political dynamics entail continuous changes of pace and can cause accelerations that go beyond institutionalized horizons. It is worth recalling, in

present and the future (between the actual future and the present to come). A mechanism that is certainly limited, but of very estimable practical relevance, is trust. Through Niklas Luhmann's study, we can understand trust as a realistic way of dealing with the issue of time.

When we cannot eliminate the insecurity of the future by controlling the course of events, we can at least try to increase acceptable uncertainty. This is what trust does. Instead of defending itself against the unpredictability of the other, trust takes the other as an alter ego, and the other's freedom of action is then made co-responsible for the future. Those who act confidently do so as if there were only certain possibilities ahead and, committing themselves to a specific future; they offer themselves to the other in the realization of a common future. That is, an individual can trust another as long as they trust in the intersubjective constitution of the world.

How does a relationship of trust occur? Trust is not something that can be demanded of another: you start by delivering it. It offers confidence by signaling to the other certain expectations regarding yourself, with the promise of fulfilling them. That is, a self-representation of the self is communicated to the other, and we commit ourselves to remain that self over time. Trust is thus a risky anticipation: one commits to a certain future behavior without knowing if the other will respond accordingly. This is a voluntary offer, and the other may or may not accept the signs of trust, preferring to keep their autonomy by keeping their distance.[83] However, once someone responds to the trust on offer, they commit in turn. They are also bound in their future actions according to created expectations. As soon as a relationship of trust is established, there is a reciprocal obligation. It does not matter if the self-representation corresponds to a real personality or has been feigned. Trust demands that participants act as if they are really what their images promise. All self-representation obligates the person to

---

the Chilean case, the disruption of the deadlines produced by the 1972–73 expectations of revolution and the anti-authoritarian protests in 1983.

83   A minister once said that a situation of "slight misfortune" allowed for the best relationship with the head of state. This might be a perception that corresponds more generally with the so-called posts of confidence.

remain the same as they showed themselves to be,[84] an image that is not static but develops through interaction. Therefore, only those who participate in the interaction can gain confidence, presenting opportunities for their self-representation to be tested and learning to incorporate expectations alien to their own image. Someone who does not expose themselves, who is disinterested in the opinion of others, may be a calculable factor, but not a reliable actor. People must be willing to respond to the trust given in order to be able to, in turn, offer trust. Conversely, someone who does not commit to other's demonstrations of trust is not trustworthy.

We can never have total and reliable information about the future. Therefore, it is necessary to overdraw existing information and bet on a certain result. Trust anticipates a certain future, but also eventual refutation. In other words, to trust is to reflect on insecurity. When a critical alternative is not weighed, we are acting based on mere hope. When we trust another, we always contemplate abuse because trust does not ignore risk, it instead offers an advantage over safe expectation. While the latter collapses at the very first disappointment, trust is more stable. By renouncing uncertainty, the tolerance barrier for insecurity increases; there may even be some indifference (those who trust require less information). Additionally, trust entails compensation mechanisms. Abuses of trust, the crossing of certain limits, are punished with the rupture of the relationship (distrust, that is).

Regarding the time problems mentioned above, trust makes it possible to reduce the complexity of the future in a double sense. On the one hand, trust in others counteracts time shortages. Thus, a deputy relies on the accurate work of the public administration to be able to gain time and meet social demands instead of reviewing official statistics. The inner workings of the democratic system rest on trust "until further notice." A parliament, however excellent its composition, cannot control all the acts of the executive power. It can, however, control its confidence in the honesty and sincerity of the executive and, at the

---

84   The divergence between self-representation and actual political practice may explain the distrust inspired—rightly or wrongly—by the Communist Party.

slightest sign of abuse, withdraw said trust (e.g., Watergate).[85] When this happens, when mistrust reigns, a lot more time is consumed because each decision requires more information that is, in turn, less reliable.

On the other hand, trust in the other limits insecurity by anticipating risks and offering a generalized punishment mechanism. No politician is unaware that an adversary can abuse their trust. Therefore, trust must be employed cautiously. If someone acted naively, the blame for any abuse would fall on them, and they would expose themselves to ridicule. However, if one trusts with awareness of the risks and another does not comply with what was planned, that unpredictability ceases to be an aggression that takes the trusting party by surprise. Disappointment is a possibility, but a specific one. Instead of focusing on countless possible options, it is enough to be prepared to cope with that frustration. This will no longer be the work of external events but can respond, punishing unfulfilled expectations.

6. Political Confidence

Luhmann's profound and substantial analysis discloses a valuable contribution when it comes to "being realistic" in politics. One way to narrow the field of the possible is to develop trusting relationships. Trusting others makes us less vulnerable to their unpredictability because we incorporate this into our expectations. Trust does not eliminate uncertainty, but it allows us to tolerate a greater degree of insecurity. External insecurity is compensated for by internal security. In this case, the problem is transferred to those internal resources that can be mobilized in case of disappointment. This would lead us to the phenomena of sanction and forgiveness, sacrifice and consolation, all of which have barely been studied in relation to political action.

There is, however, another major problem. Trust is fundamentally an intersubjective relationship that develops in social interaction

---

85   For Watergate, see "El significado de los derechos humanos para los países capitalistas desarrollados," in *Obras* I, 467, note b. [–Ed.]

through a temporal sequence (trust is offered, accepted and returned, tested and confirmed). As such, it plays a preponderant role in the relations that link political actors to each other and, above all, in the genesis of the so-called political class of a country. This is no small thing and can be decisive when a new political system is being built.[86] But even if politicians succeed in creating an atmosphere of trust among themselves, is there trust in the "system" itself? The confidence that one or another person places in this or that leader, in this or that party, is not enough. This is indispensable, as it offers the politician (the party) the opportunity to justify said commitment through a successful outcome. Let us remember that the policy is evaluated according to a criterion of success, verified ex post. Here, trust allows to bridge the temporal distance between the previous commitment and the subsequent evaluation, between the bet and the result. Confidence operates as a "term loan" with regard to the promised success, temporarily limiting uncertainty. The politician (the party) is invested with the desired future within a certain timeframe; once completed, the elections ratify or revoke the originally proffered confidence. However, elections function as a "motion of confidence" in relation to a government program or a government, only laterally expressing (via abstentionism, voting "none of the above," or voting for anti-system parties) confidence in the system.

Summarizing, let us try to specify two of the problems facing a realistic vision of democratization. Our first question is: How to create confidence within the "political class"? The problem already arises from the situation of dictatorship itself. In the absence of a public-representative institutionality, the development of relations of trust seems to be a condition for the constitution of a "political class." Initially, however, everything advises us to be suspicious, and there are plenty of reasons. Nothing encourages politicians to initiate relationships of trust among themselves except the perception that distrust often triggers negative reciprocity. Like trust, distrust

---

86 This is suggested—for the Spanish case—by the notes of E. Tierno Galván, *Cabos sueltos* (Barcelona: Bruguera, 1981). See also R. López Pintor and J. I. Wert Ortega, "La otra España. Insularidad e intolerancia en la tradición político-cultural española," *Revista Española de Investigaciones Sociológicas* (Madrid) 19 (1982).

tends to be a "self-fulfilling prophecy." Those who distrust will be treated first with leniency, then with caution, and finally with distrust, thus confirming their initial misgivings. The result is a reciprocal paralysis.

Additionally, a climate of trust between political leaders is equally relevant during the democratic process since it contributes to providing a perspective of duration. Given the public visibility of the "political scene" in democracy, the tolerance politicians display toward each other regarding the unpredictability of the other conditions the image society creates about the future's "natural" insecurity. For this reason, the distrust that the "political class" may arouse in the citizenry (with greater or lesser motive) is important. Suffice it to recall the dangers of "disenchantment."[87] Which brings us to the second problem.

The main question is: How do we build trust in democracy? The stability of the democratic system depends on society's confidence in an order. Now, what does it mean to trust an order? Trust encompasses both the "identification" of citizens with the political system and its "credibility" in the eyes of public opinion. This is based on the effectiveness of the procedures (legality), but also on a "sense of order" that allows for limits to be placed on the uncertainty of an open future. From these few indications, it is already clear that "trust in an order" has a meaning other than interpersonal trust. It is not an intersubjective relationship, as Luhmann puts it.[88] Nor is it a synonym for legitimacy. It is, rather, that substrate in which the belief of legitimacy is gestated. Order is recognized as valid because it is trusted. Conversely, an atmosphere of mistrust undermines claims to legitimacy (even if legality exists).

---

87   Paramio's thesis—"disenchantment would have been a disenchantment with politics, a rediscovery of politics as a secular activity"—highlights precisely the dissonance between the expectations of time (millenarianism) that emerged under the dictatorship, and the subsequent experience of the real time changes required. Ludolfo Paramio, "El desencanto español como crisis de una forma de hacer política," in ¿Qué significa hacer política?, ed. N. Lechner (Lima: Desco, 1982).

88   Luhmann himself indicates the difficulties when referring his conceptualization to the political system (op. cit., 58 ff.).

Despite the importance of trust processes for representative democracy, we know little about the effective connection between them. Perhaps we should explore it on the side of the so-called order value[89] that the political system acquires thanks to its duration. Over time, citizens internalize what they can and should "normally" do, make sure that everyone complies with the "rules of the game," punishing infractions, and learn which actions entail gratification. Every political system and, particularly, every democracy, rests on the development of such order security. When democracy radiates that relative predictability, even the most reluctant adversaries, the cynical and apathetic, begin to invest expectations, interests, and desires in the continuity of said order; a continuity that, in turn, is nourished by innumerable, small daily actions. These actions do not yet imply active support for democracy, or even some kind of opportunism; merely the type of conformism that is indispensable for the development of a daily routine. The consequences, however, are inordinate: since no one cares to lose their investments, whether economic or emotional, everyone is interested in preserving a lasting order.

We thus return to time as a fundamental aspect of political realism.

7. The Construction of Time in Democratization

Perhaps my initial intuition has been better outlined with this look at "everyday life": realism implies a calculation of time, but this is not a mathematical calculation. Political action, like all human action, obeys not only cognitive reasoning but also affective and symbolic reasoning. Perhaps these dimensions condition (much more than cognitive reason) our daily experiences with political time: the harassing nature of pending issues, irretrievably lost opportunities, an inescapable tomorrow, or

---

89 The notion comes from H. Popitz, *Prozesse der Machtbildung* (Tübingen: Mohr, 1968). I used it to describe the functioning of the authoritarian order in *La conflictiva y nunca acabada construcción del orden deseado*, chapter II, "Poder y orden. La estrategia de la minoría consistente," in *Obras* II, 304 ff.

that paralysis of time that produces the vision of an irreversible outcome (the fatality of destiny).

Throughout this exploration we have glimpsed the complexity of differences in temporalities. We found that the meaning of time partially depends on the affective structure of the participants. For example, whether emotional instincts demand immediate gratification or if (and to what degree) they admit procrastination. On the other hand, this is closely linked to symbolic representations of time. These may have been culled, for example, from the experience of natural life cycles (birth, maturation, death) or oriented in accordance with abstract social horizons (modernization processes), each with different patterns of periodization. Finally, we need to assign increased value to mythical images regarding the conception of time, such as the idea of progress (linear evolution), but also the idea of a cyclical time. The vision of a lost golden age ruined by the presumed actions of some maleficent group (the Jews, the Marxists, etc.), a "true world" that awaits recovery even at the price of sacrificing the present, is still powerful, and one need not mention the effects of such eschatological worldviews (whether conservative or revolutionary) on the conception of politics.[90]

A first conclusion emerges from this reflection. Politics does not allow itself to be reduced to the antinomy of rationalism-irrationalism, and a rational policy is not merely one that responds to formal rationality. This false identification leads to a narrow, if not witless, type of realism. Even as the reductionism present in such Realpolitik is obvious, it is likewise difficult to determine those other dimensions in the rational calculation of the possible.

Now, are these only dimensions "to be taken into account" via realistic calculation? This would mean restricting realism to a methodological problem of political analysis. Realism is more than a logic of calculation. By understanding realism as a critical category, we also refer to a reasoning of action. We refer to an elaboration of time. When we ask what possibilities democratization supports, what possibilities it opens, the critique of "the possible" refers us to the production of

---

90   See U. Windisch, "Le temps: représentations, archétypes et efficacité du discours politique," *Cahiers internationaux de Sociologie* (Paris) LXXV (1983).

temporalities. Seeing things from this perspective, I would draw a second conclusion.

I believe that the possibility of democracy means working politically over time and doing so in at least two ways. On the one hand, through a reconversion of the authoritarian past. To be realistic is to recognize the present effectiveness of the past. Therefore, it neither ignores nor adopts it as mere inertia. Realism forces us to update the history of the dictatorship, incorporating it into the process of democratization. For ghosts to disappear, a "past overcome" must be made present. This is the meaning of reparation (both material and symbolic) for injustices suffered and pains repressed: a restitution of the past as a history of human dignity.[91]

On the other hand, realism requires producing time as continuity into the future. Crafting a future for the democratic order means, first and foremost, building an order in which everyone has a future. So that everyone has a future (even though said future will not be one and the same for everyone), it must be conceived as the collective work of a plurality of people. Hence the need for a "certain" adjustment of different time notions, different horizons, and different temporal expectations. The same democratic institutions offer synchronization mechanisms: periodic elections, legal deadlines, administrative routines, trust control, etc. However, the effectiveness of the formal structuring of temporality lies, as we have seen, in the emotional-affective and symbolic-imaginary spheres. It will ultimately depend on these contexts whether the democratic order will be embraced as a social elaboration of a shared future. And this will depend, in turn, on how each of us responds to the issue of realism: What can we ask of democracy?

---

91 Reparation as an "act of justice" is only one aspect of the complex and painful work of learning from our past. It is worth emphasizing once again the force of time, whether as memory or as amnesia, in present action. Durkheim writes, "for in each one of us, in differing degrees, is contained the person we were yesterday, and indeed in the nature of things it is even true that our past personae predominate, since the present is necessarily insignificant when compared with the long period of the past because of which we have emerged in the form we have today." Emile Durkheim, *The Evolution of Educational Thought: Lectures on the Formation and Development of Secondary Education on France* (London: Routledge & Kegan Paul, 1977), 11.

IV

There Are Those
Who Die of Fear

1. Fear as a Political Problem

Who is afraid and of what? I understand fear as the perception of a threat, real or imagined, and I thus propose we explore fear under authoritarianism in Latin American societies of the Southern Cone.[92] There are, of course, the specific perceptions of different social groups, but there are certain "mortal dangers" common to them all. What do people perceive as a life threat? First and of course, any threat to physical integrity (murder, torture, assault). Second, whatever endangers the material conditions of life (poverty, unemployment, inflation, etc.). However, since physical-material security is the most immediate vital interest, it does not by itself explain a generalized feeling of fear. Along with visible fears, there are hidden, barely articulated ones. Fear for physical integrity and economic security stand out as the tip of an otherwise invisible iceberg. Anguish, that scattered fear without a specific object, corrodes everything; hopes crumble, emotions fade, vitality is extinguished. Cold creeps in; we become paralyzed. It is said that a life not lived is a disease from which one can die. And so, we find ourselves in deathly danger. One way to die before death comes is fear. People die from fear.

---

92 This contribution is based on a lecture given at the seminar on urban cultures, organized by Jordi Borja, the Menéndez Pelayo International University and the Barcelona City Council (Spain) during September 1985. The first version was published in *La Vanguardia* (Barcelona), November 26, 1985.

Authoritarianism breeds a "culture of fear."[93] The term, coined by Guillermo O'Donnell for Argentina, accounts for human rights violations as a massive, daily experience. We live with the imprint of authoritarianism in the form of a culture of fear. And this legacy will persist, even if the authoritarian regime disappears.

I want to draw attention to a paradoxical effect: the dictatorship hones a demand for security that in turn feeds the desire for an "iron fist." Let us look at the Chilean case. At the end of 1986, in a full state of siege, the population of Santiago was much more afraid of an increase in crime and drug use than of an increase in repression. Crime was seen as an even greater threat than unemployment or inflation, although the economic situation was seen as the country's main problem.[94] The prominent place occupied by crime and drugs is striking, but also plausible: the population could attribute the source of their anguish to a specific cause, perhaps one experienced in the flesh. By circumscribing the danger of a visible, clearly identifiable, and officially sanctioned object as "evil," fear becomes controllable. The operation is simple and decipherable. Differences are transformed into "deviation" and "subversion" and, in turn, subjected to a process of "normalization." Since it is impossible to abolish differences, these are treated as transgressions of the norm; the latter's validity is ensured precisely by instituting and, at the same time, punishing such transgressions. The high visibility given to criminality, I think, is an attempt to objectify an unspeakable horror, projecting it onto a minority and thus confirming faith in the existing order. If this were the case, if we had certainty regarding the basic norms of social coexistence, then citizen insecurity could be addressed

---

93   See G. O'Donnell, "Democracia en la Argentina: micro y macro," *Working Paper* (Kellogg Institute) 2 (December 1983). [–Ed.]

94   In a survey conducted by FLACSO in Santiago at the end of 1986, in a full state of siege, 82 percent of the 1,200 interviewees, said they were very afraid of the increase in crime and drug use; 77 percent were very afraid of the rising inflation; 61 percent of the increase in unemployment, and 64 percent of the increase in repression. In that same survey, 62 percent of those interviewed said that Chilean society required important or radical changes, with the economic aspects being the most urgent.

as a technical-administrative matter: police control would guarantee compliance with the laws. I presume, however, that such an approach obscures the underlying problem.

To glimpse the substance of the problem I propose: 1) to distinguish between criminality, defined as the transgression (violent or not) of established laws, and violence as a violation (criminal or not) of a particular order;[95] and 2) to refer to the fundamental fears of a violated order. Seen in this manner, the explicit fear of crime is nothing more than a harmless way of conceiving and expressing other silenced fears: fear not only of death and misery but also, and probably above all things, fear of a meaningless life, stripped of its roots and devoid of a future. It is on this type of hidden fears, which we all must entertain to continue living, upon which the exercise of authoritarian power is grounded.[96]

It is therefore not enough to denounce human rights violations and the forms of derangement they cause. The culture of fear is not only the product of authoritarianism, but, simultaneously, the condition of its perpetuation. By producing the loss of collective referents and destructured future horizons, the erosion of social criteria regarding what is normal, possible, and desirable, authoritarianism sharpens the vital need for order and presents itself as the only solution. In short, that which fears raise and, particularly, that "fear of fears" is, in short, the question of order: the political question par excellence.

---

95 To my knowledge, only in Brazil is there a more systematic investigation of urban violence. The aforementioned distinction is by M. V. Benevides, *No fio da navalha; o debate sobre a violencia urbana* (São Paulo: CEDEC, n.d.).

96 The similarity that seems to exist between the situations of fear here described and reflections on the postmodern condition is striking. See, for example, J. F. Lyotard, "Une ligne de résistence," *Traverses* (Paris) 33–34 (1985), and F. Jameson, "Posmodernismo y sociedad de consumo," in *La posmodernidad*, ed. H. Foster (Barcelona: Kairós, 1985).

2. The Demand for Order

North American society has a capacity for plurality that Latin American society has never had. In the latter case, all differentiation quickly becomes rebellion, fragmentation, and disintegration. In truth, there can be no plurality without reference to a collective order, and this is not conceived in Latin America as a construction. A "holistic" conception of society as an organic, hierarchically structured order has predominated since colonial times.[97] This strong idea of community has even survived the independence movements, subordinating republican universalism to the nation. The young Latin American republics rely more on the idea of the nation state (and thus a notion of community as a preconstituted unit) than on democratic procedures. Order is therefore not posed as a political problem—that is, as a collective and conflictive work. This quasi-ontological vision of order and politics has been questioned, by the way and from the start, by the exclusion of broad social sectors. The discourse of order has always been opposed by a history of invasions: the invasions of conquerors and landowners as well as of Indigenous communities, peasants, and successive forms of "marginalized peoples." The history of Latin America could be narrated as a continuous and reciprocal "territorial occupation." There is no stable demarcation recognized by all. No physical border and no social boundary provide security. Thus, an ancestral fear of the invader, the other, the dissimilar, whether "from above" or "from below," is both created and internalized generation after generation. There is fear of being expropriated by a landowner or a bank, of suffering some kind of "military occupation," or being assaulted by barbarians: the Indigenous, the immigrants and, in short, the dangerous classes. The struggle for one's own land, in the most literal sense, extends to the symbolic realm. Everyone lives in fear that the purity of their own willpower will be corrupted by others.[98]

---

97   See R. Morse, *El espejo de Próspero* (Mexico: Siglo XXI Editores, 1982).

98   Here I recall the reflections of M. Douglas, *Purity and Danger* (London: Routledge & Kegan Paul, 1966). Regarding the historical tension between the real city and the symbolic city, see Á. Rama, "La ciudad letrada," in *Cultura urbana latinoamericana*, ed. R. Morse and E. Hardoy (Buenos Aires: CLACSO, 1985).

And this danger of contamination, this generalized fear of being cornered and infiltrated, leads to a corporatist, or even privatism-based, retraction.

The greater the fear of the intruder (i.e., those who are different), the higher the defensive barriers each social group erects. This context helps us understand the situations of corporate confinement, reciprocal vetoing, and blockade that characterize politics in Latin America.

There is no such social cohesion and egalitarian ideology in Latin America like the one Tocqueville discovered at the basis of US democracy. The development of capitalism, both the commodification of social relations and industrialization, and the consequent development of an incipient welfare state, at least in the Southern Cone, have only deepened structural heterogeneity by making it more complex. Here I must emphasize that in the absence of a collective referent through which a society can recognize "itself" as a collective order, social diversity cannot be presumed to be a plurality, but is experienced as an increasingly unbearable disintegration. Hence the misgiving regarding those different others, the suspicion and even hatred of them. Having lost the certainty offered by collective referents, social differentiation can only be perceived as a threat to one's own identity. It seems, in short, that it can be affirmed only by negation of the other: the vital defense of that which belongs to *us* is identified with the destruction of that which belongs to others.

In such a climate of uncertainty, authoritarianism responds by embodying the desire for order in the face of threatening chaos. Interpreting social reality as a life-and-death struggle—order versus chaos—the dictatorship presents itself and gains support as a defender of the community and the guarantor of its survival. It asks for popular legitimacy in exchange for "bringing order back"—for imposing it: reestablishing clear and fixed limits, banishing strangers, preventing all contamination, and ensuring a hierarchical unity that assigns everyone to their "natural" place. The result is a surveilled and eventually imprisoned society.

Dictatorships promise to eliminate fear while, in fact, they generate new ones. They profoundly disrupt routines and social habits, making even everyday life unpredictable. The feeling of helplessness increases to the extent that normality disappears. Even the daily environment is seen as an alien and hostile force. When individuals realize they cannot influence their own living conditions, they also fail to take responsibility for them, and this gives rise to moral apathy. Above all, boredom grows. Life under a dictatorship is gray because nothing can excite us anymore. By not committing to anything or anyone, people lose their social roots. This rootlessness is shown in the distrust that reigns over social relations. A privatization process that drastically restricts the field of social experience takes place. In an already atomized context, such self-absorption further reduces learning capabilities. And this causes an adjustment in the sense of reality. An isolated individual has difficulty verifying their subjectivity, confronting different experiences. The boundaries between the real and the fantastic, what is possible and what is desired, become blurred and it will be difficult to draw up a realistic vision under such conditions. This lack of political realism—that is, the inability to determine the possible changes—ends up strengthening the factual power of the establishment. Dissatisfaction with the existing state of affairs becomes narcissistic, self-indulgent and, ultimately, self-destructive.

This brings us back to what seems to me to be the most politically serious effect of authoritarian aggression: the erosion of collective entities. The distance between reality itself and official history, the difference between self-valuation and social valuation is such that individuals fail to recognize themselves in collective referents. The singular life is cloistered in its immediacy; at most, there is a sum of singularities lacking a transcendent horizon (a collective imaginary or utopia) through which common life can be conceived and approached as communal work. In this manner, authoritarianism's tendency to disorganize collective identities ends up undermining its own base of legitimacy. The promise of order leads to a heightened experience of disorder, and the same dictatorship that had invoked "law and order" thus reframes the question of order. It remains to be seen whether democracy can succeed in meeting the demand for order.

3. The Authoritarian Appropriation of Fears

A historical retrospective is indispensable to understand authoritarianism in the Southern Cone not as an irruption but as the reaction to a long process. The systematic violation of human rights should not make us forget that vast sectors of the population welcomed, if not enthusiastically, at least with relief, the establishment of a regime that promised law and order. Said acceptance cannot be explained away solely based on the region's supposed authoritarian culture: this is a calculated option; the dictatorship appeared as a "necessary evil" or a "lesser evil" in the face of the uncertainty caused by the previous period of changes and social mobilizations. In which case, why do some continue to justify dictatorships, already aware of the death and violence they entail? A dictatorship only deepens fears—the anguish of losing our identity, social roots, our collective belonging. And yet, the authoritarian regime continues to muster social support among a minority in a manner that cannot be explained by the defense of economic privileges. There are other non-tangible "benefits," particularly a feeling of security. That such "security" appears completely illusory to us only highlights the political potential of fears.

Authoritarianism responds to existing fears by appropriating them, in turn a labor of ideologization. There is a quasi-theological resignification of fears that erases references to real threats, transforming them into demonic forces: chaos, communism. If the Church once appropriated qualms about the plague or catastrophes, reinterpreting them as fear of sin,[99] current authoritarianism reworks concrete fears into fear of chaos, fear of communism, etc. When society internalizes this "reflected fear" that would give it back power, brainwashing is no longer necessary. The new authoritarianism does not indoctrinate or mobilize people like fascism. Its penetration is subcutaneous: it is enough to work on fears, demonizing perceived dangers so that they appear unwieldy.

Fear of external threats is reinterpreted as fear of the enemy within. Today we no longer fear sin, but the working principle remains: guilt is added to fear. This is what characterizes the authoritarian state: instrumentalizing the fears of citizens and inducing them to feel guilty about them.

---

99   J. Delumeau, *La peur en Occident, XIVe-XVIIIe siècles* (Paris: Fayard, 1978), and his contribution "Una encuesta historiográfica sobre el miedo," in the interesting dossier presented in *Debats* (Valencia, Spain) 8 (1984).

Actualizing an ancestral panic, the dictatorship domesticates society, pushing it into an infantile state. Self-inflicted submission entails, in return, the sacralization of power as a redemptive instance. To the extent that a feeling of powerlessness is reinforced, political participation is replaced by hopes for magical solutions. Citizens should not be excluded from the political arena, but they marginalize themselves because they feel incompetent given the magnitude of the dangers. The social process appears as a godlike struggle in which an individual's opinion is completely irrelevant. Desperate, scared to death, people surrender to a higher authority which will decide for them. It is an act of faith, a kind of "fideism," which pursues salvation via the renunciation of one's own will.[100]

The instrumentalization of fear is one of the main devices with which to discipline society. It is a strategy of depoliticization that does not require repressive measures, except to exemplify the absence of alternatives. Moreover, it is enough to induce a sense of devaluation of our personal and collective capacities to effectively influence the public environment. The only thing that remains is to take refuge inside the private space with the (otiose) hope of finding a modicum of security in privacy.

The desire for order is so strong because the danger of chaos is plausible. People's "sense of order"—the thing that makes life in society and their place in it intelligible—feels threatened. They are frightened by the loss of a "cognitive map" that allows them to structure their possibilities both spatially and temporally. When everything seems possible, the danger of chaos becomes imminent. Panic spreads its double nature: a paralysis of the will, but also fascination. Power acquires the splendor of a divine halo, and the violence is not attributed to the dictatorship but chaos. Chaos is the enemy who infiltrates and subverts the established order, the mortal danger that must be defeated. The annihilation of chaos—that is, communist subversion—entails defending life. The fideistic act though which people adhere to the dictatorship is therefore a reasoned form of surrender: they prefer authoritarian power inasmuch

---

100 For a brief approach to fideism, see P. Bourdieu, "Culture et politiques," *Questions de sociologie* (Paris: Minuit, 1981).

as it embodies life struggling against death and defeat. The dictatorship, then, appears as salvation.[101]

If we do not understand this "transubstantiation" of dictatorial violence into a saving power, we cannot understand the roots of the authoritarian regime. However, these roots have been generally undervalued or ignored by democratic forces and, especially, by the left. Because of their rationalism, these groups tend to visualize fear as an obscurantist lag, a darkness that should have dissipated with the advent of light. Moreover, their ideology of progress often places so much emphasis on social change that the question of order is diluted as a practical matter, *hic et nunc*. And yet, the urgent transformation of extremely unfair social living conditions must not obscure a fundamental observation: life in society needs to be structured, and this demands institutions with their rules of the game, norms about what is valid and what is forbidden, due criteria for calculating the normal, the possible, the rational. This also requires the sedimentation of events into lasting periods, and the delimitation of public, private, individual, and common spaces. More specifically, it requires establishing social limits: that is, producing different collective identities around which to organize different experiences and options. Without such order—however tenuous the threads that both separate and bond people might be—the process of change produces vertigo and, ultimately, becomes anomic.

Vertigo is frightening. People fail to grasp a reality whose accelerated pace and multiple diversity constantly eludes them. Nothing/no one is in place anymore, and the world seems out of control. In such situations, an anxious desire for "normality" spreads. Even those who yearn for a transition to democracy subordinate change to the preservation of some degree of normality, however precarious and illusory. People prefer to know nothing regarding anything because information increases unpredictability and, therefore, uncertainty. A kind of "waterproofing" takes place whereby people seek to save their inner life, protecting it from the external world. I already pointed out this retreat into the private where we look for familiar areas that allow us to ensure

---

101 I rely on the reflections of F. Hinkelammert in, for example, *Las armas ideológicas de la Muerte* (San José [Costa Rica]: DEI, 1977).

who we are. Daily life gets reassessed. Perhaps precisely because it was so altered by the authoritarian regime, daily work acquired an unusual significance. Restoring normalcy is restoring routines, and everyday life is built on a network of norms and habits, external and internalized, visible and invisible, that make the course of the day predictable. Routine is indispensable: Who would get up in the morning if they did not know, with more or less certainty, what to expect? But this wait, due to its repetitive nature, ends up enclosed in a continuous present. As Humberto Giannini states: "[...] one waits, but without going ahead to meet the awaited. This is how routine ends up turning people's own projects harmless—they fear disturbing said routine. Psychology terms this 'pending chores,' the parasitic projects of a continuous present. Thus, routine, which maintains our unchallenged identity by avoiding the unforeseen, also keeps us away from possibilities and is no longer divisible from the vision of the route or the route itself. From such a perspective, the future appears neither favorable nor threatening: it is a parasite of the present that arrives continuously and meekly in the form of norm and normality. So is the case with the past: I am what I usually, irremediably, am."[102]

The quote well describes how routine—a vital defensive mechanism during periods of instability—becomes suffocating. Worrying about surviving prevents us from living. To live, to meet that which we expect, we need to expose ourselves. From this perspective, Giannini emphasizes another aspect of everyday life: the street. The street as a symbol of what is unpredictable, of being exposed to all possible threats ("ending up on the street"), but also a symbol of openness, of what is possible. To what extent do the streets of our city offer room for new options? Do they open possibilities for us to dream and experiment, innovate and change routes, explore new paths?

The realm of everyday life is not usually considered by a traditional view of politics. However, it becomes an indispensable aspect in our efforts to rethink democracy. The dictatorship itself has taught us how daily habits and routines condition common sense. To a large extent,

102 H. Giannini, "Hacia una arqueología de la experiencia," *Revista de Filosofía* 23–24 (Santiago: Universidad de Chile, 1984), 54.

people acquire the practical knowledge that guides their social behavior through these daily experiences. In this immediate context they learn fear and trust, selfishness and solidarity; that is, the social significance of their living conditions. Unfortunately, the debate on democracy often fails to take this "world of life" into account.

Thus, the (inevitable) distance between political discourse and life experiences causes boredom and, above all, a growing detachment from democracy.

In short, I do not believe there will be real democratization if we fail to address fears. And yet, democracy will not eliminate fear either. Moreover, the idea of a society without fear must be understood as an impossible utopia. What does seem possible is to reduce the levels of susceptibility to ambiguous and threatening situations and modify the criteria of perception. Specifically, I am thinking of the possibility of allaying our fears about the other, of their being strange and different, and of assuming uncertainty as a condition regarding the other's freedom. Because democracy means more than just tolerance. It means recognizing the other as a participant in the production of a common future. A democratic process, unlike an authoritarian regime, allows (and in fact requires) us to learn that the future is an intersubjective elaboration and that, therefore, the otherness of the other is that of an alter ego. Seen this way, the freedom of the other, which is incalculable, ceases to be a threat to one's own identity; it is the condition of their deployment. It is through the other and together with the other that we determine the framework of what is possible: what society we want and can build.

This proposal may prompt the following objection: Why hold politics responsible for citizens' fears? Are we not contributing to an "overload" of the political system and, therefore, to the ungovernability of democracy?

The is a serious objection and hard to answer. Indeed, why should politics take care of fears? Equally justifiably, we could demand that it give meaning to death and pain. And is this not an approach that contradicts the postulated secularization of politics, re-identifying them with the salvation of the soul? This would erase the distinction between politics and feelings (between authority and truth, power and love) introduced by modern politics, expanding the sphere of personal freedom. On the other hand, how can we detach ourselves from fears and desires when they are precisely the glass through which we look upon the image of our city?

Reflection on a topic of such existential import as fear has led us to the center of democratic theory: the relationship between political institutionality and social experience. Democracy presupposes a formalization of social relations. The emotional and affective weight would overload the interaction, making the presence of the other unbearable if we failed to put some distance between us. One way to establish distance is via formal procedures. These neutralize the subjective dimension; the validity of a vote or a decision, for example, is binding regardless of the personal considerations motivating it. And yet we have exaggerated the field of formal rationality to the point of identifying rational politics with the calculation of interests. For some, democracy boils down to a method of calculating costs and benefits and these conceptions show their insufficiency as soon as we try (as neoliberalism does) to achieve a self-regulating "political market" regardless of the population's values, motivations, and feelings. The dictatorship itself, despite its technocratic discourse, does not dispense with the subjective dimension. On the contrary, it is based precisely on its instrumentalization. In truth, the advance of formal rationality (progressive bureaucratization) never managed to remove politics from the world of passions. Except that, once subjectivity is excluded as a private matter, its presence frightens us, as if it were an eruption of irrationality. The subjectivity we expelled returns in the form of a ghost. In conclusion, if democracy does not accommodate fears, these will prevail behind our back, and we will then succumb to the worst of them: the desire to imagine other possible cities.

V

Democratization in the Context of Postmodern Culture

1. Creating a Democratic Political Culture

The political struggle is likewise a struggle to define the predominant conception of what is meant by politics. What does it mean to do politics? What is the field of politics? These questions take us back to political culture and this topic, already a difficult one to tackle, poses even greater difficulties when it comes to democratization processes. This is not only a question of analyzing the existing political culture(s), but of creating a democratic political culture. However briefly we might glance at the processes of democratization, we will note that the genesis of a democratic political culture is one of its central aspects. Here I want to ponder something not usually taken into consideration: the international context.

The importance of the international ideological and cultural environment in the political struggles of each country is particularly noticeable in the case of Latin American societies, whose organization and political thoughts have developed, since colonial times, under the influence of the Iberian and Anglo-Saxon tradition. We have important historical studies on this topic. The influence of Western political thought, however, is not only due to an intellectual tradition typical of the "cultural miscegenation" of our societies. These have been "capitalized" so extensively and intensively that we could not interpret national reality without resorting to the explanatory categories of capitalism. Both the external framework and the internal dynamics of Latin America are conditioned by capitalist "logic." However, anyone who has referred to the state or classes knows the sui generis character of the Latin American reality. However, if every theory illuminates some issues while obscuring others, Latin America poses even greater difficulties. The political conceptions and practices that we elaborate in our countries cannot do without the political-ideological debate in the metropolitan centers; and yet, these interpretative schemes, in turn, tend to distort our approach to the problems we face.

Let us here remind ourselves of this well-known difficulty to prevent an overly linear analysis. There is no lack of reasons for those who start from a "minimum definition" of democracy to investigate the factors that favor or hinder, accelerate or slow down the development of a democratic regime. Indeed, functionalist studies tend to be clearer and more limited. I personally find a dialectical approach that jointly addresses the forms of democratization and the historical problems of a given society more fruitful. By this I am referring to the transformations that occurred in societies under dictatorships; regardless of how we rate such transformations, the fact is that society is different. Dictatorships were not a mere parenthesis and, consequently, we cannot repeat previous forms. And yet this is not primarily an issue of new social conditions to consider, for there are continuities along with ruptures: our countries are beset by historical problems (e.g., national question or the social question) that were aggravated by the military regimes. From this point of view, authoritarianism belongs to a past cycle while expressing its crisis. Its "solution" requires new ways of conceiving and doing politics. The search for new ways of doing politics, and the elaboration of new conceptions of politics are inserted in an international context that we could term postmodern culture. To what extent does 1) postmodern culture contribute to generating a democratic political culture that 2) can respond to the historical problems of our societies?

I will not enter a debate on "postmodernity," but I want to point out two elements in our current "cultural climate." On the one hand, it expresses a process of disenchantment, particularly the disenchantment of the left, which no longer believes in socialism as the predetermined goal or in the working class as a revolutionary subject and abhors an all-encompassing view of reality. Intellectually, this entails a critique of some central aspects of Marxism and, more generally, of an entire political tradition: a critique of a philosophy of history, of the idea of the subject, the concept of totality. It is a critique that takes distance, without pretending to elaborate an alternative paradigm. The rather expressive character of postmodern culture is evidenced, on the one hand, in the emergence of a new sensibility with two striking features: the fading of affections, a cooling of emotions and, on the other hand, an erosion of historical-critical distance, flattening social life to a collage sans volume. Although these are features of a mainly aesthetic sensibility that are countered by other tendencies (the emphasis on subjectivity and, in particular, on authenticity and intimacy or the role of political-moral fundamentalism), this "state of mind," a primarily youthful one, must be taken into account when rethinking the current meaning of politics.

Put in very general and tentative terms, I see in postmodern culture the expression of an identity crisis. It reflects the lack or erosion of an articulation of the different aspects of social life that would enable us to affirm the experience of a common vital world. This said, isn't disarticulation or, to use a common expression, "structural heterogeneity," one of the great historical problems of Latin American society?

Isn't the fragmentation of the social fabric one of the most serious effects of authoritarianism? Although the problem of identity is certainly a fundamental issue in the constitution of order in Latin America and possibly one of the causes for the convulsion in the nations of Europe and North America, this is not the same phenomenon. This is not the time to address and contrast historical roots, social framework, and theoretical interpretations in either case. However, although these are different phenomena of disarticulation, these different experiences refer to a shared political problem: the elaboration of a collective frame of reference.

Although Latin American societies need to, above all, elaborate a reasonable social identity from their own (heterogeneous) modernity, the postmodern climate is not alien to them. The debate on postmodernity taking place in Europe and the United States contributes, I believe, to a reflection on the articulation of a collective order through a democratic political culture. It particularly draws our attention to two basic difficulties. On the one hand, the indeterminacy of the political space. Once this is no longer seen as a natural and/or immutable realm, questions arise regarding the limits that differentiate the political from the non-political. We must ask ourselves what belongs to politics and what to expect from politics. As these boundaries are drawn, we establish which aspects of social life can be articulated into a political identity.

On the other hand, this draws attention to the precariousness of time. What is politically possible depends on the time available and how we can use it. If we fail to produce temporal continuities, we will also fail to constitute collective identities.

2. The Indeterminacy of the Political Space

Since the 1930s and especially after 1945, Latin American societies have experienced a process of modernization with contradictory effects.[103] The dynamics of secularization and social marginalization question the foundations of the established order, even in those countries that seemed to have resolved both the national and social questions. It is within this framework that I see the "ideological inflation" of the 1960s. The search for a totalizing vision capable of unifying the social process was a response to a threat of dissolution and social atomization. Even under different or antagonistic political signs, this search for identity follows a similar pattern and what I see as three characteristic features.

1. The sacralization of political principles as absolute truth, which has a double effect: inwardly, it fosters and consolidates strong collective identities typical of religious communities. The external price of internal cohesion is rigidity in distinction, intransigence in negotiations. Purity fears pollution: the greater the ideological consistency of a group, the more it tends to demonize its adversary.

2. The sacralization of the constitutive principles of identity is closely linked to a resignification of utopia. The latter is seen as a feasible goal from which a certain "historical necessity" would emerge. The identification of utopia with a possible future then leads to a great social mobilization seeking those "irreversible changes" that will make the promised order a reality. It is an instrumental policy, referring to a

---

103   G. Germani, "Democracia y autoritarismo en la sociedad moderna," in G. Germani et al., *Los límites de la democracia* (Buenos Aires: CLACSO, 1985).

predetermined goal and, therefore, blind to the production and selection of different options. The perception of the present as a "transition" prompts abnegation and sacrificial behavior, but these easily despise the conquests of the past.

3. Utopian power rests on a notion of totality, not as an articulating instance but as a fully realized identity. The dividing boundaries between groups and classes, as well as the distinctive boundaries between the public and the private, between theory and practice, between manual and intellectual labor, between culture and politics will then appear as obsolete borders. The result is a suggestive questioning of established spaces, but also insecurity regarding the social order. Instead of elaborating a new system of distinctions, there is a tendency to extend a certain rationality, specific to a certain space, to all social life: the search for a totalizing vision leads to a sectarian/totalitarian position.

To complete and, at the same time, summarize the picture here outlined, I can only re-emphasize the religious burden this type of politics entails. All politics entail a theological dimension. In these cases, however, and to compensate for the experiences of exclusion and radical helplessness, the religious moment is accentuated in such a way that politics assumes, at least implicitly, the redemption of the soul. This is what gives revolutionary politics its mystique and, on the other hand, makes the new authoritarianism (despite its aseptic neoliberal language) a "redemptive crusade." But this is not a phenomenon specific to Latin America. If we consider the rise of fundamentalism in the United States, we see the importance of religious motivation (even as "civil religion") to counteract the feeling of uncertainty. If uncertainty is a constitutive characteristic of democracy, as some argue, the demand for certainty should occupy a privileged place in democratization studies.

It is against this background that I outline the changes pertaining to the current democratic climate in South America (I speak of a "climate" because we know little about the effective rooting of democratic convictions and behaviors). In the construction of a democratic political system and given our specific interests, two tendencies stand out. In the first place, there is a strong revaluation of secularization. In opposition to the messianism introduced by the revolutionary perspective of the 1960s and exacerbated by authoritarianism, secularization today has an exclusively positive connotation, without any further reflection on its destabilizing potential. For democratic consolidation, it is imperative that we decouple legitimacy from truth and re-establish the sphere of politics as a space for negotiation. To establish a climate of compromise, it is essential to rid politics of ethical-religious commitments, the source of previous intransigence and excessive expectations. It is, in short, about "unloading" an overloaded politics. This requires not only dismantling the search for redemption and fulfillment, but also a certain non-commitment in the values, motivations, and affections involved. The second trend also points in the same direction and is a call to realism. Reacting against a "principled" position, against a heroic vision of life and a messianic approach to the future, politics is rethought as the "art of the possible." The question of what is politically possible displaces the previous emphasis on what is necessary ("historical necessity") while opposing the impossible: to avoid repeating a past that proved unfeasible or attempting to realize an unfeasible utopia. Apart from its critical intentions, the invocation of realism is a call to the collective construction of order. Order is not an objectively given reality; it is a social production that cannot be the unilateral work of an actor but must be undertaken collectively. Hence the revaluation of institutions and procedures—that is, of the ways of doing politics beyond material contents.

Both tendencies seek to restrict the previous space of politics, seen as excessive. What would be the appropriate boundaries of the political space? We are participating in a more latent than explicit conflict regarding the limits of political space, which seems to me to be one of the privileged terrains in the genesis of a new political culture. For now, these have not crystallized into clear markings. A first step has been to become aware of the previous political "omnipotence complex" and, therefore, of the specificity of the different social fields. We can now perceive the tension between politics and morality, politics and culture, the state and politics, etc. These tensions are accepted, but not elaborated upon (not even casuistically). There is an absence of criteria. What does postmodern culture offer us in this regard?

I would like to point out two phenomena that hint at a certain contemporaneity between the democratic climate in Latin America and the international cultural context: both shed light on the difficulties of modern democracy. The call for a secularization of politics can be based on postmodern culture insofar as it implies a certain fading of affections that propitiates a cool and ironic behavior. In this sense, the international "fashion" now contributes to cooling the emotional charge of politics, reducing pressures and, therefore, allowing the political sphere to acquire greater autonomy. Such trends are likely to favor democratic consolidation in our countries. However, that is not why we enter "postmodernity." Postmodern culture does not guide a process of secularization but is its product. More accurately, it is the expression of hypersecularization. Perhaps we should understand it as an ex-post rationalization of disenchantment—a mimetic, rather than reflexive, rationalization. Put in political terms: postmodern culture accepts hypersecularization in its tendency to separate social structures from evaluative, motivational, emotional structures. That is, it accepts the liberal view of politics as a "market," an exchange of goods. What, then, about non-tradable goods? I am referring to human rights, psychosocial needs such as social roots and collective belonging, the need for transcendent references, fears, and the desire for certainty. I do not see postmodern culture reflecting on this. On the contrary, its critique of the notion of subjection (doubtless partially justified) tends to undermine the basis for rethinking politics. If we identify political rationale with the market and exchange, the problem of identity cannot be posed. This, however, is precisely one of the main tasks facing democratic political culture.

Likewise, the call to realism has, at first glance, an affinity with postmodern culture. Both reject great deeds, are sensitive to the new, the "signs on the street," and explore the political in everyday life. Above all, they de-dramatize politics. Seen this way, postmodern culture feeds political realism insofar as it fosters a new sensibility toward possibility that could help reduce the distance between political agendas and people's everyday experience. On the other hand, I do not see that postmodern culture reflects on the main problem of realism: that is, selection criteria. Once possibilities are discovered and formulated, which option do we select as the best possible? The debate about the possible refers to that which is desirable. We need this criterion to prioritize possibilities as well as evaluate the efficiency and success of political management. By which I mean that realism looks not only at what is, but also at what could and should be. It therefore requires an anticipation of the future, and this is precisely what is absent in postmodern culture. I will return later to the lack of a future, but here I advance a fundamental aspect: an idea of emancipation has been renounced. Along with criticizing determinism and a teleological view of history, any reference to emancipation (whatever its formulation) has been abandoned, which I find problematic. Apparently, postmodern culture frees itself from the illusions of the Enlightenment but it, in fact, loses track of history and, above all, the ability to elaborate a horizon of meaning. Are democratization processes not faced precisely with the task of producing a new "sense of order"? Hence the importance of political culture. If we fail to develop a new horizon of meaning, democratic institutionality will be missing its roots, an empty shell.

In short, I believe that the postmodern environment helps us demystify messianism and the religious nature of a "culture of militancy" to relativize the centrality of the state, the party, and politics in and of themselves. It also introduces a less rigid sociability and playful enjoyment to political activity. In this sense, it contributes to rethinking the limits of politics, although it does not provide criteria with which to limit the field. On the contrary, it increases the indeterminacy of boundaries and, consequently, the conflict around them, giving democratization processes both their dynamics and instability.

3. The Precariousness of Time

Today it is almost commonplace to speak of a "project crisis." After the 1960s and 1970s, which were focused on the future and, therefore, had an optimistic perspective not of the society to be attained but, above all, our capacity to build a new order, we now face two decades of failures and the era resonates as the final and delayed apogee of the notion of progress. In no country is the failure of the heroic, almost Promethean, vision of development more evident than in Chile. Neither Frei's developmentalist policies, Allende's socialist reforms, nor Pinochet's neoliberal measures crystallized into a process of sustained and stable social transformation. This does not mean an absence of changes: there were many shifts, many of them radical. And yet these were, to use historio-graphical terms, events rather than processes. We are still living time as a sequence of events, an ever more dramatic string of junctures that fail to crystallize into "duration"—that is, a structured period of past, present, future. We live in a continuous present.

Though less abrupt, the experience of the other countries in the region is not much different. Neither the purported "economic mira-cle" of the Brazilian military nor the populist reforms of the Peruvian military, not even the extraordinary resources oil once offered the gov-ernments of Mexico and Venezuela have translated into a consolidated "style." I am not merely addressing the continent's already proverbial political instability. The underlying problem is that no experience manages to create, beyond the rhetoric of the moment, a horizon for the future. Even countries with a relatively stable social order face the absence of a future. There are projections, but no projects. As soon as the present is restricted to recurring repetition, the future is, in turn, identified with something "beyond": messianism is the other face of self-absorption.

Perhaps the current crisis of projects in Latin America is nowadays more notorious because it inserts itself in an international context that considers the present as the only time available, a fact lamented by some and celebrated by others. Some criticize the lack of perspective and, therefore, of criteria that allow us to deliberately choose our future; others praise our liberation from an omnipresent foresight and an ines-capable destiny that left no room for experimentation, adventure, or gratuitous acts. The fact is that we are facing a time without horizon, whether we speak of a radically open future where "everything is possi-ble" or feel recurrently trapped by the past.

By "modernity," said Baudelaire, "I mean the ephemeral, the fugi-tive, the contingent, the half of art whose other half is the eternal and the immutable."[104] This almost hysterical anxiety for the new, the ephemeral, what is fashionable, expressly rebels against the normalizing

---

104 Quoted by D. Frisby, "Georg Simmels Theorie der Moderne," in *Georg Simmel und die Moderne*, ed. H. J. Dahme and O. Rammstedt (Frankfurt: Suhrkamp, 1984).

functions of tradition without losing the reference to the past. Only in relation to the past is modernity conceivable, while the discovery of what is modern is nourished by memory, a tension that breaks down in postmodernity. The past is erased and, consequently, so is the historical distance that gave prominence to the present. Condensing time into a single present, social life becomes a flat surface, a collage lacking perspective or an in-depth gaze: everything goes. Precisely because everything is possible, every possibility is ephemeral—instantly consumed.

In this acceleration of time, nothing is affirmed anymore; even identity succumbs to vertigo. It is in this sense that I referred to postmodern culture as an expression of an identity crisis. How can one, in fact, affirm an identity in a recurring present? It is no coincidence the schizophrenic is now evoked as an emblematic figure. The loss of identity that characterizes schizophrenia can be understood as the result of a disjointed experience in which different isolated, disconnected, discontinuous elements are not structured into a coherent sequence. A schizophrenic does not know an "I" because "he or she does not have our experience of temporal continuity either, but is condemned to live a perpetual present with which the various moments of his or her past have little connection and for which there is no conceivable future on the horizon."[105] In the absence of a sense of identity that persists over time, the schizophrenic is not only nobody, but also does nothing. Doing things would entail having a project, and that implies committing to a certain continuity. When the temporal continuities through which we select and order the different aspects of life are broken, our vision of the world becomes undifferentiated: an unlimited sum of juxtaposed elements. Schizophrenics do not "filter" the present, meaning they will have a much more intense but ultimately overwhelming experience. They will live the moment intensely, but at the price of petrifying it. In the absence of set limits to give it some dimension, the present drowns in bottomless immediacy.

---

105 Frederic Jameson, "Postmodernism and Consumer Society," in *The Anti-aesthetic: Essays on Postmodern Culture*, ed. Hal Foster (Washington: Bay Press, 1983), 119; see also "Posmodernismo: lógica cultural del capitalismo tardío," *Zona Abierta* (Madrid) 38 (1986).

4. The Creativity of Political Culture

What follows from the above for the elaboration of a democratic political culture in our region? We have seen, on the one hand, the difficulty
in determining what democratic politics encompasses, what its space
is. The identification of politics with the state or a party and an identification of the political space with the public sphere is no longer acceptable. The confinement of politics is rejected but saying that everything is
political is not an accepted fact either. Social life has become unfocused,
requiring structuring. It does not merely demand rules that distinguish
the good from the bad, the lawful from the forbidden; it needs equally
important criteria for defining the possible and the desirable, the legitimate and the rational, the normal and the efficient. The elaboration
of such criteria depends, in both form and content, on what kind of
policy we make. However, I believe these criteria are not determined,
not even in those countries that agree on the constitutional "rules of the
game." These are necessary, but not sufficient to narrow the field of what
is politically expressible/decidable.

On the other hand, we have addressed the precariousness of time.
We do not have a strong concept of time, capable of structuring past,
present, and future as historical "development," nor do we even share
commensurable horizons of temporality. Our awareness of time is
very volatile, making it difficult to agree on deadlines and synchronize
expectations. In short, our abilities to calculate and control time are
extremely poor.

Uncertainty regarding space and time reveals growing doubts about
our effective power of disposition. What degree of real influence, rational and effective control over social processes do people have today?
Gone are the days when humanity felt called to "transform the world."
The feeling of omnipotence that reigned in the 1960s has given way to
one of powerlessness. Neoliberalism is extreme, but its assault on state
intervention and the very idea of popular sovereignty is a sign of the
times. Questioning the deliberate construction of society for its own
sake does not only question democracy but all modern politics. The
faith we once placed in the strength of political will has been diluted.
However, it is not only voluntarism that disappears. There is a tendency
to downplay the importance of all political action. Latin American

society would already be too complex, too woven into an excessively rigid international context for major changes to be introduced. Even a reform government would eventually have to content itself with some "symbolic changes." That this image of unproductivity emerges from postmodern culture is a paradox, for it is precisely the culture that dismantles determinism and opens radically to explore the field of the possible that leads to a vision of the existing as the necessary.

The outlined phenomena are probably not constituent elements of a long process, but rather a kind of musical rest. And in the meantime, processes of democratization are caught in a silent beat.

VI

Does Democracy Answer a Search for Certainty?

1. The Demand for Certainty

What security does democracy offer? The debate on democracy, like much of modern political thought, revolves around security; that is, it responds to social fears, from fear of war and violence to helplessness and misery. These are at the basis of political tasks: securing peace, guaranteeing physical and legal security (rule of law) and promoting economic security (welfare state). There are hazards other than just material ones, but these are scattered and difficult to name. We perceive veiled threats that are even more violent because we feel vulnerable and without protection. This fear and abandonment question the social order.

The issue of order has specific characteristics in modern times. One can only speak of modernity, says Koselleck,[106] when the social horizon of expectations no longer finds support in past experience. As soon as society opens to the different, ceasing to be unique, people are forced to choose, at their own risk, between multiple possibilities of being, doing, thinking.

The confrontation with "the new" fascinates and frightens. Awakening has its charms when it refers to a future to conquer. Twenty, thirty years ago, we denounced the immobility of the established order because we saw an alternative. When the image of the future is diluted,

---

106 R. Koselleck, *Vergangene Zukunft*, quoted by J. Habermas in *Der philosophische Diskurs der Moderne* (Frankfurt: Suhrkamp, 1985), 22.

the new becomes a threat to the existing. The present itself loses its profile and disintegrates, gray upon gray.

It is already commonplace to speak of the fragmentation of the social fabric caused by authoritarianism. Yet this destruction, which was certainly traumatic, is not an exclusive feature of authoritarianism nor does it disappear with it. Authoritarian ruptures are inserted into a transformation of capitalism on a global scale, the development of a "new international order" through the double process of "transnational integration and national disintegration" (Sunkel).[107] It is a process of social differentiation that goes beyond the economic and covers all spheres. The now classic "structural heterogeneity" of Latin America thus becomes even more complex. Unlike the modernization process of the 1960s, the new social complexity does not have any referents. We have neither a historical memory nor a project for the future, nor a theoretical paradigm or any practical model. This air of dissolution reminds us of Marx's well-known passage summarizing the dawn of modern society: "All fixed, fast-frozen relations, with their train of ancient and venerable prejudices and opinions, are swept away, all new-formed ones become antiquated before they can ossify. All that is solid melts into air, all that is holy is profaned, and man is at last compelled to face with sober senses his real conditions of life, and his relations with his kind."[108]

We are facing a new threshold of secularization and the consequent helplessness. Everything is under suspicion: Who is the other and who are we? Not only the future, always unpredictable, is ungraspable; our existing reality becomes so too. Once the guarantees have been annulled and the established has been dissolved, everything seems possible. We settle into uncertainty under "what is possible," and it is from this uncertainty that modern democracy is born. "The essential issue," says Claude Lefort, "is that democracy is instituted and maintained in the face of the dissolution of the referents of certainty. It inaugurates an

---

107 O. Sunkel, *Capitalismo transnacional y desintegración nacional en América Latina* (Buenos Aires: Nueva Visión, 1972). [–Ed.]

108 Karl Marx and Friedrich Engels, *The Communist Manifesto* (New Haven: Yale University Press, 2012), 77.

ultimate indeterminacy regarding the foundations of Power, Law, and Knowledge as well as their respective interactions across all the registers of social life."[109]

Accepting the disenchantment of the world as a starting point, can we identify democracy with disenchantment? Current "postmodern culture" is pleased to dismantle the undoubtedly fragile certainties of yesteryear and proclaim a disillusionment that, even if justified in the face of an all-encompassing discourse, ultimately turns out to be false radicalism and crude realism.

The dismantling of false certainties is, of course, an indispensable critical act.[110] Here I am thinking of "ideological inflation," so typical of Latin American politics: the tendency to sacralize political principles as absolute truths and to guide political action according to society's global plans. Such "over-ideologization" provokes strong intransigence when it comes to negotiating compromises and modifying decisions. It is not accepted that every political issue inherently entails a conflict of interpretation. An antagonistic culture is formed in which politics is perceived as a life-and-death struggle and order as the imposition of the winning will. Underlying this violence is, undoubtedly, a desperate search for certainty. However, a critique that fails to rescue the motives of said search seems, to me, inappropriate, for criticism of a given solution does not eliminate the problem. The problem is the demand for certainty.

The current intellectual climate is marked by a kind of "deconstructionism" and, specifically, a neo-Nietzschean critique of Enlightened rationalism. The debate on modernity has the merit of rethinking the dialectic of secularization. A fertile path has opened to rethink democracy, a child of secularization in two ways. First, democracy proclaims uncertainty by instituting the popular will as the constitutive principle of order; second, it must take charge of the demands for certainty that

---

109 C. Lefort, "El problema de la democracia," *Opciones* (Santiago) 6 (1985): 84.

110 See A. Hirschman's incisive take, "On Democracy in Latin America," *The New York Review of Books*, April 10, 1986.

a secularized society provokes. Do our difficulties in institutionalizing democracy not rest upon this tension?

It is no coincidence that Gino Germani, the great scholar of modernization processes in Latin America, devoted his latest work to this problem.[111] The same secularization of society that, in the passage from prescriptive to elective forms of action via the legitimization of social change and the increasing specialization of roles and institutions, makes democracy possible, also undermines it with the unlimited questioning of everything established.

On the one hand, democracy presupposes secularization. Only a secular attitude that does not recognize any authority or norm as the exclusive and excluding bearer of truth allows a society to organize itself according to the principle of popular sovereignty and the majority principle. Secularization means decoupling the legitimacy of authority and laws from claims to absolute truth. By making religious faith and moral values a matter of individual conscience, secularization tasks politics with establishing norms of super-individual validity. It is a relationship of complementarity: moral prescriptions and claims to certainty can be privatized to the extent that the public sphere appears regulated by objective and universalist norms. In other words, claims of subjective certainty are referred to the individual courts insofar as objective criteria of certainty are shared (i.e., formal rationality). The advance of the market and bureaucracy effectively endows the public sphere with a calculability that compensates for the relativization and privatization of values. From this viewpoint, democracy is the political form of a secularized society.

On the other hand, however, secularization destabilizes democracy. The secularizing dynamic extends to all social fields and democracy itself. There are no limits other than the popular will accelerating this process. On the one hand, it subjects the material contents of politics to a systematic and permanent review. Modern democratic

---

111   G. Germani, "Democracia y autoritarismo en la sociedad moderna," *Crítica & Utopía* (Buenos Aires) 1 (1979). The subsequent debate appears in *Los límites de la democracia*, 2 vols. (Buenos Aires: CLACSO, 1985). I am particularly interested in A. Pizzorno's "Sobre la racionalidad de la opción democrática."

theories dispense with unquestioned and immutable principles of truth; the legitimacy of a decision depends on its legality. Based on such "procedural legitimacy," any rule can be revoked or modified by a new majority. Democratic procedures (regular elections, the majority principle) do not guarantee that a certain measure or programmatic goal will last over time. Consequently, the democratic transition cannot be based on a substantive pact regarding certain goals, only on an institutional pact on procedures.[112] On the other hand, formal procedures do not provide absolute certainty either. The relativism of values also contaminates and relativizes the "rules of the game." There are no "true" or "objective" procedures but contractual agreements that establish rights rather than duties, offering no guarantees in terms of an ethical obligation. A pact on the rules of the game would only be ethically binding in reference to an external norm—precisely that foundation of values corroded by secularization. Thus, the same evaluative neutrality of democratic procedures that makes certainty a matter of individual conscience simultaneously introduces uncertainty into the public sphere.

The Chilean case dramatically illustrates how difficult it is to neutralize the fear of threats, real or imagined, through formal procedures. The difficulties of "institutional engineering" refer to the symbolic world and collective imaginaries; we rediscover that politics is guided not only by interests but also passions and images, beliefs and emotions. The tearing apart of society brings to light the hidden face of politics: the fear of social uprooting, the anxiety of collective belonging, the anguish to transcend the immediacy of singular life. Democracy cannot ignore these cries of pain lest it be swept away by them.

Transition processes are a borderline case and thus clearly illuminate the central place of uncertainty. The latter provokes fears of change and conflict and, therefore, of democracy itself. At the same time, it fosters blind faith in any promise of unity and harmony, however illusory.

---

112 A. Przeworski, "Ama a incerteza e seras democrático," *Novos Estudos* 9 (São Paulo: CEBRAP, July 1984). In Chile, the topic has been addressed by Ángel Flisfisch in several pieces; see *La política como compromiso democrático* (Santiago: FLACSO, 1987).

It is not enough, then, to exorcise uncertainty, proclaiming it a democratic virtue. The demand for certainty exists and the question is, who will take care of it?[113]

Regarding this dynamic, Adam Przeworski aptly defines democracy as the "a contingent outcome of conflicts."[114] The democratic pact is not a necessary and inevitable outcome, but a possibility. It is feasible as long as it offers certain minimum assurances regarding a future respect for "vital interests." Otherwise, Germani concludes, the secularizing dynamic may well give rise to a new authoritarianism. What is authoritarianism if not an attempt to restore certainty and, specifically, to restore a sense of community in a world of unbearable disintegration? Denouncing the dictatorship and its disorder therefore implies developing new referents of certainty.

In short, assuming the uncertainty of a story without subject or end is a necessary but insufficient disenchantment. We only nurture a disenchanted vision if we disbelieve the lures of charm. Political realism should make us see that uncertainty entails the search for certainty. If democracy is born of uncertainty, does it not arise precisely as an attempt to respond to it?

2. On the Process of Secularization

Modern democracy is born alongside the disenchantment of the world. Only when society perceives its own constitution as problematic can

---

113 In a survey conducted by FLACSO and the CED in Greater Santiago at the end of 1986, of the 1,200 interviewees, 62 percent preferred to "have a clear and precise opinion beforehand" when talking about politics, while 27 percent preferred to "form an opinion in conversation" (the remaining 11 percent did not know or did not respond). Those people with a high interest in politics expected that only those with already formed judgments would address the topic.

114 Adam Przeworski, "Democracy as a Contingent Outcome of Conflicts," in *Constitutionalism and Democracy*, ed. Jon Elster and Rune Slagstad (Cambridge: Cambridge University Press, 1998), 59.

modern politics appear as society's self-conscious action. The slow secular transition from an integrally received order to a more and more
produced one is then concluded.[115] At the origin of the received order
is religion: the radical excision of the living-visible world from its foundation. The absolute precedence and alterity of religion as the constitutive principle of order makes society a kingdom of the pure past, an
immutable inheritance. The subsequent transformation of the image of
the divine, the personalization of the gods, the rationalization of mythical heroes into abstract symbols, the internalization of the origin of
the world into a "genesis," undermine the transcendent character of the
foundation. With the weakening of the external and indisputable guarantee arises the modern problem of freedom and, therefore, of certainty.

Marcel Gauchet reveals a paradox that has been present since then
and is particularly visible in our time: the more actively we produce the
social order, the more nostalgia we feel for that absolute veneration of
order, which is conceived as a situation radically beyond our control
that, on the other hand, guarantees us a firm place in its bosom. This
inviolable guarantee resides in a law totally alien to our will and, therefore, fully assumed as the best possible. The order that we internalize
as entirely received is, simultaneously, the order that allows for unre-
served consent. The order we produce, however, demands deciphering
and, therefore, we find it difficult to recognize ourselves in it. Additionally, its mechanisms overwhelm us, and, in the end, we suffer its consequences, not knowing how to control them. While the order we receive
is at the same time a destiny that welcomes us, the order we produce
becomes a future that eludes us.

This paradox hints at the field of current uncertainty: the sense of
order or, sociologically speaking, the symbolic integration of society.
Durkheim said there can be no society without a constant affirmation
of the collective feelings and collective ideas that comprise its unity
and personality. In the past, religion fulfilled the function of symbolically integrating society as a collective life. When religion no longer

---

115 See M. Gauchet, *Le désenchantemente du monde* (Paris: Gallimard, 1985). The
concept of secularization has been analyzed by H. Lübbe, *Säkularisierung*
(Freiburg: Albert Verlag, 1965).

acts as a "sacred canopy"—that system of ultimate symbols from which the purposes of social interaction were derived—by means of what referent can society recognize and affirm itself as a collective order?

The end of religion as the constituent principle of the social body marks a total rupture. Society continues to recognize and affirm "itself" through an externalized referent but is now a god-subject present in the world. Once the temporal separation of the foundation is questioned, the spatial distance is progressively reduced. Society constitutes a sense of order via a physically metaphysical instance: the state. Henceforth, the apex of the collective order resides in the state, the convergence of the constitutive foundation of social life and its material-concrete ordering. We no longer believe in a sacrosanct principle, removed from human reasoning, from whose correct interpretation the law can be deduced. Neither can we abandon any reference to a fundamental law. The self-affirmation of society qua society is still based on what Gauchet terms a "debt of meaning";[116] that is, the submission of the social order to a regulatory principle split from society, only in the form of a contradiction that becomes central: the validity of the regulatory principle is linked to the effects of its exercise. Just as the belief in a certain foundation conditions the acceptance of its material organization, so does the judgment on the existing state of things in turn condition the validity of its normative foundation. Having lost the charm of an absolute principle that is perpetually valid for all, the divisions in society (those different interests and experiences) give rise to multiple regulatory principles: a new "polytheism."

Since religion no longer operates as a mechanism for neutralizing conflicts, there is a restructuring of all social relations. If, before, the radical otherness of the foundation had excluded conflicts about what the form of social coexistence should be, now the meaning and legitimation of order are at the very center of conflict. Not only the interests of one or another social sector but the identity of society itself are permanently threatened.

---

116 Marcel Gauchet, "La dette du sens et les racines de l'État," in *La condition politique* (Paris: Gallimard, 2005), 15.

The demand for certainty comes from fear of this threat and is therefore not an individual problem. Although I can individually renounce any firm, immovable anchor in a whirlwind of possibilities and embrace uncertainty, collective life requires certainties. Specifically, certainty regarding "the collective."

Asserting its sovereignty, modern society is no longer conceived as the product of destiny and claims to own its future. It is by looking to the future (i.e., what is possible) that modern freedom is born: the deliberate constitution of society by itself. While Marx exalts self-determination as a process of social emancipation, Tocqueville glimpses helplessness. Once the principle of popular sovereignty is instituted, everything is within the reach of criticism, imagination, human will. If everything is questionable, if nothing is removed from discussion and conflict, what binds communal life?

Secularization does not merely encompass a process of deconstruction. The very decomposition of the received order leads to rearrangement, a reconstruction no longer based on divine legitimation or guided by criteria from some exemplary past. Instead of restoring a consecrated order, society must institute order from within itself. Thus, secularization makes self-identification the fundamental problem of modernity.[117] How can we be sure of "ourselves"? An attempt to specify the search for certainty is summed up in the opening of a piece by Habermas: "Can complex societies elaborate a reasonable identity?"[118] This question is, in my opinion, fundamental to democratization in our countries.

If we assume that the search for certainty is primarily about collective identity, can we elaborate a political response? Here I must recall a crucial milestone in Latin America's political development. During its independence movements, Latin American society faced the same question the French Revolution had exemplarily formulated: Is it possible to institute the social from within itself, without resorting to

---

117 J. Habermas, "Das Zeitbewusstsein der Moderne un ihr Bedurfnis nach Selbstvergewisserung," in *Der philosophische Diskurs der Moderne*, op. cit.

118 Jürgen Habermas, *Rekonstruktion des historischen materialismus* (Frankfurt: Suhrkamp, 1976).

transcendent legitimation?[119] This issue, as stressed by François Furet, underlines the basic contemporaneity of political debate in Europe and America, despite their different developments. While the French Revolution re-institutionalized the social through the principle of popular sovereignty, oligarchic power in Latin America cannot invoke this idea given the social and political conditions. Neither has it become established common sense. The new republics did not retain the monarchic principle, but neither did they make a clean break with the colonial order: they cannot be founded on transcendent legitimation, nor can they be legitimized in a democratic manner. Finally, the continent of the future only secures its identity by resorting to the past.

A "holistic" model of society prevailed in the political thought of the region, derived from the Iberian tradition.[120] This can be understood as the primacy of the whole over the parts. Unlike an individualistic society, such as that of North America, where the collective order results from the association between individuals (the social contract), Latin American society emphasizes the background (historical and rational) of the community. This tradition manages to counter the challenge of modernity (i.e., uncertainty), but does not advance a proper political response. That is, it cannot pose the constitution of order as a social production. The vision of an organic, hierarchically structured community, rests on a dualism that preserves the idea of a "common good" as the unquestionable foundation of order and, simultaneously, subjects politics to the realism of "the good reason of the state." This dualism, inherited from the Spanish Baroque and developed by the social doctrine of the Catholic Church, is still present. A democratic-egalitarian legitimation and a transcendent legitimation will coexist in a kind of staggered legitimation, invoking, in accordance with the opportunity, the "popular will" or the "common good." This ambiguity makes it easier for countries torn by social divisions to preserve a communal identity, but it hinders a secular conception of politics.

---

119 François Furet, interviewed by Massimo Boffa, in *Debats* (Valencia) 4 (1982): 112.

120 See R. Morse, *El espejo de Próspero* (Mexico: Siglo XXI Editores, 1982), and the work of Louis Dumont.

I mention this historical background to draw attention to the religious element of politics. This is not a specific Latin American trait, but here we can see more clearly how politics assumes the integrating function once fulfilled by religion. Social coexistence is reinterpreted as community through some kind of "political theology." It offers society an image of fullness in which to recognize and venerate itself as a collective order, thus stabilizing itself over time. However, it is not only the notion of the common good, but also the principle of popular sovereignty that contains a promise of final harmony. In both the liberal and Marxist interpretations, the popular will implies happiness. This split is more noticeable in Latin America, given the aforementioned "over-ideologization" of different signs. However, even in more secular societies, politics crystallizes desires and promises of a "happy ending." This secularized utopia is now decried given the disproportion between the promised goals and the available resources. What once allowed politics to assume the integrative direction of society, today causes generalized misgivings. Are we facing a new secularizing impulse that dismantles religious "residues" to inaugurate a radical realism regarding "what is possible"? Or are we witnessing an oversecularization that strips politics of its integrative mechanisms, provoking an identity crisis?

The secularization of the religious principle by politics means not only basing social integration on a "last resort" (a logical and teleological principle), but also institutionalizing that foundation in a centralized scheme. Neither is this feature exclusive to Latin America, although it is enhanced by the holistic model of a hierarchically structured order. Let us not forget, however, that this tradition endures precisely because of the difficulties of organizing the actual "people" in terms of their democratic ideas. There is no such equality or "similarity" among individuals that would allow, as per Tocqueville, to unite the community in the sociocultural sphere. On the contrary, the more acute the inequalities and divisions in society, the more pressing is the reference to the collective will, to a single and decisive instance: the One. Faced with a factional society characterized by *fronde* politics and corporatist strategies, unity is a recurring invocation of political discourse. It is the image of sovereignty. We may consider such an image unfeasible and even undesirable, and yet it seems to be a necessary fiction in Western thought. At least in Latin American societies, always torn by multiple centrifugal forces, centrality stirs much less enthusiasm than in France, for example.[121] Now, if centrality appears as a legitimate aspiration with respect to historical-social disintegration, it could also be an obsolete aspiration in regard to modern social differentiation. In truth, the process of differentiation questions any notion of centrality as an obstacle to the deployment of autonomies. Is the decentered vision, which proclaims postmodernism, a pending deconstruction to secularize a still monotheistic politics? Or will politics be able to forgo reliance on structures of centrality to shape the process of differentiation as a collective order?

I wonder, in short, about the possible limits of secularization. When secularization recovers as human that which humanity once projected toward heaven, politics takes on aspirations previously assigned to religious faith. Nowadays, this religious burden is often seen as an overload of expectations. It is suggested we enact a radical secularization of politics, freeing them from demands they could not possibly satisfy given the complexity of social relations. Only such disenchantment would enable a realistic conception of democracy. I, however, presume that social complexity demands a more complex notion of "political realism."[122]

3. Marx, Tocqueville, and the Legitimization of the Social Order

Can society be constituted from itself, creating its own normativity? One answer is precisely democracy. In this regard, we should set apart two aspects: democracy as a principle of legitimacy and as an organizational

---

121 "The Latin world has never been so goal-minded as to be in sudden need of a cosmic spiritual cure. We have never been so terribly rational as to need a pedagogy of the irrational, never so individualistic that we would now need compensatory union with the One,'" X. Rubert de Ventós, *Moral* (Barcelona: Laia, 1985).

122 See N. Lechner, ed., *¿Qué es 'realismo' en política?* (Buenos Aires: Editorial Catálogos, 1987). [Also in *Obras II*, 259–63.]

principle. Both dimensions have been intertwined and confused in the theory of democracy, from Rousseau onwards. They are certainly both related, as we shall see, but their difference will enable us to envision two approaches to the "democratic question." One trend privileges the problem of the constitution of the social order, seeking to substantiate an objective legitimization of democracy. Although few question the principle of popular sovereignty nowadays, its meaning remains controversial, and this has impacts on the modalities of institutionalization. Another trend focuses directly on the institutional organization of self-determination, emphasizing specific historical forms. And yet, every conflict about organizational reforms brings us back to a conflict over the foundation of order. Analyzing Marx and Tocqueville allows us to address the above-mentioned approaches.

Marx inherited the question of the constitutive principle of a secularized society from Hegel and the Enlightenment. Is there a substantive rationality on which to base the social order? Marx radicalizes Enlightened rationalism in two ways: the deployment of reason is conceived as praxis and praxis refers to the future of an emancipated society. All his work is, at bottom, a complex reformulation of the principle of popular sovereignty.

On the one hand, Marx still links the search for certainty to the constitutive foundation of the social order, though the constitution of the social is no longer legitimized by a divine principle but praxis. The "paradigm of production" entails a double rupture. Marx breaks with all transcendent legitimation, explaining order as a social historical product. He also breaks with the idea of a political-state institutionalization of the social and, in fact, takes the social conditions of production as the basis of political institutionality. That is, he replaces divine will with the human one while redirecting popular sovereignty toward social divisions. By making the tension between "general will" and the "will of all" explicit, Marx criticizes the illusory certainty offered not only by religion, but also by politics. This criticism does not, however, invalidate the demand for certainty. Marx accepts it as a real necessity, but one that can only be satisfied via social revolution.

The critique of capitalist society refers, on the other hand, to a possible society. What is the possible future? Following the Enlightenment's tradition, Marx hails secularization as the irrevocable advance of reason. It is this philosophy of history that makes it possible to determine what is possible: a fully rational and universal society. This society will be, unlike the extant reality, the true society. Human praxis acquires a benchmark of certainty when we identify the future with a "truth to be attained." The desire for certainty can renounce religious illusions and political ideologies because the very development of society anticipates a future of fulfillment. In a transparent society, identical to itself, uncertainty is, by definition, excluded.

It is paradoxical that a text that was fundamentally understood as a critique and dismantling of the existing system is nowadays denounced as a source of totalitarianism. In current debate, criticism of Marx tends, beyond specific objections, to get confused with the counter-Enlightenment. Enlightened rationalism is seen as the origin of "an identifying, planning, controlling, objectifying, systematizing, and unifying reason; in short: a totalizing reason."[123] If the denunciations of totalizing reason—from Nietzsche to the post-structuralists, and beginning with Marx himself—did not prevent the progressive rationalization and bureaucratization of social life, this is due, I believe, to the dialectic of secularization. The more we question the real and the rational, the legitimate and the necessary, the more we crave an all-encompassing reason that assures us of the external limits and internal structuring of social reality. The rediscovery of the social space as a "magma of differences" that can never be fully structured and institutionalized well reflects the perception of the new social complexity. The simplicity of the world, a unique nature, or rationality have dissolved. The process of social differentiation does not, however, show the radical split between the different aspects of social life. The critique of all-encompassing discourse does not imply, I believe, abandoning a notion of totality. Precisely because reality always overwhelms us, we institute society by "closing" the social universe. If we forewent a delimitation of "society," immediacy and relativism would dilute all social identity. Therefore, I find the current deconstruction of the totalizing metatheory insufficient. The reconstruction of a new notion of totality is still pending. How can we

---

123 A concise summary is presented by A. Wellmer, "La dialéctica de modernidad y postmodernidad," *Debats* (Valencia) 14 (1985).

conceive of totality in such a way as to account for plurality? It seems to me this is the fundamental problem. Both Marx and liberalism suspend the tension between totality and plurality, respectively reducing one pole to the other. I presume that the foundation of the social order will remain a "black hole" as long as we fail to articulate the two aspects of democracy: conflicting order and collective order.

Is it possible to assert "the collective" on an objective basis, or can it only be analyzed as a historical product? Seeking to oppose ideological fictions with objective certainty, Marx emphasizes the (material) legitimacy of the democratic order. On the other hand, Tocqueville is exclusively interested in the concrete modality in which democratic institutions operate. Tocqueville thus shifts the scope of analysis: the theoretical foundation of "good order" is replaced by the historical study of a "real democracy."

According to Tocqueville, the referents of certainty are cultural elaborations. Unlike an "institutional engineering" that addresses legitimation and democratic procedures in isolation from the values, beliefs, habits, and motivations of a given society, Tocqueville approaches the institutions of American democracy as a cultural configuration. In this sense, he (like Marx) understands democracy more as a social state than as a form of government. Only that his approach—less systemic, more comprehensive than explanatory—perceives culture as a constituent (and not "derivative") area of social reality. Without ignoring inequality in American society, Tocqueville relies precisely on egalitarian ideology—the similarity of feelings, beliefs, and customs—as the common sense of democracy. This sensitivity to political culture is what makes Tocqueville's thinking so modern and so attentive to the consequences of secularization. He delves, more often and explicitly than Marx, in what I think is one of the fundamental problems of Latin American democracy: What unites a secularized society so that the diversity of values and interests can develop as plurality without leading to social disarticulation?

Tocqueville poses the democratic question in direct relation to the process of secularization: "what can be done with a people which is its own master, if it not be submissive to the Divinity?" While popular sovereignty advocates an unprecedented freedom of action, religious faith sets the limits of what is possible. "Thus, whilst the law permits the

Americans to do what they please, religion prevents them from conceiving, and forbids them to commit what is rash or unjust."[124] But Tocqueville no longer thinks of religion as the radically external foundation of the social order and refers to a society of believers, not a religious one. That is, he reinterprets religion in secularized terms as a "moral-intellectual hegemony." In the absence of a right that is external and superior to the popular will (and specifically, to the majority), Tocqueville envisions the need for an "ideological-cultural cement" that ensures political institutions can be based on social experiences.

Transcendent legitimation is replaced by a "civil religion." At this point, Tocqueville moves away from the French Enlightenment and approaches English traditionalism (Burke).[125] The cohesion of American democracy lies not in the rationalist construction of order, but in historical tradition. It is the historical sedimentation of cultural patterns that leads to that similarity between people that makes them feel as members of the same community. Instead of an abstract principle, the "social contract" becomes nothing more than that historical set of common practices and criteria.

Such a factual (historical) agreement is, however, precarious given the equivocal significance of social action. Secularization has relegated certainty to the individual conscience, responsible for harmonizing particularity with universal norms. Subjective certainty thus presupposes the existence of a universalist principle. If it is the object of multiple interpretations and lacks univocal meaning, uncertainty arises again. Sensitive to the ambiguity of egalitarian ideology (which can mean individuation and anonymity, innovation and uniformity), Tocqueville rethinks the problem of the foundation of the social space.

He approaches the subject using a negative scenario: the dangers of a tyranny of the majority. Accepting that, once popular sovereignty is established, the principle of majority is the only feasible principle of legitimacy, how can we prevent the majority from doing whatever it

---

124 Alexis de Tocqueville, *Democracy in America*, vol. 1 (New York: Schocken Books, 1964), 362.

125 Véase E. Burke, *Textos políticos* (Mexico: Fondo de Cultura Económica, 1984). [–Ed.]

wants? Tocqueville glimpses the tendency of the majority not only to dominate the minority, but to absorb it. Representing the challenges of the world, the ambiguity and contradictoriness of established meanings, the minority threatens the faith of the majority: things do not have to be this way. For fear of losing their identity, the majority may desire to do more than merely express their will and try to universalize it.[126] The tyranny of the majority consists of it imposing its will as the general one.

What causes such false universalization? Does it not lie precisely in the uncertainty regarding "the general"? It seems to me that the widespread perception of the absence or erosion of a collective will is not alien to the rise of dictatorships in the Southern Cone.

Unlike Furet, I do not believe that Tocqueville "breaks with the obsession regarding the foundations of the social, so characteristic of the eighteenth century and of Marx who, from this point of view, is its heir."[127] Tocqueville also has this in mind and implicitly adopts Rousseau's approach, putting identity (general will) before plurality (the will of all). A self-image of society as a "collective ego" is the assumption under which the pluralism of American democracy is meant to operate; lacking this referent, plurality leads to anarchy and, as a reaction, to despotism. This is how Tocqueville seems to have interpreted the political development of Latin America in the nineteenth century, oscillating permanently between anarchy and military despotism.

Tocqueville criticizes Latin Americans for not knowing how to root democratic institutions in common sense: "Although they had borrowed the letter of law, they were unable to create or to introduce the spirit and the sense which give it life."[128] However, can one feasibly transplant the "spirit of the law"? Tocqueville himself assumes egalitarian beliefs and democratic customs (specific features of US society) as a fact. As we saw, he seems to share with counter-enlightenment traditionalism

---

126 R. Sennett, "Lo que Tocqueville temía," in *Narcisismo y cultura moderna* (Barcelona: Kairós, 1980).

127 F. Furet, op. cit., 115.

128 Alexis de Tocqueville, *Democracy in America*, vol. 1 (New York: Schocken Books, 1964), 185.

the idea that each historical period refers to a set of basic presupposi-tions—"axioms"of a kind that, unintelligible during that period, provide latent inspiration for the explicit beliefs and aspirations of the era. If we take democratic institutionality as a cultural crystallization, Tocqueville does not center on a fundamental problem of democracy in Latin Amer-ica: the genesis of a democratic political culture. His paradox lies in a historical approach that does not consider the problem of time.

A democratic culture is the result of a historical process. That is, its development requires time—but time is precisely one of the scarc-est resources in a democratic transition, which largely explains the successive failures of democracy in Latin America: democracy fails to consolidate because it is not given enough time to develop the cus-toms and beliefs on which institutional construction could be based. The legitimacy of democratic institutions presupposes the maturation of a democratic culture that in turn presupposes the relatively durable performance of institutions. Does this mean that, in the absence of a democratic tradition, democracy also has no future? The fact is that, in the republican tradition of Latin America, democracy and authoritari-anism are always intermingled.

Neither democracy nor authoritarianism seem capable of develop-ing the historical time required for the crystallization of a collective identity. The problem of time leads us back to Marx. He expresses, bet-ter than Tocqueville, the rupture in the conception of time: recourse to the past is replaced by an anticipation of the future.

The philosophy of praxis implies a "constructivist" vision: the deliberate creation of the future. Moreover, it tends to be a determina-tion of the historical process as a full self-realization of the individual in community: "the free association of free individuals." Underlying the emphatic affirmation of a fully rational and universal order is an idea of truth. For Marx, the critique of religion does not rule out the criterion of truth. Marx assumes the existence of a truth that will allow us to discern, even amid the present conflict of interests and interpre-tations, a collective reference that is valid for all. He adopts the idea of the "common good" as defined in substantive terms (and not merely by procedures), while projecting it into the future.

Along with his theory of the subject, the idea of a "truth to be attained" is surely one of the most objected aspects of Marxist political thought. To suppose that there is a truth that we must accomplish is seen as the very definition of a totalitarian imposition. No doubt the linking of politics and truth is problematic. I have personally and repeatedly criticized such a reference to the truth as undue sacralization of political stances, one that destroys democratic procedures. However, we cannot help but wonder why a gnostic project manages to obtain adherents in a secularized society. Probably the notions of progress, revolution, or emancipation are not only a secularization of eschatological hopes, but also a way of neutralizing the uncertainty of the future. It is an issue of giving time direction and constituting a continuity that allows us to situate current time. If the present were no more than a succession of instants, if time did not become duration, there would be no social process. From this point of view, the idea of progress as any "project" is a way of ensuring time, anticipating the future.

The projection of a "common good" as a historical goal must be very attractive in a continent that is characterized both by its communal tradition and social inequalities. Once the received order has been delegitimized, utopia seems to be the only perspective capable of transcending society's disarticulation. Hence the strength of utopian thinking in Latin American politics.[129] Such anticipation of the future, however, suffocates the present because it demands "proof" that no policy can offer, and utopia ends up being a self-destructive prophecy.

The historical experience is well summarized by Horkheimer and Adorno in the opening statements of their study on the dialectic of the Enlightenment: "Enlightenment, understood in the widest sense as the advancement of thought, has always aimed at liberating human beings from fear and installing them as masters. Yet the wholly enlightened earth is radiant with triumphant calamity."[130] The criteria of rationality and universality (which for Marx are still linked to political

---

129 On the utopian dimension of the Spanish conquest in the Americas, see M. Góngora, *Estudios de historia de las ideas y de historia social* (Valparaíso: Editorial Universitaria, 1980).

130 Max Horkheimer and Theodor W. Adorno, *Dialectic of Enlightenment* (California: Stanford University Press, 2002), 1.

self-determination and the republic) became embodied in another way of anticipating the future: technocracy.

Instrumental planning for the future has increased social control over the effects of our actions. However, it also involves the attempt to manipulate others, fixing a certain course of action in advance. Instrumental reason turns out to be as deterministic as the philosophy of history. By planning for the future, we rob others not only of the freedom to choose their future, but also of their present. The instrumental moment of action displaces the expressive moment to such a point that individuals can no longer acquire the experience of contemporaneity. And the individual who does not share a common present with his neighbor does not participate in the joint elaboration of time. Social time gets atomized and so does sociability. Given this symbolic-expressive deficit, technocratic control of the future further exacerbates uncertainty.

Technical-scientific civilization reveals itself as an unfinished secularization. On the one hand and by not resolving the demand for certainty, it permanently encourages the desire to transcend its immanence via some utopian purpose. It intends to escape the constrictions of instrumental reason by submitting to a transcendent principle. On the other hand, this same secularized society no longer admits an ultimate instance, while utopias can only be conceived as plural and as being in conflict. Fearing that the invocation of absolute truths will again provoke religious wars, Max Weber warns us that the salvation of the soul cannot be the task of politics. That said, secularization undermines every transcendent principle without eliminating the demand for some ultimate certainty. In the wake of secularization, religious hopes for happiness and final harmony are internalized by society as worldly promises because it seems unable to assert itself without a utopian referent, whether conceived in capitalist terms (the perfect market), anarchist ones (a society without ruler or law), liberal ones (rational deliberation), or Marxist ones (a classless society).[131] Democracy also rests on a secularized utopia: the so-called democratic creed. It continues to subsist

---

131   F. Hinkelammert, *Crítica a la razón utópica* (San José, Costa Rica: DEI, 1984). For the erosion of secularized utopias, see J. Habermas, *Die Neue Unübersichtlichkeit* (Frankfurt: Suhrkamp, 1985).

solely based on this faith, despite all vicissitudes. Moreover, only this creed allows us to face the adverse experiences of real democracy as challenges that may, in fact, deepen it.

In short, our secularized society does not allow us to undertake the search for certainty via some sacralized principle, but neither does it allow us to dismiss said search. The problem of the democratic order therefore seems to entail the construction of a horizon of certainty that is secular in nature.

4. A Pending Task

Can democracy respond to the demand for certainty? My question seeks to link the democratic question with the debate on modernity. Behind the difficulties of the processes of democratization in Latin America, I see a problem bequeathed by secularization itself: the difficulty for an increasingly complex society to ascertain itself as a collective order. Society is not only free to organize itself according to its own will, but also free from every time-honored prescription that previously guaranteed the validity of the established order. Meaning that, in filling the vacuum left by religion, politics must also adopt demands for certainty.

Can there be democracy without religion? Tocqueville's restlessness is much more insightful than our (severely) disenchanted society tends to believe. To safeguard a minimum core of supra-individual values, it seems indispensable that we should remove it from political conflict. Perceiving the centrifugal dynamics of emerging democracy, Tocqueville worried about the limits of popular will. His study of beliefs and customs as a "civil religion" is an initial response to the issues raised by the French Revolution.

Is it possible to institute society from within itself without resorting to transcendent legitimacy? This question remains the great challenge of democracy. Modern society must create its own normativity, its own self. How can we legitimize the constitutive rules of order without sacralizing them? We can conceive of popular sovereignty as a transcendental referent, separated from society and through which differences in society can be identified as part of a collectivity. The externalization enables the institution of a collective referent subtracted from the conflict, but for the same reason, imposed on the subjects. If we start, on the contrary, from a plurality of subjects, how can we institute a legitimatizing order principle, recognized by all? The process of social differentiation enables a conception of totality only in the plural. Plurality, however, must be produced as well as totality. And we only elaborate plurality by means of a notion of collectivity; without a collective referent, social differentiation leads to disarticulation. This is the case for Latin American societies.

Can complex societies elaborate a reasonable identity? Habermas's question[132] precisely involves the erosion or loss of the traditional referents of collective identification: religion, class, state. The complexity of social structures has eroded the promises of certainty that once crystallized in those instances. Such disenchantment, while necessary, is insufficient. If we discard the neoliberal premise of an automatic self-regulation of society, the question of order remains: the need for all individuals to recognize and affirm themselves as belonging to a community.

We have seen two ways of approaching the construction of order. Marx's aim is to discover a substantive rationality in the internal movement of society. He thus retains the ancient conception of an order founded on an objective and universal principle, but 1) defines it as a social product and 2) projects it into the future. The replacement of religious transcendence by a historical one does not only express the new consciousness of time. It responds to the need to exclude other legitimizing principles. Only the materialization of the foundation invoked in a fully rational society confirms utopia as the true totality. Conceived as a "truth to be attained," the principles of rationality and universality become an indisputable reference of identification. The problem is obvious: basing certainty on a single and exclusive foundation denies plurality.

No less problematic is an approach that replaces the problem of foundation with a rationale and ethics of action. Indeed, Tocqueville

---

132 This will be the central question of all of Habermas's work facing the German crisis of the World War II and the reformulation of critical Marxism. See J. Habermas, *La reconstrucción del materialismo histórico* (Madrid: Taurus, 1981). [–Ed.]

well apprehends the totalitarian tendencies unleashed by secularization given that totalizing reason is a "logical" response on the part of society to ensure its identity in a process of differentiation. By anchoring social cohesion to the mechanisms of cultural integration, Tocqueville's approach does not suspend plurality.

Emphasis on social experiences, however, implies a concrete-historical determination. If we address a culture determined by the historical premise of democracy, the latter becomes a contingent result. In other words, we can always desire democracy, but this will be a vain aspiration without prior cultural integration.

In both approaches, the demand for certainty is intercepted "at the level of" a social rationale (economic or cultural) without reaching the political sphere. In such scenarios, it would not be the task of politics to respond to the search for certainty. On the contrary, society already must have made sure of itself to institutionalize a democratic order. And yet, as we have seen, this is not the case with processes of democratization in Latin America. Here, the institution of "the social" passes through politics.

How do we respond politically to the search for certainty? The most frequent response is the nation state. And yet, this is only an apparent political response. In fact, the political form of the state rests on a pre-political content: the nation defined in terms of linguistics, ethnicity, or as a community of destiny. It is by means of a preconstituted unity that we ensure a "we" versus "the others." The community (national identity) is not what is properly political, but its premise.

As soon as politics is recognized as its own productivity, it is tamed by formal procedures. To the extent that secularization eroded traditional customs and consecrated values, politics is progressively subjected to devices of formal rationality. As I pointed out at the beginning, the relativization and privatization of securities is compensated for by the parallel advance of the market and bureaucracy. We cannot ignore, however, the limited scope of formal calculation. Vast sectors of social life are never articulated, neither by the market nor by means of administrative mechanisms. Moreover, the growing weight of bureaucratic and mercantile relations in political processes causes disintegrating dynamics.

Formal rationality seeks instrumental calculability and efficiency, presupposing an agreement on ends. The "rules of the game" in themselves do not offer security since their significance lies outside them, in what is often called the "spirit of the law." Whenever the regulative principle—the sense of order—is the object of conflict, controversy immediately relativizes formal procedures. It is enough to recall the Chilean process to understand that we cannot exclusively base certainty on institutions and procedures.

We need not emphasize the precariousness of the collective referents in our societies, as recurrently demonstrated by the "social question" and the "national question." Perhaps that is why charisma as a type of political production of identity is more frequent. The more or less open struggle between different constitutive principles of order can come to a truce under a charismatic leader, a physical embodiment of the nation's metaphysical identity. I am not referring to traditional *caudillismo*, but to presidential democracy. Figures such as Tancredo Neves, Raúl Alfonsín, or Alan García illustrate how democracy conquers legitimacy through adherence to the president. This is a secularized, institutionally founded charisma, but once established, loyalty to the charismatic leader becomes the pillar of loyalty to the democratic regime. We could speak of "situational charisma"[133] in the sense that a situation of helplessness and uncertainty establishes the need to believe in a leader and thus—through charismatic leadership—affirm a collective identity. This explains, in my opinion, why in many Latin American democracies, faith in authority prevails over routines and rules and is, in citizens' perception, more important than the efficiency of government management.

Charisma coexists with formal rationality. This contemporaneity belies the idea of a linear evolution of social structures of consciousness and identity. It seems more appropriate to think of an overlapping of mental structures similar to geological layers.[134] In Latin American

---

133 I borrow R. Tucker's term, "The Theory of Charismatic Leadership," *Daedalus* (Summer 1986): 745. See also S. Moscovici, *L'âge des foules* (Paris: Fayard, 1981). Always exposed to a crisis of confidence and credibility, charismatic leadership can only exceptionally (Moses) lead to the foundation of a national identity.

134 This article owes much to the stimulating studies of B. Nelson, *Der Ursprung der Moderne* (Frankfurt: Suhrkamp, 1984). For this point, see 75 ff.

society, patterns of formal rationality undoubtedly prevail: operations of generalization, systematization, abstraction, and formalization guide social action following rational-universalist criteria. It is an international standard that, once instituted, marks the mental structure in our society, however distorted its presence. This "modern consciousness," however, underlies other structures. To the extent that formal-instrumental rationality fails to ensure the symbolic-normative integration of society, a "gnostic consciousness" can emerge. Faith in the transcendent resurfaces as a substitute for the principles of rationality and universality. It is not necessary that these be fully realized, because, as Enrique Tierno Galván states, accepting the imperfect is part of the perfect installation in the finite.[135] However, there must be such referents of certainty to be able to settle in finitude. Otherwise, where modern consciousness fails to elaborate such references, people resurrect a transcendent principle to ascertain their collective identity.

In short, we cannot simply identify democracy with uncertainty. Of course, democracy has led to disenchantment and, particularly in Latin America, global revolutions must be urgently dismantled. It would be wrong, however, to radicalize disenchantment to a degree that, under the pretext of denouncing totalitarian solutions, we end up ignoring the underlying problem. On the contrary, it is precisely our critical stance toward the dictatorships of the Southern Cone that has led us to discover in authoritarianism a (false and failed) attempt to restore certainty by crushing difference. The democratization process must perforce account for this problem.

---

135 E. Tierno Galván, ¿Qué es ser gnóstico? (Madrid: Tecnos, 1985).

VII

So-Called Postmodern Disenchantment

1. A Postmodern Environment

What is the point of discussing so-called postmodernity in Latin America? Another imported intellectual fad and long acquaintance with frustration might have made us skeptical of debates that, while valid in Europe or North America, are alien to our reality. Indeed, postmodernity is a controversial notion, and it is still too early to assess the scope of the debate. And yet, the current mood certainly differs from those of previous decades and this new sensibility deserves our attention.[136] Moreover, we live in an era of transnationalization that encompasses both economic and ideological circuits; the "cultural climate" is also internationalized and the topics of European or North American debates are part (if only as fads) of our reality. Moreover, any approach will illuminate some problems while obscuring many others.

Let us therefore ask ourselves what phenomena are brought to light by this debate.

What do we mean by "postmodernity"? The interpretations are multiple and often contradictory.[137] For some, modernity has been exhausted,

---

136 It is significant for the history of social sciences in the region that CLACSO has celebrated its twentieth anniversary with the theme "Latin American Identity, Premodernity, Modernity, and Postmodernity." See *David & Goliath* (Buenos Aires) 52 (1987). No less revealing is the interest the subject arouses in neoliberal magazines; see the dossier in *Estudios Públicos* (Santiago) 27 (1987).

137 F. Jameson undertakes a brief introduction in "Posiciones ideológicas en el debate posmodernista," *Fahrenheit 450* (Buenos Aires) 2 (1987), translated

ushering a new era. For others, there is no such mutation, and this is a critique within an unfinished project of modernity.[138] In any case, it is by reference to modernity that we reflect on our situation. That is, postmodernity is fundamentally a reflection on our time. Also, and above all, the debate surrounding it, although birthed in the fields of philosophy, aesthetics, and architecture, has become a political question. Has the reforming impulse of modernity been exhausted? This is the fundamental (albeit incipient) issue, and it is from this point of view that I intend to review a possible change in our political culture.

Without a doubt, disenchantment is a phenomenon that characterizes the political situation in several Latin American countries.[139] This can seriously affect democratization processes by taking away their roots in political institutions. For this reason, political disenchantment is often valued negatively, and there is no lack of historical experience to justify this fear. There is danger in this disenchantment with democracy, and it should be analyzed more closely. There have always been periods of certainty and periods of doubt; in fact, disenchantment only appears where there previously were illusions. In this regard, there is talk of an excess of expectations democracy cannot meet. Now, more than an excess, it could be a change in the subjectivity invested in politics. It is this aspect of the "postmodern climate" that interests me. In my opinion, so-called postmodernity entails, above all, a certain disenchantment with modernity. Modernity, in turn, was defined as a "disenchantment of the world" (Max Weber). It therefore means this is a kind of "disenchantment with disenchantment," a paradoxical formula that reminds us that disenchantment is, more than a loss of illusions, a reinterpretation of longings. If so, this disenchantment called postmodernity would not be the sad end of a project much too beautiful to become reality but, on the contrary, a starting point.

---

from *New German Critique* 33.

138 See J. Habermas's well-known "La modernidad, un proyecto incompleto," in *La posmodernidad*, ed. H. Foster (Barcelona: Kairós, 1985).

139 For Argentina, see F. Echegaray and E. Raimundo, *Desencanto político, transición y democracia* (Buenos Aires: Centro Editor, 1987).

2. On Modernity

Latin America was born under the sign of modernity in a twofold sense. On the one hand, European arrival in the Americas contributed (alongside the Renaissance, the Reformation, and the philosophy of the Enlightenment) to shape modern Western thought. Their encounter with the "New World" altered the consciousness of historical time; since curiosity for the new brings so many material benefits, "the new" is constituted as a value in itself. The conquests of the Americas marked decisive milestones from which to undertake the conquest of the future. Not only temporal coordinates but also spatial ones were thrown off-center. The encounter with "the Indian"—the other—posed a new scale of differentiation that immediately led to the questioning of European identity. Their world map was modified and, therefore, the meager mental space in which the old social order was conceived was also altered.[140]

If Latin America is at the origin of modernity, on the other hand and in turn, it was constituted under the impact of modernity. The independence movements confronted our countries with the challenge of modernity as emblematically embodied by the French Revolution: How to institute society solely from the social, without resorting to transcendent legitimation? The question summarizes the issue of order as it is still addressed in Latin America. Let us therefore return to the notion of modernity, explored in the previous article, to later focus on the possible reasons for disenchantment.

By modernity, we understand the process of disenchantment with the religious organization of the world. Religious society was characterized by the absolute precedence and otherness of a divine principle that acted as an inviolable guarantee of order. This radically excised foundation and the worldly order itself were removed from human sway. Modernity entails rupture with this transcendent foundation and the vindication of social reality as an order determined by people. By

---

140 See T. Todorov, *La conquête de l'Amérique. La question de l'autre* (Paris: Seuil, 1982), reviewed by P. L. Crovetto in *Mundo* (Mexico) 2 (1987), translated by Siglo XXI Editores.

asserting their autonomy, individuals must inevitably take charge of organizing their coexistence.

Modernity is, first and foremost, a process of secularization: the slow passage from a received order to a produced order.[141] The accent is twofold. On the one hand, it is a social production of order. The world ceases to entail a predetermined order to which we must submit and becomes the object of human will. How can we take responsibility for the world when our power of influence and control is so scarce? On the other hand, there is order itself. There is no longer an absolute law or a sacred tradition that directs the human will, and people must then place limits on themselves. On what general principles can the social order be founded when everything is subject to criticism?

Questions such as these, which accompany the development of modernity with greater or lesser drama, hint at the magnitude of the challenges posed by a "produced order." Amid this revolution, whose radical nature we can hardly imagine today, the central problem of modern society is perhaps to ensure its identity—that is, to ascertain "itself" as a society.[142] It must create its own normativity from within itself. And this produced order can no longer claim any guarantees precisely because it is self-determined. Previously, the radical otherness of the foundation excluded conflicts about the form of social coexistence. Now, both the order that is and the order that should be are subject to discussion. Not only the rights of one or another social stratum, but the meaning and legitimacy of the order itself are permanently questioned. With no possible escape, modern society is inexorably self-referential. This explains both the incessant dynamic with which it tries to identify itself and the extreme sensitivity with which it reacts to any possible threat to its self-image.

Along with this radical self-reference comes modern politics. Secularization transfers to politics the integrative function previously played

---

141 For this stance, see M. Gauchet, *Le désenchantement du monde* (Paris: Gallimard, 1985).

142 J. Habermas, "Das Zeitbewusstsein der Moderne und ihr Bedurfnis nach Selbstvergewisserung," in *Der philosophische Diskurs der Moderne* (Frankfurt: Suhrkamp, 1985).

by religion. If religion once consecrated an ultimate instance upon which all the manifestations of the given order were founded, now politics is assigned a privileged place in the production of the social order. The replacement of the divine foundation by the principle of popular sovereignty doubly institutes the centrality of politics: (a) as a conscious action exercised by society on itself, and (b) a representation of society as a collective order. In general, the emphasis is on the first aspect (i.e., politics as action), but the second one is no less productive. Moreover, the fact that society recognizes and affirms itself as a collectivity is the premise for it to act upon itself. Consequently, it seems to me that a decisive question of modernity is: Can modern society politically elaborate a reasonable identity?

Here we run into two problems. I have already introduced one: How can we articulate a plurality of individual wills, unlimited in principle, into a collective will that, by definition, establishes limits? The articulation of plurality and collectivity is precisely democracy's intent. Since its inception, though, there has been a substantial gap between this theoretical pretension and its practical institutionalization. The multiplicity of existing "peoples" (i.e., heterogeneity of society) contradicts the homogeneity that presupposes the sovereignty of a people on a conceptual level.[143] That is, the idea of popular sovereignty evokes an already existing "people" when, in truth, this identity has only just been created. To be more precise: democracy (as a principle of legitimacy) presupposes an identity that democracy (as a principle of organization) can never produce as something permanent and definitive.

The second difficulty is, can politics as a partial aspect of social life "represent" society as a whole? A premise of all modern democratic theory is the possibility of elaborating, by specifically political means, a representation of unity. Such a "community" is constituted, explicitly or implicitly, by reference to a general will. Immediately, however, the fictitious and abstract character of "the general" gets criticized. Criticism may be restricted to the political mechanisms of representation (census

---

143 F.-X. Guerra, "La peuple souverain; fondements et logiques d'une fiction" (mimeo) (Paris: Seminario EHSS-CLACSO, 1987), provides a good introduction to the Independence era.

vote, etc.), but for Marx this is not a question of an insufficiency in the political field, but rather of the incompetence of politics to legitimize the social order. The problem is, how representative is politics?

These difficulties explain the various attempts to situate the question of identity in a structure other than politics and, specifically, democracy. It is enough to recall Marx's own thesis that "the anatomy of civil society must be sought in political economy," taking class as an identifying reference. Tocqueville, on the other hand, alludes to a sociocultural integration, highlighting the similarity of customs, feelings, and beliefs as the basis of American democracy. The most relevant attempt, however, is the affirmation of a national identity. Regardless of how we define the nation (as essentialist, ethnic, linguistic, or a community of common destiny), this strategy illustrates well some of the contradictions posed by modernity.

There is an initial contradiction between the centrality assigned to politics as the locus of popular sovereignty and the societal determination of identity. In the case of national identity as well as other mentioned attempts, the unity of the social process is conceived as a fact external to politics. Historically, it will be the state that carries out unification, but state action is legitimized only insofar as it "represents" a societally defined identity. This societal approach reduces the productivity attributed to politics: the collective will that is politically elaborated will always be subordinate to an ultimate instance outside politics (national unity, economic structure, tradition).

The second contradiction lies in the search for a historical identity in an eminently "futuristic" era. If modernity is characterized by a break with tradition, the question of identity, on the other hand, is projected into the past. Through a retrospective construction, the unity of social life is put before politics as a previous datum. This usually entails reducing the rich diversity of elements and alternatives to a singular, linear history from which all crossroads and discontinuities have been erased. The result is a fictitious identity based on an artificially homogenized past to legitimize the present. Additionally, this is a closed identity, with a reduced scope for modification in accordance with the innovations of the social process.

There is a third contradiction between the universalist criteria of democracy and the particularistic features of the nation state. Modern society is founded on the unlimited sovereignty and general will of the people and, simultaneously, on the institutionalization of certain values. While democracy rests, in principle, on a cosmopolitan citizenship, accepting no other limit than the recognition of the constitutional order, the national state is made up of a pre-selected population based on quasi-natural categories. In this case, the community is defined exclusively by its opposition to other nations. What is different is what is foreign. A nationalist identity consequently views differences as an (international) division of friend or foe.

We need not explain modern difficulties for society to recognize and affirm itself in more detail. It is enough to envision how the abandonment of a sacred vision and the affirmation of a profane world puts the question of identity at the center, and how this is closely linked with the democratic question. Since this has been our main concern for the past ten years, exploring the contribution of postmodern critique to the elaboration of a new theory of democracy is not irrelevant.

3. Disenchantment with Modernization

A first dimension of postmodern disenchantment is the loss of faith in the idea that there might be a theory that holds the key to understanding the social process in its entirety. Our age is characterized by suspicion of all kinds when it comes to all-encompassing metadiscourse, a mistrust stemming from anti-totalitarian intentions; behind knowledge, as with any pretense of truth, we intuit a hidden relationship of power. Postmodern criticism thus furthers the relativization of all norms. The "will to power" would be the force that structures the social magma of difference while institutionalizing a system. Counterposing what is social to society seeks to rescue the infinite complexity of "life" versus "form."

This is a well-known tension among "the moderns," as attested by the considerable discussion that characterized the turn of the century. Also, the "social system" is not a neutral structure. All criticism feeds on doubt and one must be suspicious of the power objectified in the existing structures. An indeterminate denial of all power, however, fails to discern between legitimate and illegitimate institutions. Postmodern critique approaches anarchist positions that—unless the question of legitimacy is rendered obsolete—end up as an evidentiary and ineffective rebellion. In other words: postmodern deconstruction has the undoubted merit of highlighting complexity as a central phenomenon of our society, but I wonder if it also provides us with the means to work on said complexity.

The rejection of reason is based on the existence of various rationalities—a rather banal observation when alluding to the process of differentiation proper to secularization. With the loss of unity sought by religion and metaphysics, the different social fields begin differing rapidly, each developing according to its specific rationale. The philosophers of the Enlightenment already recognized cognitive-instrumental, moral-practical, and aesthetic-expressive rationalities as separated spheres, though the acknowledgment of such differentiation was always accompanied by a search for some principle of universal validity. Modernity was conceived as a tension between differentiation and unification within a historical process directed toward final harmony. Today, the enlightened optimism regarding the convergence of science, morality, and art to achieve control of natural forces, social progress and the happiness of humanity has disappeared. The reconciliation of the good, the true, and the beautiful appears as an illusion of modernity, and postmodernity would be the concomitant disenchantment: the differentiation of dissimilar rationalities is apprehended as a split.

The break with modernity would reject the reference to totality. However, the scope of this new disenchantment remains ambiguous: Is the reference to the articulating totality of the different fields rejected because it proves itself impossible or because it is no longer necessary? Are we unable to do away with a notion of totality, albeit one considered in other terms? In my opinion, the debate on so-called postmodernity leaves a fundamental question open: Is the tension between differentiation and articulation still a practical problem or, rather, an obsolete issue?

Disenchantment always has two faces: the loss of an illusion and, therefore, a resignification of reality. The constructive dimension of today's disenchantment lies in the praise of heterogeneity. We are witnessing a new dynamic that is both threatening and exhilarating. Threatening because landscapes that were once familiar and allowed us to move with some foresight collapse (never mind said certainty was illusory; the important factor is the existence of shared references). Now everything is accelerated, and nothing is in place. Along with this oft paralyzing feeling of precariousness, the new dynamic triggers creative revulsions. Why do we assume that homogeneity favors peaceful understanding and consider heterogeneity a source of conflict?[144] For too many years we have been denouncing the "structural heterogeneity" of Latin America as an obstacle to development without considering that it could foster a much denser and richer interaction than the desired homogenization.

However, our assessment of heterogeneity was not wholly unfounded and was born out of concern over an increasingly eroded community. It is from the point of view of a threatened identity that we see heterogeneity as fragmentation—one we should reject. This is a reasonable critique because, in effect, heterogeneity does not produce greater social dynamics, unless it is complemented by some notion of community. If so, perhaps we should reformulate the problem. Instead of continuing to emphasize the heterogeneity of our societies, we should review our idea of community. In other words, our notion of community would then become the problem; more than a "crisis of consensus," we would be faced with a crisis regarding our conception of consensus.

History teaches us that the greater the fragmentation of society into segmented fields, the greater the voluntarism needed to restore organic integration. However, the will to synthesize when the objective conditions are not given cannot but be expressed as an act of violence to society. That is what our dictatorships have fundamentally been: the imposition of an organic unity on a heterogeneous and complex reality. And yet, we will only overcome authoritarianism to the extent that we arrive at a different understanding and valuation of that dispersed and eccentric modernity. That is, we lack a theory of modernity that recognizes the existence of diversity, its value and the need to give it a formal, though never substantive, coherence.[145]

---

144 For a suggestive confrontation with Asian thought see M. Maruyama, "Diferentes paisajes mentales," *Letra Internacional* (Madrid) 5 (1987).

145 X. Rubert de Ventós, "Kant responde a Habermas," *Fahrenheit 450* (Buenos Aires) 2 (1987).

The contribution that the "postmodern climate" brings to the debate on democracy lies in this shift of focus. Historically, suspicion of heterogeneity as a threat to social integration has extended to the political field. Latin American democracy has always been traversed by a distrust of plurality as an undue questioning of national unity. In recent years, authoritarian experience and postmodern culture, reinforcing each other, question the seemingly univocal meaning of said unity. Ethnic and cultural pluralism, the diversity of economic structures and political-ideological tolerance are now starting to be appreciated. In other words, social differentiation is positively revalued rather than simply identified with social divisions and inequalities. A new sensitivity to "fair differences" is emerging. This is the postmodern contribution, so to speak. In Latin America, however, it is not limited to a praise of heterogeneity. Here, the revaluation of heterogeneity cannot fail to reference the question of order. How do we distinguish between legitimate diversity and illegitimate inequalities?

By criticizing the "great narratives," the discussion readdresses the ordering of social life as a central theme. What alternatives does it offer? Because of its rejection of notions of totality, it is not concerned with the institutionalization of the collective. Moreover, postmodern disenchantment is often expressed precisely as a loss of faith in the state. The state is perceived, above all things, as an apparatus of domination, always suspected of seeking totalitarian control. A distrust of the "philanthropic ogre" is certainly justified; where the state takes on tasks of collective responsibility, it tends to liquidate individual ones. However, in its rejection of the statist disposition, postmodern culture tends to dismiss the very question of the state. Its anti-institutionalism ignores the symbolic dimension of the modern state. Once the divine foundation has been eroded, society is obliged to create a new instance that allows it to structure its divisions; the state will be the referent through which people recognize and affirm themselves as a collective order. This representation of the "whole" through the state is questioned nowadays, either in theoretical terms or because of the process of secularization itself.

For Niklas Luhmann, for example, the functional differentiation of modern society leads to a set of subsystems, the state being one more of them and lacking any privileged status to represent the social system as a whole. "No system of functions, not even the political, can take the place of hierarchy and its summit. We live in a society which cannot represent its unity in itself, as this would contradict the logic of functional differentiation. We live in a society without a summit and without a center. The unity of society no longer comes out in this society [...]. Systems of functions can only legitimate themselves. That is, no system can legitimate another."[146]

Robert Bellah comes to similar conclusions from another perspective. Once a public and sacred sphere, politics also suffers from the progressive advance of privatization and secularization. "Such a privatized and secularized politics, though celebrated by many political scientists, seems unable to stimulate not only patriotism but even respect. Being of uncertain legitimacy itself it cannot supply social legitimation and instead becomes the source of widespread cynicism and desaffection."[147]

In our countries, too, the metaphysical halo radiated by the state has disappeared; today we find the patriotism of nineteenth-century theater, painting, or poetry that exalted the state as the embodiment of national unity anachronistic. The current state ends up reduced to one of the three powers, the executive, which in turn bears more and more the stamp of bureaucratic machinery. From the standpoint of collectivity, the state becomes a certain administrative unit that is threatened by the very state's privatization. To the extent that the state becomes a "political market" of specific interests, the citizens may not recognize in it a res publica. The symbolic dimension of the state that, whether as a bureaucracy or as a market, now appears exclusively guided by a formal-instrumental rationality, is vanishing.

Here we come to a turning point in understanding postmodern disenchantment. That all-encompassing discourse that certain interpreters of postmodernity attribute to a planning, controlling, objectifying, and systematizing reason (i.e., totalizing reason) is nothing but formal rationality. In my opinion, the problem is not so much reason under the Enlightened tradition as much as the identification of reason with

---

146 N. Luhmann, "The Representation of Society within Society," *Current Sociology* 35, no. 2 (1987): 105.

147 R. Bellah, "Legitimation Processes in Politics and Religion," *Current Sociology* 35, no. 2 (1987): 95.

formal rationality. The discussion highlights the differentiation of the various aspects of social life without paying enough attention to the formal rationality that crosses the specific rationale of each field. This leads to a kind of "systematic integration" imposed behind the backs of citizens. Social demands are often administratively absorbed by the state bureaucracy even before they enter the political arena. Thus, the political-parliamentary debate appears as an irrelevant "theater" in the face of the absolute predominance of formal rationality. This rationality is undoubtedly essential yet does not ensure the articulation of the social process by itself. That is why a politics entirely guided by a calculation of means and ends will fail. According to Luhmann, politics is incompetent when it comes to representing the whole of society, but this failure is that of formal rationality. Bellah points to this when he addresses the privatization and secularization of politics. Because this form of rational-formal politics is currently predominant, disenchantment must be linked to it. It is not a disenchantment with politics as such, but with a certain way of doing politics and, particularly, a politics incapable of creating a collective identity. Inverting the viewpoint, I do not see, in the postmodern praise of heterogeneity, a rejection of any idea of collectivity but, on the contrary, an attack on the false homogenization imposed by formal rationality.

Seen this way, postmodernity is not opposed to the project of modernity as such, but to a certain modality of it. And not a minor one, incidentally. It is a disenchantment with that process of "rationalization" that Max Weber considered characteristic of modernity. Weber conceives the rationalization of the world as a system of complementarity.[148] Once the unity pursued by religion was lost, the relativization of values forced its privatization. Social life can only be organized as peaceful coexistence if faith, moral norms, and aesthetic tastes are relegated to the limits of a private forum as a matter of individual conscience. The privatization of subjectivity is complemented by the formalization of the public sphere; politics, law, economics are subjected to a formal,

---

148 I base this on K. Otto Apel, "The Situation of Humanity as an Ethical Problem," *Praxis International* (October 1984): 257 ff. See also the introduction in R. Bernstein, ed., *Habermas and Modernity* (Oxford: Blackwell, 1986).

value-neutral rationality. This dualism between the public and private sphere, between procedures and values, is undoubtedly an emancipatory act. There is nothing worse than a moralizing power that demands not only obedience, but love and faith. Individual autonomy takes shape with the separation of politics and faith, of power and love. This promise of autonomy with which modernity begins is, however, soon contradicted by the irresistible advance of the market and bureaucracy. The "rationalization of the world" leads, again, to a closed system.

What Max Weber still sees as a rupture is subsequently conceptualized without the slightest degree of bewilderment. Little by little, a monist vision of capitalism crystallizes. In the concept of "modernization," modernity is reduced to the deployment of formal rationality. The social process is seen exclusively in terms of functional elements that ensure systemic equilibrium. Political modernization is then defined in an ahistorical manner by the development of the various capacities of the system (symbolic, regulatory, extractive, and distributive).[149] The functional requirements of the "system" replace the old categories of sovereignty, representation, will, etc., politically neutralizing the question of order. Democracy is "cleansed" of all harshness and resistance to formal rationality, to the point that all pathos is also eliminated. The moral commitment and affective bonds on which the democratic order rests are then weakened and, finally, the citizenry cares as much for one political regime as another.

In short, our current disenchantment refers to modernization and, specifically, to a managerial-technocratic style of doing politics. I think this interpretation is supported by some visible trends such as the concern for human rights. More than a vindication against the state, these are a questioning of a state that only manages to respect the plurality of values by excluding them from the political sphere. The distinction between politics and morality is not in question. The issue is how they are split and the consequent reduction of politics to a value-neutral rationality. Another example is the interest in everyday life. To speak

---

149 For this issue, see D. Lerner and J. Coleman in *International Encyclopedia of the Social Sciences* 10; and G. Pasquini in N. Bobbio and N. Matteucci, *Diccionario de política* (Madrid: Siglo XXI, 1982).

here simply of "privatization" would be to accept the aforementioned dualism between the public and private spheres when, in fact, the concern is that this dualism should be broken. Again, the separation of the two areas is not in question; what is rejected are the quasi-ontological limits cloistering political activity. Finally, let us remember the demand for radical pluralism. I mention it because this mandate is not content to merely claim a plurality of political actors, or a plurality of rationalities differentiated according to their various areas. The demand is radical in that it points to a plurality of rationalities within the same political field insofar as it rejects a single "political rationale." This is expressed in the "informal politics" introduced by the new social movements with their reluctance to institutionalize and formalize. This reaction can become premodern and even irrational, to be sure, but it is not an inevitable course if we know how to read the underlying desires.

The examples cited seem, to me, expressive of postmodern disenchantment. Our societies want to be "modern," of course, but we must not confuse modernity and modernization. This is, I stress, a disenchantment with modernization and not with modernity. What reveals an illusion is the claim to formal rationality as the principle of totality. In this sense, the term "postmodernity" is misleading. On the one hand, it implies a rupture, but only with a certain modality of modernity. That this modality is hegemonic does not imply, however, that we cannot conceive and develop the project of modernity in some other way. This is precisely the challenge posed by the current debate. On the other hand, we cannot speak of a rupture insofar as the noted disenchantment does not abandon the tension between differentiation and articulation that, as we saw, characterizes modernity. Postmodern disenchantment has not made the underlying problem disappear. On the contrary, the examples mentioned indicate a rejection of the segmentation of the various aspects of social life while failing to formulate an alternative notion of the collective. The problem, then, is present in its absence. We cannot, I believe, work the complexity of modern society without some kind of collective reference.

Postmodern disenchantment therefore contemplates, in my opinion, a double challenge that invites us to 1) rethink the project of modernity and, to do this, 2) emphasize the articulation of social differences. What it proposes is, in short, a reversal of approach: instead of asking ourselves, based on a supposedly given unity, how much plurality we support, so-called postmodernity consists of assuming social hetero- geneity as a value and questioning ourselves about its articulation as a collective order.

4. Disenchantment Regarding Redemption

Another dimension of our current disenchantment is a loss of faith in progress. This is a direct reference to modernity and its characteristic modification of our awareness of time: the modern era ceases to pay tribute to some exemplary past and defines itself for the future. Time accelerates, quickly devaluing any acquisition, while the new is conse- crated as a value in and of itself. The avant-garde, an emblem of novelty (whether artistic or political), displaces tradition.

Faith in the value of novelty turns progress into a central factor. The idea of progress makes it possible to structure an open future, neu- tralizing the leakage of meaning through a teleological construction: by believing in a sense of history we ensure, above all, the meaning of the present. We see here the effects of secularization which, in addi- tion to abolishing the sacred vision of the world, must find a channel for hopes of a better life. Also secularized are the heavenly promises of harmony and happiness, now projected toward the human kingdom and, specifically, to politics. Hence the pathos of progress. Let us not dismiss it, for it also nourishes democracy. It is faith in a freer and fairer society that makes it possible to justify sacrifices and overcome repeated inadequacies. If the idea of progress creates illusions, it also relativizes disappointments. (Also, if the disappointments were final, who would believe in democracy today?) A radical disenchantment is unbearable because, in the end, it is that of a utopia—a fully autonomous society, identical with itself. Consequently, the current debate on postmoder- nity does not escape the question of tomorrow: once the illusions of progress have been criticized, what hopes can we summon? Thinking about the importance of a political "creed" for the affective roots of democratic institutions, we must review the disenchantment that we thematize as postmodernity from this angle. Postmodernity postulates an exhaustion of secularization; one where the innovative capacity of society would have spread and accelerated to such a degree that it makes progress routine and finally empties it of content. The differentiation of all fields advances incessantly, but in this infinite range of novelties it is increasingly difficult to appreciate something genuinely "new." Accustomed to an endless sequence of innovations, the eyes get tired of déjà vu. The changes are marginal and predictable, forming a chain of iterations. The future ends up diluting in the present and ceases to have value. The promises of a new society are like a fata morgana that dissolves as soon as we try approaching. An illustrative, though little thought-out, aspect of this phenomenon is the resignification of social-ism in recent years. For many decades socialism was, despite recurring criticism, a symbol of social progress and, as such, an alternative to cap-italism. Suddenly, in a short period of time, it ceased to be perceived as an alternative. What happened? Perhaps, more than a strictly political phenomenon, what we have is a cultural turn: the idea of progressive emancipation seems to have lost its meaning. Instead, the image of an eternal return becomes attractive. Postmodern discourse expresses this new mood, denouncing progress as an illusion.

Here, too, postmodern disenchantment has a double face: the dis-mantling of illusory progress translates into praise of the present. Of course, I see this revaluation as positive. We have lived the present as a mere prelude to the future for too long, sacrificing even already con-quered freedoms for the sake of a "promised land." Disenchantment recovers the present, providing it with a dignity of its own.[150]

This means, above all, to renounce any "forward flight." By aban-doning a futuristic perspective that approaches problems exclusively through some model of a future society, we open ourselves to existing tensions and contradictions. These lose their pejorative connotation. We have already seen how postmodern culture revaluates heteroge-neity; it makes it possible to confront social complexity without try-ing to immediately reduce it. Today, rather than tolerating a singular discourse (a common or majority-based one), we seek to promote a

---

150 See, among others, J. Ramoneda, "Una teoría del presente," *Letra Internacio-nal* (Madrid) 6 (1987).

multiplicity of meanings without presupposing some ultimate instance. From this point of view, uncertainty is a distinctive feature of postmodernity. Despite this new provision, there is a limit because we assume the absence of certainties. Beyond a certain point, disenchantment ceases to be a beneficial loss of illusions and becomes a dangerous loss of meaning.

It seems reasonable to assume that the material conditions of life provide hard nuclei of meaning, like the structuring of time in the past, present, and future. We cannot do without such a construction of continuities and discontinuities lest we get devoured by an infinite present.

What is madness but such an absence of limits? As per the slogans of some European youth circles, we are going through "mad years" again. Graffiti stating that there is "no future" or that "everything goes" speaks of a deranged world. The statements are interconnected: if "everything goes," there is no way to imagine a tomorrow; and if we have no notion of the future, we lack perspective to choose between the multiple possibilities of the moment. Indeed, everything becomes possible. Postmodern destructuring reflects, consciously or not, a "project crisis." On the one hand, the future is seen more as a result of the unintended effects of human action than as a deliberate construction. In other words, the future is not merely open, but essentially opaque; politics could intervene occasionally, resolving minor conflicts, but not direct the course of history. If our will is blind, why be interested in politics? On the other hand, there is a project crisis because our notions of a desired order have been blurred. Neither capitalism nor socialism, left nor right offer a "model" that summarizes the majority's aspirations. Longings seem to vanish without crystallizing in a collective imaginary. In short, it seems we do not know what we can do, or even what we want. So-called postmodernity might then refute not just the future, but even history itself. Deep down this would be the beginning of "posthistory" (A. Gehlen).

There are those who settle into disenchantment and rationalize it as a new value. While seemingly radical, this attitude is profoundly conservative: it prefers to adapt to the supposedly natural course of the world. It seems that the misfortunes to which our dreams have led effectively censored our desires. Disenchantment breeds boredom, and fatigue besets us. If we look at ourselves, we will echo the words of César Vallejo: "I tell you, life lies in the mirror and you, the originals, are death. [...].

Dead you are, not having lived before. Anyone would say that, not being now, in other times you were. Truly, you are corpses of a life that never was. Unhappy fate."[151] Vallejo stated there is no life without dreams. Life always dreams of a better life. We are in want of another future, but what future? What do we find desirable?

This feeling of precariousness and bewilderment appears thematized under the name of postmodernity. Like disenchantment with modernization, disenchantment with progress does not eliminate the underlying problem. The question of a better life remains. And an adequate interpretation of disenchantment must account for this. In my view, disenchantment with a future is fundamentally a loss of faith in a certain conception of progress: the future as redemption.[152]

The belief that we can save our souls through politics is a substitute for the religious vacuum left by secularization. This gives rise to a process of "de-transcendentalization" that transfers eschatological hopes to human history and projects them into the future as the purpose of social development. The future is then condensed into utopias conceived as feasible. From this confusion of the imaginary and the empirical, of the ideal and the real, we manufacture illusions of a happy ending and eternal harmony. In the name of such feasibility (and, perhaps, proximity) all sacrifices are justified, and the idea of redemption fundamentally operates as a mechanism of legitimation: we affirm ourselves, against all existing vicissitudes, projecting ourselves toward a safeguarded future. However, all politics rest on such illusions. The astute Machiavelli understood this: society requires illusions, not as acts of "Machiavellian" deception, but as a project for the future that enables it to ascertain its fleeting present. Illusion is, paradoxically, an element of certainty: we secure our identity through promises of perpetuity. If politics, then, is always based on such motivational beliefs, what sets the paradigm of redemption apart? The search for redemption points to a fullness beyond history separated from every empirical condition of existence.

---

151 C. Vallejo, *Trilce*, poem LXXV.

152 See J. Whitebook, "The Politics of Redemption," *Telos* 63 (1985), and its reply in *Telos* 69 (1986); also see F. Feher, "El paradigma de la redención," *Leviatán* (Madrid) 28 (1987).

It knows no mediation between the present and a radically different future. The expectation of the new is exceeded to such an extent that the future has value only as an absolute discontinuity. Redemptive policies will thus often lead to an aestheticist and moralizing vision of politics, if not terrorism. What distinguishes the belief in redemption from other political cultures, then, is faith in a total rupture and the advent, *ex nihilo*, of an integrally different order. The goal is not to change existing conditions but break away from them.

Our enchanted view of salvific ruptures goes hand in hand with a monistic view of social reality. Here I am thinking of approaches that see capitalism as an inexorable ratiocination of alienation, a one-dimensional system from which one cannot escape except by exiting it completely. The revolution would be that leap into a new order, one just as monolithic. If the monist vision results in a revolutionary strategy, when postmodern culture conversely abandons the idea of a single rationality it likewise renounces a strategy of rupture. If we consider that the social process is crisscrossed by different rationalities, its transformation can no longer demand "breaking with the system" but reforming it.

Here, perspective opens to redefine reformism. As usual definitions, reformism and revolution have the same goal (a classless society) and differ regarding what path to take. The issue is, as they say, strategic: it has become clearer that these are two very different approaches. Why not think of reformism as a disenchanted conception of the social process? To reform society is to discern competing rationalities and strengthen those tendencies we think are best. The result will not be a pure and definitive order. On the contrary, our societies will remain as contradictory and precarious as life. And, for this same reason, ongoing creative processes.

In short, disenchantment can be politically very fruitful. Postmodern sensibility fosters an experimental and innovative dimension in politics: the art of the possible. This reevaluation of politics, however, rests on one premise: a renewed awareness of the future. We rely on political creativity only to the extent that we have a perspective of the future. Seen in this manner, the problem is not the future, but the ideas we build about it. A better future is not simply around the corner within the reach of faith or science. Neither is it an "unripened grape" we should ignore. Perhaps, as Rubert de Ventós said, we lack the courage to understand that "the grapes are ripe and beyond our reach; that they are desirable and unattainable; that there are problems we cannot solve but should continue to consider."[153] In this regard, our disenchanted postmodernists could well renew the critical and reforming impulse of modernity.

---

153 Xavier Rubert de Ventós, "Kant responde a Habermas," *Fahrenheit 450*, 2 (Buenos Aires: Grupo Fahrenheit, 1987).

Acknowledgments

The texts gathered here have been published in several social science journals in Latin America and Europe. Some of them also appear in the collective works *¿Qué es 'realismo' en política?*, Buenos Aires, Editorial Catálogos, 1987, and *Cultura política y democratización*, Santiago, CLACSO, 1984, both of which I compiled.

I wish to thank Enzo Faletto for his incisive comments on the paper "De la revolución a la democracia," originally written for *Mondoperaio* (Rome, January 1986), and republished by *Leviatán* in Spain, *Esprit* in France, *Opciones* in Chile, and *La ciudad futura* in Argentina, between 1985 and late 1987.

"Estudiar la vida cotidiana" is an unpublished text written in 1984 based on reflections that inspired my *Notas sobre la vida cotidiana*, which were published as *Materiales de Discusión* 38, 50, 53, 54 and 57 by FLACSO-Chile.

"El realismo político, una cuestión de tiempo" was presented at the second meeting of the Theory of the State and Politics group at CLACSO, Buenos Aires, 1984. It was published, alongside the other papers presented at this meeting, in the aforementioned *¿Qué es el "realism" en política?*.

"Hay gente que muere de miedo" is based on a lecture I gave at the seminar on Urban Cultures, organized by Jordi Borja, the Universidad Internacional Menéndez Pelayo and the Barcelona City Council in September 1985. It was initially published in *Vanguardia*, Barcelona, in November 1985.

I wish to thank Guillermo O'Donnell for his nuanced comments during the writing of "La democratización en el contexto de una cultura posmoderna." It was presented at the seminar Il consolidamento della democrazia in Amèrica Latina, organized by the Istituto per la Cooperazione Internazionale Politica, Economica e Culturale de Roma, in January 1986. That year it was published in *Politica Internazionale*

(Roma) and *Leviatán* (Madrid); in 1987 in *Mundo* (Mexico) and the aforementioned *Cultura política y democratización.* "¿Responde la democracia a la búsqueda de certidumbre?" was presented in the seminar Democracia, socialismo y totalitarismo, organized by the École des Hautes Études en Sciences Sociales and CLACSO Paris in 1987. It has been published in Spain, Italy, and Brazil in *Zona Abierta*, *Progetto*, and *Lua Nova*, respectively.

"Ese desencanto llamado posmoderno" was first published and presented at the CLACSO conference on Identidad latinoamericana, premodernidad, modernidad y posmodernidad in Buenos Aires, 1987.

I wish to thank FLACSO for their authorization to publish this new edition with Fondo de Cultura Económica.

The Shadows
of Tomorrow

The Subjective Dimension
of Politics

First published in Santiago, LOM Ediciones, 2002
Translated for this volume by Victoria J. Furio, 2023

For Sofía

Author's Note: Four of the texts [in this book] have been previously published. In this instance, I have introduced only minor changes.

The text on the erosion of political maps (Chapter II) is based on the lecture I presented at the conference, "Politics of Antipolitics," organized by the Vienna Dialogue on Democracy (Vienna, July 7–10, 1994). The English version was published in A. Schedler, ed., *The End of Politics* (London: MacMillan Press, 1997), and the original version in R. Winocur, ed., *Culturas políticas a fin de siglo* (Mexico: FLACSO/Juan Pablos Editor, 1997).

The study on our fears (Chapter III) was delivered on the occasion of the inaugural conference of the *Asamblea General de la Facultad Latinoamericana de Ciencias Sociales* [General Assembly of the Latin American Faculty of Social Sciences-FLACSO], in May 1998 in Mexico, and published in *Perfiles Latinoamericanos* (Mexico) 13 (1998), and in M. Villa, *El miedo, reflexiones sobre su dimensión social y cultural* (Medellín: Corporación Región, 2002).

In collaboration with Pedro Güell, we wrote the reflection on the social construction of collective memories (Chapter IV), which I presented at the Social Science Research Council workshop in Montevideo (November 1998). The article was originally published in the magazine *Esprit* (Paris) 258 (November 1999). The Spanish version was included in A. Menéndez-Carrión and A. Joignant, eds., *La caja de Pandora: el retorno de la transición chilena* (Santiago: Planeta/Ariel, 1999).

The fifth chapter was presented and published by the Museo Nacional de Colombia in *Museo, memoria y nación*, comp. G. Sánchez Gómez and M. E. Wills Obregón (Bogotá: 2000).

The first and last chapters are unpublished works; the introductory essay on "The Naturalization of the Social" is a byproduct of discussion in the UNDP Human Development team in preparation for the 2002 report and for a debate with Tomás Moulian ("El loro de Flaubert y el búho de Minerva," *Rocinante* [Santiago] 28, February 2001).

Introduction

What do my fears and desires have to do with politics? And conversely, what could I expect from democracy that would give meaning to my experiences? I realized very late how intertwined my queries about politics were with my personal biography. At the time, it was the issue of order. By raising it, I wanted to give an account of life during the dictatorship, but without knowing it, I was responding to my previous experience of disorder. Having been born in Germany on the eve of the war, changing countries several times, I am sensitive to the loss of ordering referents. Living in the midst of uncertainties, the bonds of belonging and rootedness tend to be fragile. This was how I learned, although instinctively, that the question about order does not only allude to an institutional or structural problem. Above all, it entails the emotions, beliefs, and images that guide us in everyday life.

In the movement of '68, I discovered that feelings are not a matter confined to the personal realm. But it was the leaden years under Pinochet which showed how enmeshed subjective experience is with the political order. I believe that since then my reflection has revolved around social subjectivity. For many years now, and ever more explicitly, I have devoted myself to exploring the subjective weight of politics. My book, *Los patios interiores de la democracia: subjetividad y política*,[1] pulls together a set of variations on the topic. And the texts gathered together here continue to probe the relationship between subjectivity and politics.

Why is the subjective dimension of politics of interest? My concern derives from an implicit premise. If we believe politics to be what I once

---

1   Fondo de Cultura Económica, Santiago, 1990. (Also included in volume III of these *Obras*, 117–228 [-Ed.]).

called "the conflictive and never-ending construction of the desired order,"[2] social subjectivity provides the incentives that fuel that process of construction. It presumes, however, that politics actually contributes to producing society. Upholding the "constructivist" nature of modern politics is not out of place in an era that tends toward the "naturalization of the social." Today the sensation abounds that the current state of affairs is a natural fact which does not admit alternatives. They would have us believe that we are subject to an authority that we have not created. Contrary to a society which refuses to acknowledge the human origin of the law that it urges us to obey, the modern struggle to "be a subject" is still valid. We can only speak of politics when order is understood to be a human creation. Therefore, I would like to begin my reflection on the politics of subjectivity by objecting to the "natural aura" which conceals the social production of our ways of living together.

> He has two antagonists: the first presses him from behind, from the origin. The second blocks the road ahead. He gives battle to both. To be sure, the first supports him in his fight with the second, for he wants to push him forward, and in the same way the second supports him in his fight with the first, since he drives him back. But it is only theoretically so. For it is not only the two antagonists who are there, but he himself as well, and who really knows his intentions? His dream, though, is that some time in an unguarded moment—and this would require a night darker than any night has ever been yet—he will jump out of the fighting line and be promoted, on account of his experience in fighting, to the position of umpire over his antagonists in their fight with each other.[3]

Kafka's parable, which I have taken from a text by Hannah Arendt summarizes human anguish between past and future. On the one hand, past experiences, whether passive routines or exceptional events, set the

---

2   See the book of the same title published by Santiago Ediciones Ainavillo in 1984, found in volume II of these *Obras*, 267–421.

3   Hannah Arendt, *Between Past and Future: Six Exercises in Political Thought* (New York: Viking Press, 1961) 7.

goals that we truly desire. On the other, faced with an unknown future, we are led to search the past for lessons that help to understand it. And then we dream of being beyond that tension: not outside of time but being able to choose which past we take on and what future springs out of nowhere. But we cannot escape the cross-fire. What I might be able to be always carries the mark of what I have become. Not only does the past cast shadows, so does tomorrow. They are the forces that keep us from imagining something new, another world, a different life, a better tomorrow. It could be argued that there is nothing better than imagining other worlds in order to forget how painful the world we live in is. That is what Baudolino, Umberto Eco's character, thinks before he understands that imagining other worlds also ends up changing this one. The texts that follow deal with such difficulties and challenges.

The subjective dimension of politics has received little attention from contemporary political theory. This reflects the process of de-subjectification that the social sciences have been promoting for quite some time. The contrast with the sixties and seventies is substantial, when Latin American social sciences contributed to equipping the changes with intelligibility and meaning. Their contributions were often erroneous, plagued with dogmatic premises and illusory proposals. Nonetheless, they provided clues that stimulated the debate regarding the direction and meaning of those transformations. Today, we miss the "mental maps" that allow us to shed light on the world in which we live. It would suffice to see how the coordinates of space and time have changed and, consequently, certain basic guiding criteria. And that redimensioning particularly affects political action. In the second chapter, I point to some reasons why politics no longer are what they were. One of the transformations has to do with the codes of interpretation that allows people to structure what is real. Criteria such as left/right, reform/revolution, state/civil society were some of those qualifying tools that helped to interpret the complexity of society. Now, a false "realism" seeks to dispense with all "ideological discourse." Where the wise and smooth workings of the "invisible hand" of the market reign, ideas are superfluous. My interest, on the contrary, is to reformulate our interpretive codes. It is a necessity as much for the politics that seek to chart the country's path as for those who seek their place as participants in a shared world.

It is true that situations of uncertainty and contingency prevail. And feelings of abandonment and helplessness emerge out of the confusion. How does politics respond? Given that a truthful government cannot promise its citizens security and certainty, it attempts to vent the pent up anguish through repeated campaigns against crime. But it is not the danger but rather the sense of vulnerability vis-à-vis the unknown Other that produces fear. Some fears are due to concrete acts of urban violence or the threat of joblessness. Others are vague fears that have no rhyme or reason. There are unspoken fears and fears that can be conjured up among all. There are those who are afraid to confess their fears and those who appropriate and manipulate them. The third chapter addresses this. Based on the empirical results presented in the *Desarrollo Humano en Chile 1998* report, we can see some of the experiences that trap us: fear of the Other and of social exclusion, the secretive fear of meaninglessness. Emotions like these are the ones that condition our expectations about what a democratic order can and should produce. That is why, I say, naming the fears is an exercise in democracy. We must take responsibility for the dark side of daily life if we wish to prevent a populist discourse from embracing them and leveraging the injured subjectivity of the population. It is true that neo-populism recognizes people's fears; but only "one at a time" as individual cases, not as a common cause and joint action. But a list of personal problems never shapes a public sphere. Something more is needed.

Fears about the future originate in the past. And dreams of the future speak to us of unfulfilled promises from the past: what could have been but was not. Of what we have lost and what should not have happened. To remember is to refresh our experiences. But, as René Char's aphorism says, our heritage is not preceded by any testament. We can no longer resort to a hallowed tradition which names and transmits, selects and values that past "that is worthwhile" to preserve. Not only the future, also the past is open to a (re)construction. When at the invitation of Elisabeth Jelin[4] I started writing about collective memories with Pedro Güell, we did not want to solely shine a light on the silences that surround the Chilean dictatorship. The reflection on the politics of

---

4   E. Jelin, *Los trabajos de la memoria* (Madrid: Siglo XXI, 2002).

memory in Chile allows us to argue two additional theories. First, the thread that links the past—and therefore, the way in which we built the memories—with the present and our current capacities to contend with the future. Second, the nexus that weaves together the manner in which we structure social time with the way we organize our coexistence. The fourth chapter attempts to show how the production of temporal horizons is intertwined with production of the social order. And to remember, conversely, that the way to shape our means of coexistence has to do with the temporalities that guide us. I have added a short chapter with some ideas that had not been included.

A statement by Zygmunt Bauman[5] summarizes quite well one of the current dilemmas. The increase in individual liberty, he tells us, tends to coincide with an increase in collective impotence. Today, the individual gains an unprecedented degree of autonomy while collective action is restricted to successive expressions of targeted interests. This phenomenon indicates how limited the "freedom of choice" is that the individual enjoys. Long before they exercise their right to choose freely, a large part of the matters relevant to their daily life have already been decided. This applies as much to the consumer who voices their preferences in the market as to the civic right to choose different options of social organization. How can the individual autonomy that the society preaches be achieved given the subjective conditions that the society itself promotes?

To the feeling of unease and impotence I will respond with two theories which arise out of the studies of the Human Development Programme.[6] On the one hand, the degree of individual autonomy is conditioned by the level of autonomy enjoyed by the society. On the other, the society's capacity to intervene in its own development depends on its own self-image. In other words, only a society that has a strong image of the "We" as a collective actor feels it has the power to determine the country's path. And we develop such an imaginary

---

5   Z. Bauman, *En busca de la política* (Buenos Aires: Fondo de Cultura Económica, 2001).

6   United Nations Development Programme, *Desarrollo humano en Chile 2002, Nosotros los chilenos: un desafío cultural* (Santiago: UNDP, 2002).

of the "We" as we have successful experiences of collective action. So, who are "We"? The "We" would be the mortar that links individuals in a community. Cornelius Castoriadis[7] discovered the precise definition: "we are an autonomous community composed of autonomous individuals. And we can observe ourselves, recognize ourselves, question ourselves in and about our deeds." In the final chapter, I present signs of the weakness of the "We" in Chile and its influence on the precarity of social capital and the affective rootlessness of democracy.

It is the task of politics, I have said, and one of its most noble tasks, to embrace people's desires and woes, anxieties and concerns, and include their experiences in the public discourse. In this manner, providing space for subjectivity, politics gives the person the opportunity to acknowledge their everyday experience as part of life in society. So, what has politics done to name and interpret what is happening with us? Little. Consequently, we have the so-called crisis of representation. The gap that is created between society and politics has to do with the difficulty in accepting and processing subjectivity. This is not the raw material that precedes social life; it is a cultural construct. It depends, therefore, on the way in which society is organized and, in particular, the way in which politics shapes that social organization. Nonetheless, I ask myself, if the political system has "antennae" capable of seeing and hearing, apart from the noisy demands, the whispering and silences of the street. That politics has become a self-referred system is not news. But there is more to it than that, I believe. Although politicians may be well aware of people's concrete problems, they do not manage to translate them into public debate and political will. It would seem that social matters are no longer a coherent whole. What I mean is, the very concept of "society" seems to have been called into question.

Can we ask of politics what society does not offer? The studies on human development in Chile would have us believe that societal experiences have become more sporadic. Every day we see the deterioration of the *animus societatis* in different settings. To this "negative individualism" there seems to be a barely perceived underlying event: the erosion of the collective imaginaries by which a society recognizes itself as a

---

7   C. Castoriadis, *El avance de la insignificancia* (Buenos Aires: Eudeba, 1997), 96.

community. Once again I cite Castoriadis to describe the trend. "Current society does not accept itself as a society, it puts up with itself. And if it does not accept itself, it is because it cannot maintain or forge an image of itself that it can affirm and value, nor can it generate a project of social transformation that it can subscribe to and which it would want to fight for."[8] While the contemporary individual seems to endure society as an alien and unjust burden, a "naturalized" and "armored" society drives out critical thinking. But a society that does not have questions about itself, that does not talk about the meaning that current and future coexistence could have, takes away from politics its fundamental purpose. More precisely, it relinquishes politics as a collective effort to build a community of citizens and is satisfied with managing daily affairs.

Publishing a book is my way of showing gratitude for the affection received and repaying the pleasure of good conversations. I thank all those with whom we share in the Human Development Programme: Eugenio, Rodrigo, Soledad, Carola, María Luisa, and with special fondness, Pedro Güell. We have a good time because we learned from the old Greeks that for friendship (civic) "there is nothing better than to have food cooked on the same fire and shared at the same table. The banquet is a communion that produces a oneness of being among the diners, a type of consanguinity."[9] Let me add the wine, and I will greet my brothers and sisters at the annual symposium. Indeed, the texts attest to other friendships spread out around the world; in particular, those extended to me in Mexico. For a traveler like myself, writing helps to temper time and distances. Here I will only name Klaus Schroth in remembrance of those who, in one way or another, are part of my life. And to my children Paula and Javiera, Tomás and Paula: thank you for the love that you give me. I hope that these notes can be useful to them and the new generation that is building the future. Going a step further, I dedicate the book to my granddaughter Sofía Leighton, who dreams of the day after tomorrow.

Santiago de Chile, July 2002

---

8   Ibid., 31.

9   J. P. Vernant, *Los orígenes del pensamiento griego* (Barcelona: Paidós, 1998), 90.

I

The Naturalization of the Social

Our everyday experience seems to be ever more restricted to a narrow and immediate realm. Of course, we buy imported goods and listen to music from the United States; we use the internet daily and find out about world events from CNN. In a nutshell, we know we are inserted into globalization. What is more, we have internalized it as a "national reality." And, despite this, we live it as a faraway process. By speaking of the economic system or "model," although it may be in a simplistic way, we are conveying how strange social reality has become. Apart from the microsocial sphere, we contend with society as a distant and hostile fact, removed from any deliberate intervention by human beings. We are acquainted with the process of alienation typical of capitalist development; yet, through globalization, the divide between the person and society seems to be growing. In what follows, I will set out a brief reflection on the "naturalization of the social," understood as the transfiguration of the social order into an apparent natural order.

I would like to very briefly point out some links that this process has with the development of social theory. The argument stems from this premise: social theory is a cultural product. I am assuming that the social theory represents a story that society tells about itself. If that were the case, focusing on the forms of conceptualization would allow us to see the reasons that have led to considering the social as a nature removed from human will. My argument, based on Giesen and Hinkelammert,[10] will first present two historical events specific to the advancement of the social sciences: the de-subjectification of reflection

---

10   B. Giesen, *Die Entdinglichung des Sozialen* (Frankfurt: Suhrkamp, 1991), and
     F. Hinkelammert, *Cultura de la esperanza y sociedad sin exclusión* (San José, Costa Rica: DEI, 1996).

and the de-materialization of the social. Then, along the lines of Alexander,[11] I will deal with the way in which said theoretical construction contributes to the naturalization of the social.

1. The De-Subjectification of Reflection

The narrative concerning social reality has a historical backdrop that is worth remembering: it takes shape in the eighteenth century when nature begins to be conceived of as something eternal and immutable. Displacing metaphysics, the enthronement of nature as the objective referent of human action gives rise to the modern sciences. Their objective is to fathom the laws of nature by observing the facts. Based on the facts, the inductive method and the quantification of the events allows for establishing causal relationships. By working with those relations of causality, science acquires a new characteristic: its usefulness. From then on it would be the task of social analysis to translate the causalities observed into an instrumental means-end action.

This process creates not only the distinction between nature and the realm of social action known to all. In addition, it ends up assimilating society into nature. The old idea of a social order, assessed according to moral standards, is substituted by the notion of an abstract and impersonal system. The social is understood as an objective structure which will be the premise (not necessarily conscious) of human action. The split is thus established between object and subject, between structure and action, between system and worlds of life. The consequences are far-reaching: the subjectivity of persons, their values and emotions, are cast out of scientific reflection. Social research is placed under the methodological imperative of a neutral act with respect to values. In short, an objectification of the social takes place along with a de-subjectification of reflection.

As a result of the above, an absolutization of instrumental reason occurs. Truth and value become separate realms. Truth, referring to

---

11   J. Alexander, *Sociología cultural* (Mexico: Anthropos/FLACSO, 2000).

the validity of a theory, would be different from value, derived from an interpretation of the world. In scientific terms, judgment bears exclusive worth over facts, and facts are taken to mean the events that can be measured in their causal means-end efficiency. Franz Hinkelammert emphasizes a dual reduction: a) from "objectivity" to de facto judgments, and b) from de facto judgments to means-end efficiency. As a result of this operation, rationality is restricted to instrumental rationality. Only action that complies with the criteria of means-end efficiency would be rational. Such a definition of what is rational makes the goals of action an abstraction and also, the possible effects. Hinkelammert illustrates this reductionism by means of a small example: what would you think of a person who efficiently cuts off the branch of a tree, but without taking into account that they are sitting precisely on that branch? The efficiency of the pruning says nothing about the rationality of the actor.

Neoclassic theory conducts a similar abstraction in economic thought. In the name of scientific objectivity it only accepts de facto judgments and reduces those judgments to a means-end relation. All other judgments would lack scientific legitimacy. Therefore, the consequences that are destructive of employment or the environment, which tend to have the means-end market efficiency, are excluded. The economic theory treats those facts as unintended "external effects" which do not pertain to the formal rationality of the process.

A conclusion is evident from the above: a latent restriction exists of the possible alternatives to the established order. The first step was already mentioned: define the rational as solely that proposition that fulfills the means-end efficiency. The second step consists of transforming the decision—perhaps an option fulfills those criteria of efficiency—into an objective judgment. That is achieved by defining it as a technical decision, since it would not be assessing the goals of that alternative. That is, a) the possible social alternatives are reduced to the principle of efficiency, and b) the operation is considered an impersonal act, because it would not involve a value judgment. Only the options judged rational are viable and legitimate. And only those that represent an efficient means to achieve a given end would be rational.

In sum, applying an approach that reduces the social to a means-end efficiency signifies denying people the power of decision about the goals of their action. Ultimately, it means rejecting politics as a conscious construction of the social order.

2. The De-Materialization of the Social

The process of abstraction takes place in various fields. In that of aesthetics, for example, the ideal of a faithful representation of reality is abandoned in favor of a self-reflection on the color (impressionism), the forms (cubism), or the interiority of the artist (expressionism). Art tends to become more autonomous as a specific field the same way that the economy separates itself from the usage value of goods and the way that formal law makes an abstraction of concepts of justice. It would seem that, today, the social tends to dematerialize itself in the sense that the attempt at an "objective" portrayal of the social reality is relinquished. What is real would no longer be a matter of knowledge but of interpretation. And the interpretation of social reality would be subject to a multitude of competing codes.

In the twentieth century, the distinction between the individual and society, theory and empirical reality, nature and history, takes a new turn. Individual subjectivity and social action, causality and progress are no longer solid and indisputable referents of reflection. The suspicion remains that neither the individual subject nor the society represents those "basic units," which, like the elements of nineteenth-century physics, establish an order. Currently, the prevailing opinion is that in the growing social and functional differentiation it has become difficult to determine the "unit" of society. "Economy, culture, state and solidarity can be considered only as different 'codes' by which to evaluate and construct actions and the opportunities for action. Money, law, solidarity and truth shape those codes or means of interaction. They no longer delineate social groups, organizations or societies among them, but rather determine the functional sense of a particular social context."[12]

---

12   B. Giesen, op. cit., 134.

The differentiation and multiplication of the interpretive codes of social reality facilitate a type of return to Darwin's theory. Just as in the natural sciences the primacy passes from physics to biology, in the social sciences empiricism and functionalism are displaced by an evolutionist theory of the systems. Returning to the Darwinian perspective, it approaches the evolution of a particular system in relation to its surroundings. Evolution interests us not so much due to the changes but for its capacity to endure. The duration of a system would be regulated through a "natural selection" that depends to a greater or lesser degree on adaptation to the environment. Applying this neo-Darwinian view to the social process, the evolution of the "species"—the society—would depend on the constant adaptation to the external conditions.

Here is where the so-called naturalization of the social appears. Given that the codes do not correspond to certain social groups, their evolution can seem to be a "natural selection." It would be "natural" if only the system capable of the best adaptation to the setting survived. In this manner, the development of society is identified with the self-reproduction of the system. And that very same natural selection would regulate the "struggle of the species for survival." In short, the people better adapted displace those less adapted.

This process of "natural" reproduction (in the sense of an automatic self-regulation) excludes the subject and intentional action. The social process would not be responding to any intentionality. It would have neither direction nor central thrust. Subordinated to the spontaneous dynamic of self-regulation, the social structure would be nothing more than a sequence of temporary constellations. But such a process is hard to bear. We know that there is no social life if coexistence lacks a certain degree of duration. A social structure that seems fragile, temporary, and even chaotic, prevents interaction. People will only relate insofar as they perceive their situation to be somewhat normal, visible, and calculable. This is precisely what the naturalization of the social process offers: a safe and inviolable order. The need to stabilize a reality that seems to be elusive in its constant mutation operates therefore as the necessary premise for interaction. We would have to lock in an order "as if" it were set in stone and self-regulated in order help people develop strong and predictable relations among themselves. An old mechanism seems to be repeated: human beings project the norms that govern their social relations to the firmament of the natural laws.

3.   Theory as Cultural Production

The theory of society is a social construct. This formulation rests not only on accumulated knowledge but also includes beliefs, fears, and aspirations. Often overlooked is the fact that social theory is a moral fact; it involves a judgment that values the present with respect to its past and a desired future. And it is a symbolic system that interprets reality, but also grants it meaning and purpose. It converts what is real into an object of fear or one of desire. As Jeffrey Alexander points out, "social theory must be considered not only as a research program, but rather also as a generalized discourse, of which one very important part is ideology. As a structure of meaning, as a form of existential truth, scientific social theory operates, in effect, in a non-scientific manner."[13] In this sense, the theory of society itself is a cultural construct, permeated by numerous dimensions.

In assuming that social theories are a cultural product, we are stating that they can operate as symbolic representations of society. The theories—as long as they are symbolic reconstructions—confer meanings and purposes to the various aspects of social life. Today, Alexander asserts, the theories seem to be constructions that 1) hinge on a binary code, and that 2) make reference to the distinction between the sacred and the profane.

With regard to the first point, it suffices to consider the principal trends that followed one another during the second half of the twentieth century to discover the essential role of the binary code. In the fifties and sixties, modernization theories had as a central theme the distinction of modernization versus traditionalism. Later, the neo-Marxist approaches of the sixties and seventies stressed the capitalism versus

---

13   J. Alexander, op. cit., 65.

socialism dichotomy. In the eighties and nineties, it was replaced by the thrust of modernity versus postmodernity.

These antinomies rest on a historic vision that makes the contemporary era a topic of discussion in relation to the past. Traditionalism, capitalism, and modernity characterize an order of the past that could—and should—be superseded by a new social constellation, which could be called modernization, socialism, or postmodernity. The theories mentioned go well beyond an "objective" interpretation of society: they recount a dramatic history that calls on people to take sides; they foster a teleological vision of the social process that identifies the changes diagnosed with progress in the society. We must opt for the future, since it will be better than the past.

Regarding the second point, we should focus on the mythological function that these distinctions fulfill. By classifying the world according to the criteria of the sacred and the profane, a referent is put in place that orders the social while also giving guidance on how to experience and think about life in society. In order to fulfill that role, social theories tend to adorn modernization, socialism, and postmodernity with a sacred halo. They are the Good to be obtained. At the same time, they attribute the ills we suffer to traditionalism, capitalism, and modernity.

When the social theories symbolize certain elements of the social reality as sacred principles, they carry out a "naturalization of the social." Sacralization and naturalization are, as I see it, two equivalent ways to guarantee the constituent rules of the social order, removing them from public discussion. For a long time, the state was the almost metaphysical entity that—placed outside society—enshrined the fundamental principles of the order. Now, to offset the "technification" of the state, the market acquires a sacred halo. The market symbolizes "something" beyond a mechanism of social coordination. It embodies the sacralization of specific principles: efficiency, productivity, competitiveness, profitability. They remain vested with the moral authority necessary to legitimize the "imperatives" of the market and justify the social costs. At the same time, those sacred laws allow one to denounce people's efforts to deliberately build their future as the Evil that stalks the established order.

If this line of reasoning were plausible, then we would have to submit social theories to a cultural critique. We would have to spotlight the interpretive codes that order our way of social living and generate the collective imaginaries regarding that coexistence. Above all, we should pay more attention to the symbolic representations inherent to the theoretical formulation. We could then discover the symbols and images hidden in the social production of the order and that, therefore, prevent people from becoming subjects of their destiny.

The Erosion of Political Maps*

In Latin America, as in other regions, a sort of antipolitics is gaining influence and even political power (Collor, Fujimori, Menem) which, without openly questioning democracy, is profoundly altering its exercise. These new, anti-political phenomena represent more than simple "deviant cases"; they form part of a more general process of redefinition and restructuring. We are witnessing not only political changes, but a change in politics itself.

The situation in Latin America forces us to revise two tactical premises which have been implicit in the processes of democratic transition. Our defense of politics in opposition to authoritarian antipolitics had implicitly identified politics with democratic politics. Yet as soon as the "business" of politics re-emerged, its democratic character faded away. Thus we must again ask ourselves an ancient question: What is the meaning of democratic politics? That question compels us to reconsider yet another premise. Early in the transitions from authoritarian rule we took for granted that democracy would be our point of arrival. However as we moved ahead with this process we believed was leading us to democracy, our goal shifted like a *fata morgana*. We discovered that the journey of democratization does not lead to an unequivocal destiny, fixed once and for all.

There is a deep uneasiness with modernity as we usually understand it: as the normative reflexivity and the political steering of societal

---

* This text belongs to the chapter "Politics in Retreat: Redrawing Our Political Maps," published in Andreas Schedler, *The End of Politics? Explorations into Modern Antipolitics* (UK: Palgrave Macmillan, 1996). It was translated by Andreas Schedler with the aid of Jane Schroder and Marcela Ríos. An initial draft was published in Spanish under the title "Los nuevos perfiles de la política," *Nueva Sociedad* 130 (March–April 1994).

processes. The impression prevails that contemporary processes of transformation escape our control. Overshadowed by the antinomy between democracy and authoritarianism, the tension between modernity and modernization has been ignored for many years.

The struggle against authoritarianism served to revalue democratic regimes, but at the same time it dried up all reflections on political dynamics. We have forgotten that democracy is a historic movement whose meaning we must bring up to date with changing circumstances. It is true that any epoch is tempted to view itself as an exceptional period, and thus as the end of history. But later on contexts change, and things are read differently—not because new "truths" appear but because reality itself changes.

I wonder if the new panorama does not also change our very way of looking at politics. We find ourselves in the midst of a diffuse struggle which is still at the larval stage with regard to how we understand democracy and democratic politics. Such political conflict should not astonish us. It is part of all major transformations which modify the institutionalized forms of conducting and of conceiving politics. In fact our malaise with politics can be explained neither by an economic crisis nor by a political one. The economic hardship of Latin American countries, which is rooted in foreign debt and structural adjustment measures as well as in the enormous social costs stemming from them, is notorious. Nevertheless there exists a broad-based agreement both on the need for such economic reforms and on the urgency to reduce social inequalities. We are not facing a political crisis in the usual sense in which ideological polarization and partisan mobilization generate conflicts that overwhelm democratic institutions. On the contrary, it seems to me that this discomfort is not so much related to economic and political-institutional problems as to a new "cultural climate."

The relationship between politics and culture is not the only significant element for understanding democracy. In fact it is not even a matter of high priority. But it allows us to visualize the fact that the current uneasiness with democratic politics is crystallizing into a new perspective. The usual images of politics, and therefore traditional expectations with regard to political action, are more and more difficult to replicate under the new conditions. They are maintained by inertia while we seek to form another idea of politics and democracy, which is more concordant with everyday experience.

If we further reflect on this intuition, we arrive at the basic parameters according to which we preconceive politics. The new context alters the dynamics of political institutions and actors. Yet it seems to me that, beyond those political changes in a narrow sense, one of the greatest challenges for Latin American democracies lies in the area of political culture. This encompasses not only beliefs and preferences gathered in public opinion surveys, but also symbolic representations and collective imaginations—in other words, those bits of "evidence" people do not make explicit because they consider them "normal" and "natural." It is in this cultural sphere that we form our images of politics as well as our prejudices about societal problems and their possible solutions.

A "culturalist" approach is usually thought to be more problematic and controversial than other approaches. One recent example is the interpretation offered by Charles Maier, who deciphers the current discontent with democracy as a moral crisis.[14] It is easy to agree with the cautious and subtle way he describes the symptoms: a sudden sensation of being disconnected from history, the disaffection with the *Nomenklatura* of any ideological sign, and a recurrent skepticism toward the doctrines of social progress. Even though I share his intention, I nevertheless fear that the notion of a "moral crisis" may lead us not to a renovation of ethical-normative principles but to an explosion of irrational altitudes. When the usual guidance criteria fail and tensions become unbearable, returning to the moral trenches appears attractive; it substitutes simple and pure convictions for the complex process of developing and selecting alternatives. History has taught us too many times the unfortunate consequences of pretending to save morality by denying evil. In order to avoid any confusion of politics with the salvation of souls (Max Weber), I prefer to use the well-known metaphor of the map.

At the present, political processes resemble a journey without a compass. Since democratic politics lacks a pre-established objective, the traveler needs maps which order reality and offer orientation. The

---

14   C. Maier, "Democracy and its Discontents," *Foreign Affairs* 73, no. 4 (July–August 1994).

metaphor of a map refers to the coordinates of space and time which we use to represent social reality. Maps help us to delimit space, establish hierarchies and priorities, structure boundaries and distances, determine goals and design strategies. In essence, maps help us to visualize things in their proper proportions. The maps we are using, however, have become obsolete and disproportionate. Things are no longer where they used to be, and the scales have changed. And the more details we add to these outdated maps the worse things get, because the only thing we achieve is to create false confidence. It is better to realize that we are living not only through a crisis of ideological maps, but also through an erosion of cognitive maps. We have to revise our political cartography.

The crisis of ideological maps is evident everywhere. After the excessive ideological polarization of the 1960s and 1970s, we have welcomed the decline of ideology as a sign of realism. Instead of subjecting reality to a prefabricated scheme, social complexity is accepted. In the absence of interpretative clues, however, this complexity turns out to be unintelligible. We now discover the relevance of ideologies as maps for reducing the complexity of social reality. Indeed the antagonism between capitalism and socialism has given rise to simplistic interpretations and ill-fated dichotomies, but it has operated as an effective scheme for structuring political positions and conflicts throughout this century. The fall of the Berlin Wall (to use a symbolic point of reference) brought about the collapse of this scheme, and with it a whole set of milestones vanished, a whole set of focal points for political classification and for the structuring of reality. Thus, in the absence of all the customary points of reference a familiar landscape offered, politics is perceived as disorder.

To my understanding, politics in its modern conception aims at the deliberate construction of a societal order. Once divine principles and ancestral traditions are lost, politics takes their place as the privileged authority for bringing order into social life. In modern, secular societies, where nothing is fixed or predetermined, politics is expected to establish and to assure "law and order," and not only in legal terms. In a more fundamental sense, politics is also called upon to guarantee the moral and cultural ordering of communal life, to create a framework of reference shared by citizens in all their plurality. The difficulty of fulfilling this task can be observed with particular clarity in political parties. Their main job is to offer interpretive schemes and practical options which allow citizens to order their values, their preferences, and their fears, and to integrate them into collective identities. Because of the profound transformations worldwide, parties and party systems are no longer able to develop such keys of orientation, and the temptation arises to impose some kind of "national unity" through populist or plebiscitarian invocations. In fact, feeling dispersed and unprotected, people long for the absolute certainties and immutable identities of the past. In this context we can understand the current disenchantment with politics and the citizenry's lack of identification with parties not as opposition to democracy, not even as a rejection of the parties, but simply as the result of a distressing absence of interpretive codes.

We can observe a deeper cultural transformation which is underlying this ideological crisis. A restructuring of our cognitive maps is underway, that is, a restructuring of the mental coordinates and interpretative codes through which we make social processes intelligible. This is perhaps one of the most significant features of our time, the erosion of shared interpretative codes. The contested meaning of democracy is an illustrative example. The lack of intelligibility reinforces a climate of uncertainty which cannot be resolved through more information. In politics as in economics, accumulating data only increases the weight of the unknown. Uncertainty can only be absorbed through intersubjective links which allow us to tame the vicissitudes of the future.

1. The Spatial Transformation of Politics

The processes of globalization and segmentation that characterize our times are accompanied by a profound restructuring of the political realm. In the first place, the scales of politics are changing. Dimensions, proportions, and measures are becoming altered and politics, as a consequence, displaced and dislocated. The former congruence between the political, economic, and cultural realms delimited by national boundaries is dissolving. Economic, cultural, and administrative processes are being integrated on a supranational level, while the integration of citizens barely reaches the national level. We have all seen how internationalization redefines the actors involved in politics, the political agenda, and even the institutional framework of politics. The recent free trade agreements (Mercosur, NAFTA) limit the latitude and the political options available to the respective countries. This has stabilizing effects, but also adverse ones. The sphere of popular sovereignty, and hence that of citizenship, becomes vague. Issues of major social impact are removed from the public agenda, while others of scant relevance are magnified. This lack of proportion creates doubts about what can be expected from politics. It becomes impossible to determine the value of politics.

Another aspect worth highlighting is the phenomenon of shifting boundaries. On the one side, boundaries become more tenuous and porous. The massive flows of migration, the rapid circulation of cultural moods, and the relative uniformity of consumption habits all break down old barriers. However these new commonalties, expanded almost compulsively, do not mean that we share a common culture. Therefore, on the other side, some boundaries become more rigid and controversial. Collective identities are always based on distinctions from others, and today differences are more rapidly drawn and also more easily perceived as threatening aggression. This triggers fears of conflict and provokes a strong desire for stability. In this situation of diffuse and shifting boundaries, politics faces obvious difficulties in expressing, connecting, and ordering the existing universe of unstable, overlapping, or antagonistic identities.

Changing distances also contribute to the destructuring of the political realm. On the one hand, the extension of transnational circuits to very diverse spheres reduces distances. The international integration of political systems has increased considerably during the past years, even though the mechanisms of political regulation are weaker than in other spheres and often inoperative. We need only to recall the new roles played by the United Nations, the Organization of American States, and the Group of Rio. Interaction has increased, and bonds have multiplied, which, for better or worse, restricts the field of political action and generates continuity. On the other hand, however, internationalization has given birth to processes of segmentation that widen distances within each society. Thus socioeconomic inequalities intensify, and political distances increase, although in a different way than in previous cases of ideological polarization. Initiatives for decentralization weaken the links between national and local elites while, in general, old clientelistic networks successfully adapt to the new environment. Gaining predominance are new mediating mechanisms (such as television) that generate rapid and immediate yet volatile bonds since they are based on shared emotions as opposed to shared interests.

The different elements just mentioned allow us to visualize the spatial restructuring of politics. They are too contradictory, however, to pin down the direction of these changes or to circumscribe the emergent space with any precision. I propose, therefore, that we proceed by approaching two basic points of reference in the new context: the expansion of the market and the redimensioning of the state.

Modernity has brought about the transition from a natural, given order to an artificial, produced one, and it has enthroned politics as the sphere responsible for organizing social life. Yet in recent times this idea of politics has been questioned in the name of self-regulation. As during the era of Polanyi's Great Transformation,[15] the "laws of the market" are once again seen as representing the constitutive principle of social organization. In recent years the attempt to substitute politics with the market as the privileged means for regulation and coordination has undoubtedly found its maximum expression in neoliberalism. Nowadays it is easier to discern two aspects that have been frequently confused in the generic use of the term. On the one hand, neoliberalism promises the affluence of market societies and hints at the fact that our countries have no choice other than to adapt their economic structures to the new modalities of the world market. On the other hand, Latin American experiences disprove a core assumption of neoliberalism. The market on its own neither generates nor sustains social order. Structural adjustment programs that ignore political-institutional consensus building reinforce the disarticulation of society. The high levels of poverty and social inequality represent only the most dramatic expression of the disintegrative force of free markets. Even the international financial agencies have modified their previous positions. They now

---

15   K. Polanyi, *La gran transformación* (Mexico: Fondo de Cultura Económica, 1992; originally published in 1944).

assign high priority to political factors as key factors for the viability of economic programs.[16] And still the political reconstruction of society encounters enormous difficulties.

Due to the very violence with which market mechanisms have been imposed in Latin America, they have acquired a momentum of their own which is difficult to regulate. One of the new market societies' most notorious features is the expansion of the market to non-economic spheres. In particular, the political field is literally taken over, even if the consequences are not in line with the idea of a self-regulating society. On the contrary, the uncontrollable advancement of a capitalist market economy tends to subvert the public order. Instead of giving citizens greater freedom to choose and instead of making political decisions more transparent, the enthronement of market rationality basically consecrates commercial criteria—money as the general means of exchange—to the detriment of the traditional ethos of politics as public service. This alters the communicative structure of democracy. Deliberation and debate are replaced with the exchange of goods and favors, and political negotiation increasingly resembles trade and business practices.

The imprint that market society leaves on politics should not lead us to demonize the market, whose advances, after all, are based on a transformation of the state. In fact, underneath the rhetorical surface of urgent calls for state reform, its reorganization is already underway, and little attention has been paid to its implications.

Critics from the left who oppose the state's authoritarian face and critics on the right who reject its intervention into social and economic affairs find common anti-statist ground. They jointly create an anti-state atmosphere in which the state is viewed as nothing more than a necessary evil. In Latin America we have gone from one extreme to another—from state idolatry to contemptuous anti-statism that ignores the very nature of the state. In fact the role of the state continues to be one of the most controversial issues.

Rescaling the state's productive activity, the administrative structure, and even public services has been inevitable. It has represented a

---

16   See, for example, Banco Inter-Americano de Desarrollo, *Reforma social y pobreza* (Washington, DC: BID-UNDP, 1993).

step of adjustment to changed conditions, which we may welcome to the degree that it promotes social creativity. Nevertheless any modernization of the state apparatus will produce ill-fated results if the state's symbolic significance is ignored. It will lead to situations of "modernization without modernity." The current discussion often overlooks the role the state plays in shaping public morality, the universe of symbols, and the so-called national culture. As the state codifies linguistic and legal norms and homogenizes bureaucratic procedures and socialization in schools, it guarantees common forms of perception and reasoning as well as shared milestones of memory and hope—in other words, that common sense through which people communicate. The state embodies the symbolic unity of social coexistence without which society would not be able to recognize itself as such, that is, as a collective order.

The de facto redefinition of the state currently underway contains the risk of oversimplification. We may look, for example, at privatization policies in Latin America. Even if we accept their economic soundness in numerous cases (while others are difficult to assess in the medium and long term), there is no doubt that a strategy of massive and indiscriminate privatization undermines the institutional order. I am referring to structural changes in the relationship between the public and the private, and more specifically to transformations of the public sphere. The predominant approach dissolves the notion of "public goods" by reducing its attention to economic competitiveness and efficiency. An "open market" not only implies that access is restricted for many. More importantly it means that commonalties, spheres of shared interest, are diluted. Hence feelings of community lose their content. They become empty shells. Even social policies, which after all aim at compensating for the increasing social inequalities, employ strategies which focus on target groups without any reference to overarching collective identities.

In this way economic privatization generates a privatization of behavior. New ways of life based on individualist strategies emerge. They are rational and creative in adapting to competitive relationships and in taking advantage of market opportunities. But they do not assume collective commitments. On the contrary, they weaken the public sphere and hence the shared experiences, the affective bonds, and the practical knowledge upon which any institutional order rests. As a consequence the new social relationships, as successful as they may be on an individual basis, increase uncertainty as well as the perception of risk and threat. Against this backdrop the recent social explosions in the region are not so much an expression of prevailing misery. Rather they represent a demand for public spheres of collective self-recognition.

The experiences just described make it necessary to review carefully fashionable propositions for strengthening civil society. No matter how relevant civil society may be, I believe it is important to emphasize the fact that civil society by itself, without reference to the state, does not generate societal order. Unilateral approaches risk ending up as leftist versions of market apologies.

Neither the strength of market society nor the downsizing of the state represent factors external to political dynamics. On the contrary, politics actually contributes to the limitation of its own sphere. This self-restraint of the political realm is likely to be a decisive experience for people. And perhaps it makes it easier to understand their loss of confidence in politics as a means of regulation and direction as well as their symmetrical trust in the decentralized coordination of private individuals, that is, in the market.

2. The Temporal Transformation of Politics

Maps not only represent reality, they also provide orientation. Tourists may use maps as "travel guides." This brings us to the notion of time. In order to approach the temporal dimension of politics, I believe it is fruitful to consider two points of tension. First, political time moves between the poles of change and continuity. In our modern, future-oriented societies, politics is in charge of constructing the future. It represents the instrument citizens dispose of in order to create the future instead of falling victim to it. Modern politics is not only action; it is also innovation. Since building the future means building something new, it values social change more than the status quo, renovation more than conservation. At the same time, however, politics must create continuity. It is only through their endurance that institutions may acquire moral force, a normative foundation. Citizens expect politics to be solid and consistent, regardless of being grounded on fragile relationships such as trust. Faced with the ancestral trauma of chaos as well as with recent experiences of violence and disintegration, politics bears the responsibility of assuring that the community persists, that it survives beyond the futility of the singular life. We can observe the difficult balance between innovation and duration in the ambiguities of democracy. Contrasting with the tyrant's arbitrariness, democracy establishes laws that restrain citizens as well as public officials in the future. However, together with the rule of law, the principles of popular sovereignty and majority rule imply that nothing is irrevocable and that every decision may be revised. Hence the difficult management of time.

Second, the contingent nature of decision-making puts the political task of formulating desired objectives under a heavy strain. As the "art of the possible" politics is called upon to reconcile the desirable with the necessary. I would like to highlight the difficult elaboration of societal goals at this point. In reality agreements on objectives are as important as those on procedures in the game of democracy. Politics aims not just at constructing the future. It wants to construct it deliberately according to a certain project, an image of a desired future. Moreover, in essence all politics justifies itself by means of references to a better tomorrow. The "aura" of politics lies in this promise. By delimiting the horizons of "what is desired" and "what is possible," democratic deliberation serves as the modern, cooperative and institutional method of managing societal uncertainty. Yet, though the most noble aspect of politics lies in the formulation of social objectives, its daily exercise is ruled by contingency and constraint, that is, by a limited "menu" of uncertain options. In everyday politics, necessities (real or apparent) often leave little room for choices. The "necessary" always presents itself with great urgency. There is no time left. And often this scarcity of time dramatically limits the range of available alternatives.

There are two phenomena which, in my opinion, clearly illustrate the current awareness of temporal factors: information technology and ecology. A widespread fascination exists for the world of computers and its steady stream of innovations. Underlying this fascination is an eagerness to gain time. Yet the acceleration of time turns things into fleeting events. The new discoveries—which are actually successive developments of the same product—fail to produce anything qualitatively new. It seems to be a hallmark of our epoch that its advances fail to generate new horizons. The prevailing slogan is "more of the same." This pattern of unlimited consumption contrasts, however, with the notorious interest in preserving the environment. Alongside the admiration for the quick and transient comes an increasing concern for conservation—but conservation in relation to nature. In other words the current desire for permanence is no longer based on a consciousness of history. Rather, time is taken as being natural and therefore, reified notions of natural time are crowding out older concepts of historical time.

Our consciousness of time no longer relies on tradition. Nor does it rely on the revolution of the status quo. Instead it withdraws into a permanent present which freezes history. The relationship between past, present, and future, through which we try to understand social processes as historic processes, is weakened by the overpowering irruption of an omnipresent present. There seems to be no other time than the present. On the one hand the ghosts of the past are watching us. Despite all our efforts to create memory, history vanishes into thin air, only to survive in the form of mythical visions. Without a doubt the past continues to have its effects on the present, but it is no longer available as practical experience. On the other hand the future dissipates. It turns into a simple projection of the current state of affairs. Therefore the course of events loses relevance as well as depth. It becomes flat and shallow. When the future is reduced to electoral timetables, statistical projections, or negotiation schedules, the very notion of the future becomes insignificant.

The culture of images, which is so characteristic of our times, illustrates well how all that is solid melts into instants, substitutes, and simulacra. When time is consumed in a voracious repetition of fleeting images—just like a video clip—reality evaporates and at the same time becomes overwhelming.

The acceleration of time prevents the political system from elaborating societal goals and thus from opening up common horizons, a shared future. Promises for a better future are reduced to improvements for certain sectors. They may provide important benefits to specific social groups but they lack any reference to joint projects. Even allusions to concepts of order that would transcend immediacy are missing. Politics consequently fails in its mission to construct shared frameworks of reference.

Under the impact of the market, politics loses some of its vital dimensions. Instead of discovering and formulating the citizenry's self-determined goals, politics tends to confine itself to reacting to external challenges. The calculation of given opportunities becomes a substitute for reflecting on desired states of future. The public agenda therefore resembles an outdated inventory more than a guide for discussing alternatives for the future.

The retraction of the temporal dimension provokes a crisis of leadership. Politics confronts more and more difficulties in making sense of the future and conferring meaning to societal processes. To my understanding this contributes decisively to the loss of the interpretative codes mentioned above. To a large extent, political leadership consists precisely in offering mental maps that permit the citizenry to recognize itself as a community of citizens.

With the erosion of interpretative codes, the future ceases to be intelligible and predictable. And it is no longer subject to common action. Citizens experience the loss of political guidance as a loss of perspective. Their collective imaginations no longer manage to anticipate the course of events, and therefore all notions of order shrink to the here and now. Because of this lack of perspective, the situation seems out of control. And abandoned in a world without clear boundaries, people lose confidence in politics.

To the degree that its governing capacity is weakened, politics becomes more and more similar to business management. Of course improving public management is a prominent task in Latin America, and we should therefore avoid confusing the two concepts. Management is based on instrumental rationality, on the choice of proper means for ends which are given, while defining those ends is the task of politics. However, as I have already pointed out, politics encounters manifest difficulties in discussing and selecting the objectives of social development in our times. In losing its reference to societal goals, political action is increasingly reduced to economic management. In our internationalized economies no policy can ignore such data as productivity, inflation, investment and exchange rates and so on. However managing macroeconomic constraints is not the same thing as elevating macroeconomic equilibria to guiding normative principles of political action.

Political society finds itself more and more constrained by the economy through "technical imperatives." It is definitely healthy that politics now respects the dynamics of other societal spheres and refrains from pretensions to control economic processes (remember, for example, recent experiences in Latin America and Eastern Europe). But in doing so, tasks which are specifically political are often relinquished. A kind of naive veneration of the market places an unduly high value on economic efficiency to the detriment of other vital dimensions of societal coexistence. This coexistence depends on "hard" economic data as well as on "soft" changeable constellations of symbols and collective imaginations. Politics degenerates into a self-referential activity when it fails to take these cultural aspects of a democratic "community of citizens" into account.

3. Redrawing Our Political Maps

Our incipient inquiries into the meaning of democracy and democratic politics lead us to a double phenomenon. We can observe a certain "neutralization" of democratic politics as its capacity to order and direct social processes is questioned and even paralyzed. It would be erroneous, however, to blame democratic institutions or politicians for this regressive process. To my understanding, the problem lies in the cultural realm. Underneath the retreat of politics, we find a loss of perspective, a loss of cognitive means to make the present intelligible and to guide the construction of a common future. And to the extent that politics loses its dynamic force, its image becomes blurred. The current disenchantment with the institutionalized forms of democratic politics is linked to the crisis of orientation and the loss of purpose that we have discussed. People no longer know what to think of politics. Today, politics tends to confine its responsibilities to such an extent that one is forced to ask startling questions about the residual meaning of democracy. This uncertainty affects our ways of conducting politics. If we do not know what to expect from democracy, we can easily develop distorted views of what is feasible in politics. This also has consequences for the way we evaluate democratic politics. If politics no longer sets the course for societal development, its value becomes ambivalent or undecidable.

In the current context of major transformations, politics is suffering from an apparent deficiency. If we want to adapt ourselves to the new situation, we have to redefine politics. We have to update the maps we formerly used to determine the importance and the meaning we ascribe to democratic politics. This is a practical exercise, not an academic one. And it is also a cultural exercise if we comprehend political culture as production and reproduction of "the political." I am referring especially to the interpretive codes through which we structure and orient political life. With the erosion of ideological and cognitive maps, the cleavages which have provided structure to the political world fade away. It would be shortsighted, however, to confuse the loss of political creativity we are experiencing, and which is reflected in the reigning mood of political malaise, with depoliticization. Quite the contrary, politics is facing a process of transformation.

As we have seen, recharting political maps implies the reformulation of spatial coordinates.[17] It also means redefining the scales we operate with. Currently the use of small-scale maps predominates. Such maps provide us with meticulous information. For instance they enable us to identify in detail the exact location actors occupy in the political space. However this type of map generates too much information. The informational excess it produces makes it difficult to discern which points are significant and thus creates obstacles to the design of medium- and long-term strategies. What we need are large scale maps, which are more useful for approaching a globalized field, for reconstructing relationships between multiple levels, and thus for establishing workable criteria of orientation.

A second factor involved in processes of cartographic restructuring is symbolization. Maps operate as symbolic representations of reality. Through them we find out what is "real" and what is "possible." They form a symbolic universe which has undergone a complete

---

17   Credit for the mapping criteria must go to Santos Boaventura de Sousa, "Una cartografía simbólica de las representaciones sociales," *Nueva Sociedad* 116 (November–December 1991).

transformation. The weakening of the state, once in charge of representing society, reflects a generalized erosion of collective symbols. It is around these symbols that conflicts over the meaning of democratic politics focus. To the degree that the democratic order loses its symbolic density and consistency, the people's bonds to and their identification with democracy will weaken. Redrawing our political maps therefore presupposes the restoration of democracy's symbolic force as a collective enterprise.

All maps are based on a projection of space starting from a central axis. This structure inevitably highlights some points while marginalizing others. At present our standard map, which is based on the centrality of politics, is being put into question. Today the international bipolarity has collapsed, the national framework of politics is crumbling, and processes of globalization and fragmentation are reaching startling heights. This intersection of critical processes is destroying our former certainties regarding the proper place of politics. At this point we do not even know what the central political issues are. Political positions appear as "collages" in which different and contradicting elements are juxtaposed in fluid kaleidoscopic configurations. Hence strategies of minimal consistency and durability no longer exist. We must therefore attempt to recompose political perspectives which restore our ability to establish priorities. This leads us to the temporal dimension and with it to the notion of the future.

As we have seen, the acceleration of time has undermined our images of the future. Without horizons we confound the existing with the necessary, and the generation of alternatives is blocked. To a large degree this explains the anachronistic impression democratic politics conveys. It appears outdated. Incapable of formulating objectives that would transcend immediacy and thus reduced to an uninspiring choice of lesser evils, politics is held hostage by contingency. However, while this "omnipresent present" raises questions about the steering capacity of politics, it does not eradicate the concern for the future. The longing for a better tomorrow continues to exist. It may take regressive forms (as in different types of fundamentalism) and feed anti-political movements which are incompatible with liberal democracy. But it may also advance the development of democracy. For that to happen, however, we need to rethink our notion of time and, in particular, our idea of the future.

One final observation: reconstructing cognitive maps means reconstructing the rationality currently in use. Since the Age of Enlightenment, modernity has strived to illuminate darkness with the radiance of reason. In reality, however, any theory or concept illuminates some aspects and leaves others in the dark. In our perplexity we may recur to a different, perhaps less "illuminist" experience of everyday life. We may turn off the lights until our eyes become accustomed to the darkness and then spot the shadows. What I wish to say is: perhaps we should temporarily suspend our familiar conceptions in order to visualize the emergent contours of new democratic realities.

III

Our Fears

In 1998 the United Nations Development Programme (UNDP) presented a study on Chile that substantially impacted the public debate. The stinging sensation came from a different perception regarding the Chilean process. A dimension normally not considered gained visibility: people's subjectivity. Subjectivity matters. We do not know how much or how, but life teaches us that it is as real and pertinent as the demands of socio-economic modernization. Only if we reckon with the existing tension between the rationality inherent in modernization and people's subjectivity can we make the changes underway result in human development.

Subjectivity is a complex phenomenon which encompasses values and beliefs, mindsets and practical knowledge, norms and passions, experiences and expectations. Here I will return to an aspect I had dealt with earlier: fears. Fears are a powerful motivation in human activity and, in particular, in political action. Whether acute or subcutaneous, they condition our preferences and behaviors as much as or more than our longings. Through them, with greater or lesser acumen, we learn about the hidden side of life. Below I will present three types of fears that, I believe, can be gleaned from the *Desarrollo humano en Chile 1998* report. Based on the empirical results set forth there,[18] I can identify three phenomena:

Fear of the Other, who is usually seen as a potential aggressor;
Fear of exclusion—economic and social;
Fear of meaninglessness stemming from a social process that seems to be out of control.

---

18   United Nations Development Programme, *Desarrollo humano en Chile 1998. Las paradojas de la modernización* (Santiago: UNDP, 1998).

1. Fear of the Other

People's fears have a distinctive expression: fear of the criminal. Crime is perceived as the primary threat that triggers the sense of insecurity. Without disregarding the high crime levels in all Latin American cities, it is noteworthy that the perception of urban violence is much higher than the actual level of criminality. Therefore, it does not seem appropriate to reduce public safety to a "police problem." The image of the ever-present and all-powerful criminal is probably a metaphor for other aggressions that are hard to grasp. Fear of the criminal seems to strengthen a generalized fear of the Other. Various considerations fuel that mistrust of the outsider.

Poor Memory

Our fears have history. Sometimes a very recent history: the current sense regarding a criminal is not far from what "extremist" or "informant" signified yesterday. Chile's traumatic experience has left unhealed wounds. The thick veil of silence does not make them disappear. Fear of the fears of the past is so great that we disavow them. It is impossible to live without forgetting, but we are not even conscious of how compulsive our forgetfulness is. We have a poor memory, said Marco Antonio de la Parra.[19] In the next chapter I will return to our fear of memory. We do not know what to forget, what to remember. We are insistently advised to "look to the future." But that is not enough. Our expectations are laden with past experiences, of their fears and hopes. To create a future, first we must remember.

How many years have we spent surrounded with fears? Chilean history is permeated with overflowing fear. Fear that the torrent of subjectivity will sweep the institutional dikes away. The weight of the night does not seem to have dissipated. The stifled conflicts remain current. Any occurrence can activate the ghosts of the past. Perhaps we distrust the Other because we fear conflict. The Other represents a threat of conflict. Not only the threat of physical aggression: daily life in a competitive society is also aggressive. When concerns grow about "what is

---

19   M. A. de la Parra, *Mala Memoria* (Santiago: Planeta,1997).

ours," fears about the "invader" increase. As Carlos Franz says,[20] "our walled-in city-society confesses one of its most primitive fears in its urban literature, perhaps one of the cornerstones upon which we found our coherence: the fear of invasion." The fears speak of us. Is not the fear of the aggressor a fear of our own aggressiveness? Perhaps we distrust above all our own abilities (psychic and institutional) to manage conflicts. If by democracy we mean the institutionalization of conflicts, its functioning depends on our capacity to address and resolve conflicts. Have we learned to tolerate, negotiate, and resolve the struggles of opposing interests and differences of opinion?

Coming to terms with history entails confessing our vulnerability, the precarity of the material conditions of life and above all, the precarity of our coexistence, of our identities, of our ideas and categories. A precarity at odds with the "obsession with success." In a country where everyone wants to be a winner, it is not easy to admit to being vulnerable. At most, we complain about the problems that prevent greater successes; we rarely ask ourselves about the criteria for success. We too easily confuse the results obtained with results that are possible. We go from "the system works well this way" to the fallacious conclusion that "the system only works well this way." It silences doubts and uncertainties, but also critique and innovation.

Fears are dangerous forces. They can provoke aggressive reactions, anger, and hatred that end up corroding day-to-day sociability. They can produce paralysis. They can induce submission. Fears are the easy prey of manipulation. There are "fear campaigns" that seek to exploit and hijack the fears in order to discipline and censor. The vaguer the fears, the more tempting it is to exorcise them through dramatic invocations by security forces. Sometimes security takes the form of prison: don't do this, don't say that, better not to think. Is it not possible for us to feel secure in the realm of freedom?

Fears as well as security are both a social product. They have to do with our experience of order. Any event can become a vital threat when we do not feel welcomed and protected by a strong and friendly order.

---

20 C. Franz, *La muralla enterrada (Santiago, ciudad imaginaria)* (Bogotá: Planeta, 2001), 75

What is, however, the experience in our immediate surroundings? The neighborhood and city are usually lived as something foreign, harsh, and lacking emotional importance. If we do not feel appreciation and pride in our closest habitat, we are not likely to appropriate the social order as something valuable that belongs to us. The fragility of the social order has to do with a style of modernization that does not root itself in the public's subjectivity. In short, we must talk about the fears, take them out of the dark, give them names. Only then will we be able to share the fears, define them, and contend with them.

The Fragility of the "We"

If the outsider causes alarm, it is because we do not trust our own strengths. The more fragile our "We," the stronger our fear of Others. Modernization breaks with the narrow stately world of the past and opens broad "contact zones." Transactions grow, but that does not necessarily create social ties. Most of the relations tend to be anonymous and fleeting. We hardly know our neighbor. We see day after day how the processes of secularization, differentiation, and commodification of modern society, fostered by globalization, undermine collective identities. The normal contexts of trust and meaning are weakened. The family, school, company, neighborhood, and the nation are no longer obvious places of integration and identification. The new public places—shopping centers, soccer stadiums, rock concerts—provide new rituals but do not form bonds of social cohesion. The "tribes" increase mobile and flexible clusters, which share emotions, symbols and selective interests, but lack the authority and duration necessary to provide stable norms and beliefs.

With the erosion of collective identities, individual identities are also hindered. Is it not paradoxical that the individual—the pillar of modernity—would lose their normal setting of insertion? Between the thirties and the sixties "organized modernity"[21] afforded the individual a normative, cognitive, and organizational framework to structure their place in the world. Its crisis (addressed as postmodernism) makes the

---

21   P. Wagner, *Sociología de la modernidad* (Barcelona: Herder, 1997).

socialization models, the distribution of roles, life plans falter. Our "I," freed from the "We," finds itself in a type of societal weightlessness. It is no longer solely about fear of the Other; it is fear of oneself. Insecurity sprouts from within me.

The self-sufficient and rational individual continues to be the foundation of liberal democracy and daily coexistence. But which individual are we talking about? The prevailing discourse about the individual proves abstract. The emphasis on the individual as the "unit" of social life has not been accompanied by a reflection concerning the actual process of individuation. What is the net balance, seen in historical perspective, of this civilizing task? The promise of individuality, advanced by modernity, seems to be revoked daily by the frightened, isolated, anesthetized individual in our society. In speaking about our fears, we must also talk about the difficulty of being an individual in the midst of a "negative individualism."[22]

The precarity of the "We" exacerbates the withdrawal to the home. The family appears to be the last refuge against the hostile forces of the environment. It represents not only the principal support in case of economic problems; it is usually also the (almost) sole reserve of meaning in the face of the moral and emotional dilemmas. Especially in the middle and lower sectors, the family depends exclusively on its own economic and normative resources for contending with a multitude of tasks: from illness and labor precarity to the dangers of crime, drug addiction, or teenage pregnancy. Internal tensions are added to the external demands generated by the entry of women into paid employment. Couples can no longer fall back on the inherited roles. In such circumstances, the home becomes a fortress besieged by all the insecurities, and the family begins to bear a significant overload. And to make matters worse, it is assigned the responsibility of socializing the norms and values that hold together community life. In an era in which the family undergoes so many changes, the call to defend "traditional family values" not only proves to be empty: it also hinders the reformulation of the meaning of family in the new context.

---

22   A. Giddens, *Modernidad e identidad del Yo* (Barcelona: Península, 1995).

The Erosion of Social Bonds

The commonplace side of fear is the "mistrustful society." Insecurities generate pathologies in the social bonds and, conversely, the erosion of daily sociability accentuates the fear of the Other. It is no coincidence that the region shows the greatest social inequalities in the world, along with the highest levels of mistrust. The situation is reproduced in Chile, where eight of every ten people do not trust others. Indeed, how can trust be built when the great stories, national identities, hallowed traditions, family scenes from childhood fade away? Undoubtedly, community life goes on through many networks of interaction, formal and informal. Every day we repeat acts of trust and establish some cooperative relationship. At the same time, however, we presume that others are aggressive, selfish, impudent, and ready to step over corpses in order to achieve their goals.[23] In other words, the presence of associative networks at the microsocial level seems to be a misfortune due to their absence at the macrosocial level.

The image of the mistrustful society shows the lack of trust in ourselves, in the strength of our bonds. In the case of Chile, the erosion of the social bond has historical reasons. But in addition, it reflects the effect of the current modernization strategy. It increases the independence and free choice of the individual, who gains new opportunities for initiative and creativity. It shatters old restraints, but without creating a new concept of community. The speed of the process and the expansion of the market to extra-economic realms (such as education, health, or social welfare) tend to severely modify our view of society and the cultural meaning of "living together." An individualistic vision of the world, of its opportunities and its risks, prevails. Simply stated: the processes of individuation lead to processes of privatization. Privatization of standards and behaviors, privatization of risks and responsibilities. It weakens integration in community life and—as fear of crime shows—leaves the individual helpless. The social bond represents a wealth of knowledge and customs, of practical experiences

---

23   Facultad Latinoamericana de Ciencias Sociales, *Representaciones de la sociedad chilena*, 4 vols. (Santiago: Flacso, 1997).

and mindsets that a society accumulates, reproduces, and transforms throughout generations. It is a country's "social capital."[24] And, just as all capital, its development requires a favorable environment: active bonds of trust and cooperation, fluid conversations on matters of common interest. It requires the participation and coordination of countless organized actors (from Rotarians to neighborhood associations) and informal groups (rock bands, Alcoholics Anonymous, literary groups). To a fair degree, the production of this social fabric defines the organizational, managerial, and innovative capacity of a country to contend with international competition. It generates a "climate of trust" much required by the market. That very same market, however, drives competitive and flexibility trends in social relations which tend to destroy solidarity linkages. This loss of social networks is usually more marked in the more vulnerable sectors of society. The outcome is paradoxical: the same strategy of modernization that demands strong social capital can weaken it and, on the contrary, heighten social inequalities.[25]

2. Fear of Exclusion

Our fears are basically expressed in our social relations. But they are equally present in people's relation to the functional systems. Chileans recognize that their overall situation, their educational, labor, social welfare situation, etc., is better than that of their parents. In fact, the country's modernization expanded access to jobs and education, improved health indicators, established the individual procurement of social welfare; in sum, it streamlined the operation of various systems. Nevertheless, people are mistrustful. They do not believe they will have adequate education and training. Even those who have jobs are afraid of being excluded from a very dynamic and competitive labor market. Hence, to be excluded from

---

24   R. Putnam, R. Leonardi, and R. Y. Nanetti, *Making Democracy Work: Civic Traditions in Modern Italy* (Princeton: Princeton University Press, 1993).

25   United Nations Development Programme, *Desarrollo humano en Chile 2000: Más sociedad para gobernar el futuro* (Santiago: UNDP, 2000).

the health and welfare systems. Excluded from the consumption of goods and services in a society in which social status and self-esteem are closely linked to lifestyle. In short, people fear being excluded from the future.

Deficiencies of the Systems

People's distrust regarding obtaining protection against misfortunes and actually being able to take advantage of the best opportunities is not baseless. I would like to highlight three factors that cause a sense of abandonment and impotence.

The principal deficiency lies in the *unequal access to the functional systems*. The possibilities for people to access the essential goods (education, healthcare, or social welfare) are heavily conditioned by their socioeconomic level. Inequalities in income become demeaning when they hamper obtaining basic levels of health and welfare. Comparing their own sacrifices with the obscene wealth of others, the feeling of an unjust treatment springs up, of contributing more to the society than what one receives from it.[26] In the case of Chileans who live in a situation of poverty (one of every four), they are not even in a position to choose and make the most of the opportunities and risks of modernization. Such inequalities in fundamental aspects of each one's life undermine the "discourse of equality" as a frame of reference to develop legitimate social differences. The issue is not trivial. The republican motto of "liberty, equality, and fraternity" is being stealthily altered. Well then, what is left of liberty when the other intrinsic principles of order are hacked off? If the social bond is no longer based on the values of equality and solidarity, liberty is reduced to a selfish individualism.

Another deficiency comes from the *excessive monetarization of the problems*. Money is an effective mechanism for formalizing social flows and extending chains of action. Monetarization opens up possibilities by reducing social complexity, making it comprehensible and manageable.

---

26   G. Campero, "Más allá del individualismo. La buena sociedad y la participación," in *Construyendo opciones*, ed. R. Cortázar and J. Vial (Santiago: Cieplan/Dolmen, 1998).

An abusive monetarization, on the other hand, closes possibilities; it excludes persons without financial resources from essential services. But in addition, it excludes occurrences not translatable into prices. Commodification does not value the meaning of a word, the affective importance of something; it is insensitive to demands for recognition, inclusion, and protection. Therefore, it does not manage to adequately process the demands for work, education, healthcare, or social welfare. These demands, beyond their material relevance, bear a heavy symbolic weight for people. I am thinking about the feelings of dignity, identification, and integration that previously generated work, now greatly weakened in the new organization of companies. In today's Chile, the privatization of certain public services, redirected to private and individual contracts, tends to eliminate the symbolic dimension without providing an equivalent compensation. Of course, it is not the market's job, no matter how efficient it is, to create bonds of belonging and roots. The Chilean state, in turn, continues to be the primary agency for social policies but lacks a narrative capable of representing its activity. Therefore, even when the benefits improve, people do not feel welcome and protected, recognized and respected as participants in a community.

Furthermore, the sense of vulnerability has to do moreover with *new types of threats*. Society itself is producing ever more risks. For example, mental illnesses and nervous disorders generated by the current lifestyle. Or the insecurity caused by the disintegration of work through subcontracting, subsidiary procurement, part-time work, self-employment or consultancies. Our societies may be more or less prepared for "natural" misfortunes but have trouble dealing with the transformations underway and the proper protection mechanisms. This is due, in part, to the prominence of the market. The latter usually anticipates problems insofar as they can be translated into prices but does not consider the costs and social responsibilities (of reconversion or unemployment). Consequently, people feel forced to participate in a "development model" which, in turn, does not take responsibility for the ensuing problems. The result is usually a mixture of disempowerment, anger, and disconnection.

In particular, the disconnection seems to become a survival strategy. In order to defend themselves, at least subjectively, from the various exclusion mechanisms, people withdraw into their individual worlds.

252 ON DEMOCRATIC POLITICS

When they assess—as with television zapping—the different options offered, without committing to any, they manage to momentarily enjoy a sense of controlling their destiny. The pleasure (or illusion) of the disconnection may be a valid strategy for an individual, but I wonder about its effect on social integration.

The Self-Referencing of the Systems

Fear of exclusion is closely linked to a fundamental trait of current society: *the growing autonomy of functional rationales.* As social rationalization advances, systems appear to acquire a life of their own, become independent of the subjects, and exclusively adhere to their internal "logic." The process has two sides. On the one hand, the possibilities of availability or social intervention actually seem to decrease. It is well known and confirmed that political control of the economic system has strict limits. Nonetheless, we should ask ourselves, how steadfast and inescapable are such rationales? Perhaps the supposed "iron cages" are convertible conventions, that is, modifiable by social accord. In fact, public assets and whatever a society defines as such are subject to political intervention. Let us define, then, the limits on system autonomy when we define the limits of politics.

At present, however, the "system rationales" set themselves up as true "de facto powers." The neoliberal discourse "naturalizes" the changes underway.[27] The "logic of the market" illustrates the transfiguration of a "system rationality" into a type of natural fact, supposedly immovable, imposed behind people's backs. The social order tends to be lived as a natural order. The political system is also evermore self-referred and impervious to external influences. People feel that their fears and desires, their motivations and feelings do not count at all, that they are merely agents in an abstract apparatus. This points to the other side of the increasing autonomy of the systems. The consolidation of an abstract logic tends to annihilate real life, toss aside the thousand folds of subjectivity, eliminate the debris of experience, what was not but could

---

27   P. Bourdieu, *Contre-feux* (Paris: Liber, 1998).

have been. It whitewashes the memory of the losses. And, looking to the future, it tends to reduce the possibilities of what is feasible within the framework of the given, to reduce subjectivity to its usefulness to the functional systems. Subjectivity produces and requires such structural channels but is not limited to them. Individuals cannot freely utilize the functional rationales, nor can the systems manage to completely appropriate the subjectivity. Exploiting subjectivity also has a limit. Subjectivity always produces an extra-systemic surplus, a *plus* that goes beyond any institutionalization. What happens to that surplus, with that subjectivity denied? I would like to deal with a frequent interpretation that attributes the feeling of insecurity to an "excess of expectations" by people. Seen in this manner, social malaise would be nothing more than the mental reflection of an insufficient modernization. Therefore, we should stop criticizing the "model," assume its inevitable contradictions, and hit the accelerator: more things in less time. In reality, however, it might be more complicated than voluntarisms of all sorts tend to admit.

The commitment to a strategy of economic growth at all costs presumes that the demands of Chileans and the satisfactions sought are found in the same realm—the market—when perhaps they operate in different registries. Are we not dealing with expectations that, at least in part, cannot be satisfied by the market? Let us take work, for example. Employment represents not only the primary source of income, but also the realm in which people have a vital experience of what is dignity, recognition, and inclusion in a collective task. Therefore, job precarity—beyond its effects on remunerations and unemployment—affects this basic experience of individual and social identity. The excessive flexibilization of labor relations affects many other spheres because it teaches the individual to distrust their neighbor and avoid affective commitments outside their immediate circle. When the relationship is temporary, why get involved in something that does not concern you? Hence, the flexible and temporary work relationship tends to promote tendencies of disaffection in other areas, from the couple's relationship to support for a democratic government.

The 1998 UNDP report argues in favor of another approach: to consider the tension between people and the functional systems as a relation of complementarity. This can take various forms. One of them, the most widely known, is the one epitomized by the state. From the 1920s to the 1970s, the state was the preferred entity for mediation between the subjectivity (increasingly differentiated) and the demands of economic modernization. With this historical backdrop it is understood that despite the success of the privatizations, no matter how dynamic private initiatives may be in Chile, the calls for an active state persist. Ultimately, it defends a form of community that was able to articulate social demands and economic regulation in a context of legitimacy for everyone. That "community" was shattered to pieces in the globalization process and, surely, there is no going back. But we cannot dispense with "something" in common that allows us to structure social coexistence. What makes a diversity of social relations a "society"? A plurality of human beings demands a shared world, says Hannah Arendt,[28] and this is the task of politics. Those who ignore that construction of "community"—a community of citizens—nullify the cultural and symbolic dimension of politics. I have insistently repeated this point which is usually systematically avoided in the current debate. It is there, however, that our "way of life" is currently at stake.

3. Fear of Meaninglessness

The most diffuse of the fears is the fear of meaninglessness. It emerges from a combination of new experiences: stress, the rise of drugs, the persistence of pollution, aggressive treatment, and traffic jams. A combination of irritants that lead to the feeling of a chaotic situation. This impression is heightened by a globalization experienced as an extraterrestrial invasion. Daily life, accelerated at a dizzying pace by thousands of pursuits, an endless succession of upheavals, and a constant transformation of the labor environment and of the urban landscape, leaves people gasping to process the changes. Reality is no longer intelligible and seems out of control. In the midst of the whirlwind, what is the meaning of life?

The vanishing of all that is established is not new. Our society has seen great migrations along with the revolt of the rural world and no

---

28   H. Arendt, *La condición humana* (Barcelona: Seix Barral, 1974).

less radical regroupings around mines, industries, and major cities. Modernity is a history of breakdowns and reconstitutions of customs and traditions, social identities, and collective representations. Successive modernizing waves allowed people to free themselves of obstacles and restrictions, but they also meant rootlessness and atomization.

Is the current process different? The changes create new opportunities: a global perspective of reality opens up, legitimate differences are able to be expressed, thinking breaks out of orthodoxy, and new networks of social interaction emerge. All of this is true, but let us not be blind. New paths open, but also unknown abysses. And we cannot celebrate some without pondering the others.

In the second chapter I showed how the restructuring of the space-time coordinates disoriented us. The change of the millennium was accompanied by a transformation of our mental maps. At the same time, the reserves of affection and meaning that society had placed in its institutions have been weakened. So reality overwhelms the established order. We are in a world of moving and temporary referents, characterized by contingency. Apparently everything goes, everything is possible. In this context, the fear of the Other and the fear of exclusion increase in likelihood.

Tolerating Uncertainty

Subjectivity is deprived of its usual referents while it takes over new arenas. Such tension is intrinsic to modernity; we cannot eliminate it. All human life inevitably includes more or less significant degrees of uncertainty and all social change increases it. The processes of secularization, globalization, differentiation, and individuation shake up the established certainties. And as contingency grows, it becomes more difficult to generate new certainties. The hopes of controlling the uncertainty through technical advances have dissipated; they themselves manufacture new uncertainties. We live in a "society of risks." [29]

---

29 U. Beck, *Die Risikogesellschaft* (Frankfurt: Suhrkamp, 1986); U. Beck, A. Giddens, and S. Lash, *Modernización reflexiva* (Madrid: Alianza, 1997).

A society is modern when it learns to manage uncertainty. This entails, first of all, *constraining the realm of uncertainty*. Legal conventions and social institutions, the symbolic and cognitive representations, are means of restricting it and extending some calculability to coexistence. Since the 1920s, the organization of interests, the restructuring of guidelines for action and consolidation of a social state were an effective means of assuring that predictability.[30] To the degree that the social conventions are relaxed, arguments are trivialized, and reality itself becomes "virtualized," managing uncertainty becomes problematic. This is the new development, and it is here (and not in the mere presence of uncertainty) that the challenge lies.

It is hard to define the uncertainty, for the simple reason that we lack specific language for it, among other things. We lack a codification of the uncertainty. We barely have a meager "economic code" to illustrate the various shocks in international finance, in the fluctuations of the stock market or the exchange rate. There is no wording, however, for the everyday uncertainties. Without categories to ponder and define the uncertainty, we tend to look to people's behaviors for direction. The absence of appropriate criteria is hidden by adaptation to the existing state of affairs.

Magnified by the mass media, a tacky conformity sets in as an antidote for the "fear of the void."[31] Second, the challenge consists of *increasing our tolerance of the uncertainty*. If we cannot avoid it, how do we make it bearable? There seems to be an anthropological threshold which, when crossed, allows uncertainty to eat away at identity (individual and collective). However, an exceptional mechanism exists to raise the walls of tolerance: intersubjective connection. As people deal with uncertainty as a shared problem and develop networks of trust and cooperation, they are able to construct a framework of certainties. The Other becomes, more than a "calculable factor," an indispensable partner in building a common future in the face of trials and tribulations.

---

30   R. Castel, *Las metamorfosis de la cuestión social* (Buenos Aires: Paidós, 1997).

31   O. Mongin, *El miedo al vacío: ensayo sobre las pasiones* (Buenos Aires: Fondo de Cultura Económica, 1993).

Intersubjective connection presumes shared meanings, not just a private communication between the parties. The social linkage is set in particular language, in normative assumptions, and interpretive codes. In other words, it makes use of a particular coding, produced and reproduced in the public sphere. When public space is weakened, communicative structures necessarily deteriorate and hence our ability to decipher reality. In fact, it is difficult for us to reflect on what is happening to us. It is difficult to establish the register of the conversation, specify the qualifying categories, discuss ambivalences, clear up misunderstandings. Communication is filled with noises, interferences, and doubts. What is unspoken (such as fears) mixes together with the unspeakable (the mystery) and is covered by a thick cloak of silences.

Constructing a Future

Our fears can become productive if they help to translate deficiencies into tasks. Ultimately, fear of the meaningless clamors for a future horizon. Tomorrow always signifies a prospect of meaning through which we can place the present into perspective. Precisely because it is fleeting and irreversible, life cannot be encapsulated by immediacy. Closing off future horizons is death. The 1988 plebiscite operated from this symbolic context. The slogan "Happiness is Coming" challenged Chileans' subjectivity, linking two great passions: fear and hope. In an environment dominated by fears, it invoked hope in the future: something that does not yet exist, but could. It invoked an emotional bond and affective commitment to a future to be created. Political action was fed by this anticipation.

What prevents us from dreaming? The *Desarrollo humano en Chile 2000* report reveals a symptomatic fact: a blockage exists in the formulation of collective aspirations. It is difficult for us to create and believe in some dream for the future, beyond the best wishes for family well-being. Do we not have dreams? Do we dare not express them? Perhaps we do not want to dream for fear of the dreams spawning nightmares.[32] We know changes give rise to conflicts and that the conflicts can shatter

---

32 United Nations Development Programme, 2000, op. cit.

order, hopes, and the sense of life itself. Until we come to terms with and work on that experience, all projections into the future will be fearful. As we have seen, not only the present but also the future require that we reclaim the past. We can learn from the past. We should promote a learning process that allows us to overcome inertias while also updating our meaningful traditions. Safeguarding freedoms won grants the right to change what was established. In fact, it is just as important to steer clear of repetitions as it is to maintain historical continuity. History can be a source of confidence: we who were able to do so many things together have reasons to continue building the future together.

We are always building a future. But we do not always know what horizon we seek, what kind of country we want, what kind of world we desire. We lack imagination based on sound reasons. We lack codes of interpretation that enable us to order reality, narrow down its complexity, and determine the meaning of the changes. In order to chart a future horizon, we have to understand the existing processes: specify what they have that is necessary and what is optional. Only then can we weigh the degree to which they are subject to intervention and social regulation. It is in this framework that alternatives are constructed. Viewed favorably, there is a future (and not just an inevitable destiny) when there are alternatives.

The construction of a future presumes—as so stated—an emotional and affective bond. It is in a particular context of fears and desires that the proposed alternatives acquire (or do not acquire) meaning. Only a future that embraces the burdens, doubts, and dreams of the present will be appealing. It is not enough that a future be possible; we must possess the motivation to want to attain it. We must have passion. However, just naming the passions causes suspicion. And we have ample reasons to fear explosions of irrationality and fanaticism. But are not such occurrences precisely the reprisal of a subjectivity that is not institutionally channeled? By playing off reason and passion, we doubly truncate reflective action.[33]

---

33   R. Bodei, *Geometría de las pasiones* (Mexico: Fondo de Cultura Económica, 1995).

The future is envisaged as a promise. That is why a policy that looks to the future is laden with promises. Not only do they help to identify "the possible," but also to identify ourselves as "We." Envisioning the possible encompasses more than a projection of what is materially feasible. It entails a reflection regarding what is socially desirable. Especially in times of high risk, when the range of the possible has become so broad, it is essential to outline perspectives. It is what delineates the promise: it drafts criteria to discern, among all the possibilities, those that allow us (everyone) to live better. Of course, the frustration from so many unfulfilled promises teaches us to be cautious. Nevertheless, the "meaning of life" for each one of us demands a future in which we are not afraid of the Other, do not fear exclusion, and—stated in the affirmative—enjoy a beneficial environment so that living together has meaning.

IV

The Social Construction of Collective Memories*

Memory and oblivion are social constructions that are constantly being crafted and reformulated. This process occurs in the framework of another, broader, social and cultural construction: the social production of time. As part of this production process, memory and forgetting, the present and the future act and are arranged as symbolizations of that great work of collective action that we call history.

"Modern times" are characterized by the dual process of differentiation and linkage between the past, present, and future. By positioning the present in tension between the past and the future, modern society can distance itself from the contingency of the immediate and contend with reality as a malleable order. The central argument of the chapter is situated in this context: modern memory operates precisely in the connection of past and future as part of this dual process: production of time and the social order.

The process has specific connotations in the case of Chile. On the one hand, the Chilean transition to democracy arranges a particular linkage between the times subject to its initial constraints. In the name of governability a possible future is stressed at the expense of a past filled with conflicts. But silencing the past does not eliminate social divisions. The past repeatedly bursts onto the scene, undermining the political construct of consensus. Poor memory does not enable a strengthening of the social bond and the ability for collective action. Furthermore, the prevailing means of modernization, viewed as a quasi-spontaneous result of independent market forces and private interests, obscures the link between the social order and collective action. The result is the

---

* In collaboration with Pedro E. Güell.

weakening of the perception of time as a space in which society constructs its future. In both cases, the outcome is a highly contingent "presentism" and a blocking of future aspirations.

1. Construction of Memory, Production of Time

Memory is a way to distinguish and link the past in relation to the present and the future. It does not refer as much to the chronology of events that have remained fixed in the past as to its significance for the present. Remembrance is an act of the present, since the past is not something that happens once and for all. What is more: it is only partly a given. The other part is fiction, imagination, rationalization. That is why the truth of memory does not lie as much in the accuracy of the facts as in the narrative and their interpretation.

Memory is an intersubjective relationship, developed in communication with others and in a particular social setting. Consequently, it only exists in the plural. The plurality of memories comprises a battlefield in which one fights for the meaning of the present in order to define the materials with which to construct the future. In the light of the present, memories select and interpret the past. Some things are valued, others rejected. And those retrospective views change; one day they shine a light on one aspect which will hide another. The same events can be treated in very different fashions. The uses of memory can justify the repetition of the past as well as legitimate the transformation of the present. But the different uses are guided by the same compass: the future. It is in thinking about the future that the past is reviewed and reshaped. Remembrance establishes continuities and fissures and is itself a temporal flow.

The social construction of memory is set in a more general process: *the construction of social time*. We must "historicize memory" and situate it in a particular social concept of time.

For many centuries, social time was not very differentiated. Past and present were intertwined without major discontinuity in the same galactic distance to the cosmic time (experienced as an eternal repetition of the same thing), or in the reference to a predetermined eschatological time as an absolute future (experienced as awaiting the Last Judgment). Around the year 1500 the awareness of "new things" modified the vision of time and only at the end of the eighteenth century was the distinction between past, present, and future established as discontinuous times of the same process: history.[34] Our social time, is, therefore, a relatively recent construct. It was through this operation that modern society adopted the past as a product of human action while distancing itself from the contingency of the present and the future. A distance that allows for considering them to be open times, that is, available and malleable.

The modern organization of time establishes, first of all, a strong link between the parts of the triptych. Past, present, and future, being different, only acquire meaning through their reciprocal relationship. Second, it is a complex relationship in that there is no unanimous determination about the "before," regarding the "after," nor of the "tomorrow" regarding the "today." The past does not automatically determine the decisions of the present nor do the latter predetermine the evolution of the future. Similarly, the future does not provide absolute guidance for shaping decisions about the present.

Third, as a result, the relation between past, present, and future represents a problematic construction. There are different ways to look at and sense each one of the three times and, in particular, to tie together the threads, faint or hefty, between them. And ultimately, the construction of the social order and its meaning depend on that delicate weave. Our way of experiencing the social order has to do with the way in which we situate the present in the tension between the past and future. Transformations in the prevailing notion of time necessarily modify the structure and function of memory. A thought-provoking example occurred in the passage from the Middle Ages to the modern era.[35] There, in passing from the "traditional society" to the "modern society" focused on the future, the "immemorial memory," which transmits the

---

34 R. Koselleck, *Vergangene Zukunft* (Frankfurt: Suhrkamp, 1979). Spanish version, *Futuro Pasado* (Barcelona: Paidós, 1993).

35 J. Le Goff, *El orden de la memoria* (Barcelona: Paidós, 1991).

hallowed traditions, repeats what our ancestors did and said, and institutionalizes venerable rights and customs, disappears. An *active memory* appears, formulating a "past-present." Memory is transformed into the depiction of the possibilities open to us and of the paths that are forbidden as a result of the lived experience. It is yesterday's people who prevail in us by force of circumstances, Durkheim asserted. As every person knows from their own biography—also valid for countries—considering certain historical facts, not all destinies are still possible. The past conditions future paths. The institutionalist approach has particularly highlighted the role of this *path dependence*[36] in the institutional and economic performance of the new democratic order.

Memory is the tool with which society displays the materials, sometimes fruitful, sometimes sterile, that the past contributes to building its future. We are currently witnessing a significant change in the temporal coordinates which order our social living. As the well-known study by Koselleck[37] shows, the modern era is characterized by a temporal acceleration which creates a wedge between the field of people's experiences and their horizon of expectations. Experiences quickly become obsolete while, on the other hand, expectations for the future grow, increasingly detached from the present reality (utopias). This acceleration becomes a radical shift in our lives. The new technologies associated with the process of globalization and the crisis of ideologies in history have led to a delinkage between time and space; time is compressed to the point that we all seem to be living in the same flash of time no matter where we are. Time as a flow tends to disappear, setting us in a *timeless time*[38] whose effect is the absence of an intrinsic connection between the events which could endow them with a meaning beyond themselves.

We are living, as I said earlier, in an "omnipresent present." On the one hand, the present loses future prospects. Not only does faith in progress enter into crisis in the face of the "risks fabricated" by the

---

36   D. C. North, *Instituciones, cambio institucional y desempeño económico* (Mexico: Fondo de Cultural Económica, 1993).

37   R. Koselleck, op. cit.

38   M. Castells, *The Rise of Network Society* (Oxford: Blackwell, 1996).

post-industrial society. The very notion of the future seems to vanish. The concept of postmodernity is disputed, but points to a trend: "what is new" has become problematic. On the other hand, the present loses historical depth. We might ask ourselves whether the shrinking future horizon also drags along with it a contraction of the past, or if, on the contrary, the vanishing of the future causes an appreciation of the past. The two possibilities are not mutually exclusive. We are probably witnessing a heavy blurring of the past and—for that very reason—a remembrance in search of its tracks.

This is the context that is defining the functioning and meaning of oblivion and of memory today; and our relation to the future is also framed in them. A first possibility is *to forget the past*. This can be lived in two ways. One, it could be lived as a loss. Two judgments that Hannah Arendt usually cites[39] bear witness to this. As a result of the loss of tradition, "our heritage was left to us without a testament" (René Char). Consequently, we lack criteria to contend with the future: "When the past no longer illuminates the future, the spirit walks in darkness" (Tocqueville). But oblivion can also be experienced as an act of liberation: "Without forgetting it is quite impossible to live at all" (Nietzsche). Sometimes history becomes a burden that threatens to crush the present (like the long history of struggles in the Balkans). The weight of the dead crushes the living. So it is time to "free the future of its past." In other words, we must process/select/eliminate the past to make way for the new.

The second possibility—*remembering the past*—also has two readings. It could be an acknowledgment of what was lost. Like the song says: "the shame of having been and the pain of no longer being." A type of "wistfulness" that takes on the pain and the vulnerability. But it could also be a nostalgic reading which—considering the present woes—remembers the happiness of yore. The two possibilities are not mutually exclusive—memory and forgetting form a pair. Marc Augé says it so beautifully: "Memories are crafted by oblivion as the outlines of the shore are created by the sea."[40]

---

39 H. Arendt, *De la historia a la acción* (Barcelona: Paidós, 1998).

40 Marc Augé, *Oblivion* (Minneapolis: University of Minnesota Press, 2004), 21.

2. Chile: The Politics of Memory

In the Southern Cone countries (as in Central Europe and South Africa), the transition to a democratic regime calls the past into question. But the ways of doing so can be different since it depends on the concrete dynamics of each specific process (more or less rapid, with greater or fewer splits). The military defeat of the Argentine dictatorship is not the same as Chile's constitutional plebiscite. Moreover, it is not the same if the collapse of a dictatorship is experienced as a defeat or as a liberation. The sociopolitical context determines the ways in which collective memories review the past. The struggle of the various collective identities to recall their respective histories harkens back to a realm of representation in which to recognize oneself and to be recognized. In turn, the possibilities and scopes of that struggle are marked by the form and dynamics of that realm. The dispute over the memories goes back to politics as the "staging" of the possible memories. Every society has more or less explicit *politics of memory,* that is, the framework of power within which (or against which) society develops its memories and forgettings.

Let us suppose that the collective construction of memory operates in a dual tension: the relation between past and future, as well as the relation between the political construct and social formulation. We will analyze these processes in the case of Chile. A presentation (with extremely broad strokes) of the political struggle regarding the past will serve as the backdrop for reflecting on the anguish of collective memory at the societal level. We will present the "politics of memory" through 1) the future envisioned at the start of the transition; 2) policies regarding human rights; and 3) their subsequent questioning.

The Chilean Transition

The process of democratic transition in Chile is characterized by having taken place

1)   in the politico-legal framework established by the Constitution of 1980;
2)   in an expanding capitalist market economy;

3) with Pinochet continuing on the political scene (as commander-in-chief of the army and lifetime senator); and
4) with a fairly stable bipolar distribution of the political forces.

It was a "negotiated transition" in the sense that the armed forces acknowledged the validity of a democratic regime and the political parties acknowledged the procedures established by the 1980 Constitution.

The first democratic administration, headed by Patricio Aylwin, faced three priority tasks: 1) consolidate the democratic regime; 2) reform the economy to link growth and social equity; and 3) prosecute the human rights violations. The numerical order represents an order of priorities corresponding to a feasibility assessment. Unable to contend with the three tasks simultaneously, the government coalition prioritized the consolidation of democracy. In essence, it was banking on politics, that is, it believed that the mechanism of the "political game" would open up their field of maneuver. This was confined to "the possible": what could be achieved through broad agreements. The so-called democracy of accords required negotiated and gradual reforms that would not harm the vital interests of the parties. In this manner, governability understood as conflict prevention was enthroned as the guiding principle. Under the dominion of this imperative, a number of issues were withdrawn (de jure or de facto) from political decision-making.

This context shaped a certain organization of social time. The present is "strapped" by the legal and economic continuity with the past. At the same time, the present sought to free itself from a past of conflicts that divide society. However, it was not forgotten, precisely because of the recurring presence of the inherited conflicts. Given these difficulties in handling the past, political action is shifted to the future. "One step at a time" and "focus on the future" are the slogans of all the political parties. The attempt is to assure governability through a shared future. The "politics of consensus" maps out future prospects based on two pillars: representative democracy and market economy. This policy assures a climate of peace and tranquility longed for by all. At the same time, however, consensus conceals a variety of interpretations regarding the meaning ascribed to democracy and market. More than a consensus about a shared future, Moulian affirms,[41] it is a shared fear of reliving past conflicts.

The Politics of Memory

Similar to other experiences, post-authoritarian Chile faced the "justice or democracy" dilemma. The strong tension between memory and future present in this dilemma, as well as the narrow framework available to contend with it, explains the successive reformulations of the politics of memory in the Chilean transition.

Identifying the re-establishment of democratic coexistence as the primary objective, the Aylwin administration dealt with the past within a perspective of national reconciliation. It therefore considered truth and justice as conditions for a pardon. The governability viewpoint that marks "looking to the future" also encompasses the past. Accordingly, the demands for truth and justice were framed within "to the extent possible." The possible has its limits.

The search for truth paved the way for the Rettig Commission's *Truth and Reconciliation Report*. It is a "monument of memory." The process culminates with Aylwin's speech in March 1991 in which, in the name of the Chilean state, he asks society for forgiveness. But the gesture saw its scope limited by the reticence of the armed forces, who do not contribute information, neither institutionally nor anonymously, on the detained-disappeared. The subsequent assassination of Jaime Guzmán puts an end to the effort. The ritual of reconciliation fails.[42]

Unable to be resolved through the symbols of forgiveness, society's wounded memory seeks justice through the legal path. This prompts the filing of numerous lawsuits for human rights violations and, among other things, the conviction of General Contreras, the head of the Dirección

---

41   T. Moulian, *Chile actual: Anatomía de un mito* (Santiago: LOM Ediciones/ Universidad Arcis, 1997).

42   P. Güell, "Opfer und Menschenrechte: Die rituelle Dimension der Suche nach Versöhnung in Lateinamerika," in G. Ammon and Th. Eberhard, *Kultur, Identität, Kommunikation* (Munich: Eberhard, 1993).

de Inteligencia Nacional (National Intelligence Directorate-DINA). At the same time, there was an attempt to ascertain the conditions that long ago led to the social conflict and institutional breakdown. Building the future (consolidation of the democratic order and a more equitable economic development) becomes the premise for overcoming the past. That requires time. Time for the most acute pain to ease, the feelings of hatred and fear to dissipate and the affective investments in the future to prevail over the debts of the past. These debts must be settled someday, but the postponement of that deadline can facilitate addressing the past without destabilizing effects. The speech was a triple success: it narrowed down the differences in the heart of the political elite, deactivated the subjective components of memory and, in effect, proscribed the past as a topic of social conversation.

The Irruption of the Past

In Chile, memory imposes itself. The detention of Pinochet in London and his indictment exposed the vicissitudes of the Chilean transition. The accompanying dilemma becomes obvious: it attempts to construct the future while leaving behind a past experienced as an obstacle. But the lengthy judicial battle clearly shows that the present does not allow for crafting a shared future without taking responsibility for the divisions of the past. Memory in Chile is a Pandora's box that one is afraid to open in order not to affect the hard-won coexistence, but is impossible to contain, exploding over and over again.

"The past is fruitful—Todorov declares—not when it feeds resentment or triumphalism, but rather when it bitterly induces us to seek our own transformation."[43] The weakness existing in the Chilean transition's politics of memory regarding giving the past its rightful place in the construction of the future democracy has various origins. I will name two. On the one hand, the fear of conflict is apparent in the population, frightened by traumatic experiences. According to a survey by the Psychology Institute of the Universidad Católica, only 1.4 percent

---

43   T. Todorov, *El hombre desplazado* (Madrid: Taurus, 1998), 85.

of Santiago residents interviewed claim that no human rights violations took place. Half of them believe that torture was a common practice of the security forces. In other words, a "historical fact" exists, acknowledged by everyone. Furthermore, eight of every ten interviewees felt that the economic development during the military regime in no way justifies the violations. At the same time, however, according to a national survey by the UNDP,[44] two-thirds of those interviewed maintain that in Chile "there are more things that separate us than unite us." And for half of those persons, speaking about the past damages harmonious coexistence among Chileans. Remembrance becomes a portrayal of the conflicts.

The fear of conflict finds its counterpart in the principle of governability. In addition, the public discourse denies space and language for processing the past and ends up suppressing the grieving process. With governability understood more as the absence of conflicts than a collective way of processing them, the politics of memory does not contribute to chasing away the specters of the memory: that is, that the remembrance creates an uncontrollable conflict. People do not see in the political realm the symbolic representations that could serve as a mirror to give the past a name and in so doing, take charge of it. Lacking words and symbols to give an account of the past, they opt for silence. And memory opts for taking charge of people through the pathway of fears. In essence, the population is asking the political system for a "neutralized" image of a society without a past, in which, however, it cannot find itself.

3. The Social Construct of Silence

The politics of memory and people's relation to the conflicts of their past constitute a framework in which a particular form of remembering and forgetting is built and rebuilt.

---

44   United Nations Development Programme, *Desarrollo humano en Chile 2000: Más sociedad para gobernar el futuro* (Santiago: UNDP, 2000).

Poor Memory

The top of the list in processing an authoritarian past is *justice*. It is true that Chileans do not mention human rights among the country's priority problems. Nevertheless, they have formed an opinion about the violation of human rights. Even during the dictatorship, according to a 1986 Facultad Latinoamericana de Ciencias Sociales (Latin American Faculty of Social Sciences-FLACSO) survey, 71 percent of those interviewed believe that it is a concrete problem, while only 18 percent of them feel that it is propaganda against the government. Despite the difficulties faced by the first democratic administration, public opinion does not change regarding human rights. In 1992, another FLACSO survey indicates that six of every ten interviewees are in favor of knowing the truth and carrying out punishment; 18 percent prefer to know the truth and give amnesty, and 13 percent feel that the problem has been overcome. The trend has been confirmed by other studies over the years. Recently, according to the survey by the psychology institute referenced, only 25 percent of those interviewed prefer to consider the issue of the detained-disappeared resolved and to forget about them. The expectations for justice have therefore been documented.

However, justice is only one aspect of the collective experience of the dictatorship stowed in one's memory. Another is the *psychological experience* inflicted on each individual. Of course, the opinion polls cannot give an account of these processes, and it is not easy to assess their significance at the societal level.[45] Qualitative studies[46] indicate that September 11, 1973, is lived by Chileans as a breach that—in both personal life as well as that of the country—marks a categorical division between before and after. The interpretation (justifying or accusatory) of the coup varies, but they tend to understand it as an irruption that disrupts everything. All of a sudden, extreme situations that seemed impossible

---

45 E. Lira and M. I. Castillo, *Psicología de la amenaza y del miedo* (Santiago: ILAS/Cesoc, 1991).

46 X. Tocornal and M. P. Vergara, "La memoria del régimen militar," *Documento de Trabajo* 35 (Santiago: Centro de Investigaciones Sociales/Universidad Arcis, 1998).

formed part of the normalcy of daily life. The breach is experienced as "something" unspeakable, ultimately inexplicable. It represents a social trauma. This traumatic experience continues throughout the military regime, remembered as a long period of fear and polarization. "State of siege" and "curfew," raids and arrests, blackouts and informational censorship conditioned the new routines for Chileans. A "culture of fear" is generated whose disciplinary effects have lasted to this day.

The level most relevant to our issue lies in *historical consciousness*. Marco Antonio de la Parra[47] speaks of a *poor memory*: there is memory, but it is broken up, partial, and poor. A fragmentation of the memories predominates which prevents people from reconstructing a path of much consistency. Images are juxtaposed as *flashes* without establishing a sequence. People do not want to talk about the past, they want to forget but cannot fail to perceive the daily presence of that past. A *memory in spite of...* reigns. Unintentional memory that filters in through the recesses of consciousness like an annoying and continuous noise.

Poor memory, for most Chileans, is usually an *ordinary memory*, that is, not dramatic, having not suffered deaths or tortures, but neither does it disregard them. A memory of daily pain and fears, without a legitimizing discourse, which accepts what happened as part of what is "normal and natural." A normalcy which, in the absence of visible blood, does not allow for reflection on its damage. This ordinary memory transforms people into a type of spectator of a far-off shipwreck. Analyzing the sense of the metaphor over the centuries, Hans Blumenberg[48] shows the current watershed moment: if the shoreline once provided an illusion of safety, now the distance between the spectators and the shipwrecked is vanishing. Chilean memories seem to be made up of *silences*. The writer José Donoso liked to talk about the "thick veil of silence" that has covered Chile for a long time. Silence has slowly installed itself. It obeys no order, has no slogan. A silence that is not forgetting. It knows the stories but remains silent. Perhaps a way to express the unmentionable; perhaps a strategy for struggling with contradictory

---

47   M. A. de la Parra, *Mala memoria* (Santiago: Planeta, 1997).

48   H. Blumenberg, *Schiffbruch mit Zuschauern* (Frankfurt: Suhrkamp, 1979).

emotions. A silence that makes a gesture of courtesy among strangers and seeks complicity among friends. A surrogate of conversation. But the silence is not merely the absence of words. It is also active: the silencing. It does not have to be a deliberate action; sometimes it is merely an omission. Some motives foster that silencing.

Forgetting History

We still have not put together the history of a consciousness torn apart. On one hand, the distant past comes to us by means of an "official history" (and as such, already cleansed of all critical junctures) firmly rooted in the collective memories. On the other, the recent history is the subject of deep divisions. Opposing views linger regarding the significance of the reformist administrations of Frei and Allende, as well as of the military government. There are conflicting assessments of the content and forms of their policies. Obviously, the three administrations expressed different values and served different interests. This means that Chileans were affectively involved with emotions that were at once strong and different. There was no politico-ideological neutrality nor affective indifference. Everyone felt at one time or another hatred and joy, hope and fear. This mobilization of passions not only could not be channeled within democratic institutionality, but also could not be recounted in the frameworks of a common history. The passionate division lacking language to discuss it provided an excuse for the military coup and ended up being leveraged by it, this time under the most severe form of division between the victors and the defeated.

If the dictatorship repressed the mental and emotional processing of what was happening to us, the advent of democracy in 1990 marginalized it. With the failure of the initial major effort, the official discourse tacitly refused to process the past.[49] To the extent that the correlation of political forces seriously limited "the possible" in truth and justice, "the possible" was projected into the future. This decision, based on an "ethic of responsibility," relates not only to the real constellation of power (of

---

49   J. Bengoa, *La muerte: Transfiguración de la vida* (Santiago: PUC, 1998).

the de facto powers) but also to public opinion. For the latter, the end of the dictatorship is the end of the repression but not of the fear. Let us not forget that the entire society is permeated by the fear of conflict. The acute, sometimes pathological sensitivity to conflicts reveals the force of memory. A subcutaneous but real presence. The mutual conditioning is glaring: a certain assessment of the possible and feasible glosses over the conflicts of the past at the same time that, on the other hand, the memory of the conflicts, in its traumatic state, hinders a dynamic perspective of the future.

The primary consequence seems to be the *loss of historicity*. We have been left without history. That is valid for individuals and for the whole of society. At the individual level the blurring of biographies seems frequent; lived experiences are juxtaposed piecemeal, without forming a path. As a result, those experiences become foreign, kidnapped by greater forces. Nor is society able to see itself in a history. There is too much of a rush to forget a past for which, ultimately, no one, for a variety of reasons, feels like an heir. Too much of a rush to stabilize a decent coexistence to re-examine the values of community life. An understandable urgency: Did not all postwar societies quickly hush their damages and pain? But that rush comes at a price: it hampers placing things in perspective. The difficulty of formulating a future project is attributed to the urgency of the problems, when, in reality, it is the lack of perspective that creates the urgencies.

The result is a mis-encounter with reality. Stripped of its history, of the traits and testimonies of human action, social reality loses all affective proximity. How can I feel the established order as my own when all my footprints have been erased? Why should we feel pride in the country and its development when we are not part of its history?

The Swift Transformation of the Social

Memory and oblivion are two sides of the same coin. Not only memory, but also forgetting is a social construction. We can speculate on some sociological reasons for forgetting. In the last twenty years, Chilean society has undergone a profound transformation. This structural change, induced by the expansion of the market economy and the authoritarian template of social relations, was concealed by the preeminence of the dictatorship. It barely became clear to the public with the advent of democracy. Its primary feature is the transformation of social bonds and our way of life.

Internalizing market criteria changes people's habits and attitudes, without overcoming the legacy of fears and mutual mistrust. The obvious result is a privatization process. The privatization of public services is accompanied by the privatization of behaviors. Fear of Others corners us inside the home, and the withdrawal to the home restricts memory to the family album. Meanwhile, public spaces are transformed, and normal communication structures are impoverished. The fragmentation of Santiago's urban fabric is emblematic of a segmentation of spaces for social encounter and conversation. And where a strong social bond does not exist there is no support or material to build collective memories.

We have heard of "memory through forgetting,"[50] but perhaps what Chileans have is a "silent memory." Silence is not the equivalent of forgetting. The past is present, but hushed. It does not speak, it has no voice. In essence, it is a matter of collective memories that they have not been able to reflect upon in order to name the processes underway. It seems plausible to assume that the transformations in progress are so meteoric and of such a magnitude that it is extremely difficult to account for what has happened. In other words, *the gap between the present and the past may be much greater than the distance between the democratic order and the dictatorship.*

Memory and the Future

The politics of memory is more than managing the past, and its effects go beyond our relationship to the conflicts experienced. It is part of the social construction of time, and the manner of relating to the past frames the possibilities and meanings of the future.

---

50   Steve J. Stern, "From Loose Memory to Emblematic Memory: Knots on the Social Body," *Remembering Pinochet's Chile* (Durham: Duke University Press, 2004).

The Vanishing of the Future

Sufficient emphasis has not been given to an aspect of current Chilean society which could, however, have serious consequences. We are referring to a certain blockage of dreams.[51] We are not sure if Chileans are concealing their aspirations, if they are unable to verbalize them, or if they fear that dreams may turn into nightmares. In any case, they usually express little hope for the future. A discourse of despair prevails, either due to disillusionment with the state of affairs, or due to giving up on even wanting a different society. In the absence of collective projects, aspirations remain limited to individual propositions. The desire for a "better tomorrow" seems to be limited to the private realm, the family and job prospects.

The drastic shrinkage in horizons has various causes. The phenomenon possibly shares in that global movement of restructuring called "postmodernity." The loss of tradition, the de-linkage of space and time, the end of the bipolar world, globalization and the weakening of national identities, transformations in the identity of the "I"—all of this impedes an intentional construction of the future.

In the case of Chile, the vanishing of the future refers back in a special way to the relation between future and past. One with a double meaning: a weak notion of the future weakens the reading of the past and, conversely, the silencing of the past takes away abilities to create a future horizon. The combination of the "Asian crisis" and the "Pinochet *affaire*" during 1999–2000 illustrates the mutual conditioning. After years of strong and sustained growth, suddenly the financial upheavals display their vulnerability when faced with an "external shock." The future reveals an arbitrariness that escapes one's own grasp and abilities. The efforts made seem to be in vain in light of the financial setbacks. In this context, the silence around the military regime also seems like a futile sacrifice. In spite of his "good behavior," Pinochet has once again invaded the daily lives of Chileans, demonstrating that the divisions of the past have not disappeared.[52]

---

51 United Nations Development Programme, 2000, op. cit.

52 A short story by Maupassant, "The Necklace," sums up the situation. "Its protagonist, a young woman of modest means, borrows a diamond necklace from a wealthy friend in order to go to a ball; to her misfortune, the necklace

Memories of the Past Future

The relationship between past and future varies according to the present point in the chronological timeline. There are different futures: the "present future" of today, which is the "future present" of tomorrow. And also the "past future," which, yesterday, was envisaged as future. So, the blurring of the present future is related to the *past future*. There is a "memory of the future"—the memory of "what could have been"— that conditions the expectations of the present future.

The blockage of dreams that we ascertain in Chile is, in part, a product of our memory. A memory that links the past (dictatorship) with a past future (coming of democracy). Frustrated expectations exist regarding two desired futures. First, with the prospects opened up by the *promise* of the 1988 plebiscite: "Happiness is coming." An effective slogan that counters the "leaden years," a call to affections. The promise of a change, if not of living conditions, at least in the way of living. A change in the way of living, breathing, relating. This heralded future does not materialize. The twelve years of democracy signified extraordinary improvements on many levels, including economic well-being. In contrast, human relations were renewed less and, hence, the realm in which happiness is born.

Second, the *expectations for justice* documented in the surveys cited above are postponed. Insofar as General Pinochet's trial and the search for the bodies of the detained-disappeared dragged on for months and months, the wait is frustrated and a negative learning sets in: there are human rights violations, but there will be no culprits. It is a perverse social learning: "since the Other is not accountable for his actions, don't trust him." The widespread distrust reproduces the climate of general

---

is stolen from her. She thereby decides to return it and turns that restitution into a matter of honor. She borrows an enormous sum of money and buys an identical necklace. For the rest of her days, she is deeply distressed by the payment for the debt incurred. Long afterward, now in her waning years, she reencounters her former protectress and, with great pride, confesses the incident to her. 'My poor friend, the latter exclaims, those diamonds were imitations, the necklace was worthless.'" (Cited by Todorov, op. cit., 82, to illustrate the post-authoritarian gloom in Central Europe.)

suspicion, so typical of the authoritarian period. A past understood as a history without responsible subjects leads to an orphaned future—we are not masters of our history nor of our destiny.

One possible lesson is giving up on the desired future: it would be the "sour grapes" syndrome. You should not wish for the impossible. But another conclusion could also be reached. The image of "what could have been" could likewise nurture the dream of "what could be." The mind (like the culture) is a palimpsest on which many marks are super-imposed. Lastly, all memory is the memory of other memories.

The Normative Power of the De Facto

When reality is presented as the quasi-automatic result of variables that are not managed by the social subjects—think of the market, globaliza-tion, the macroeconomic balances—and is presented as successful, then it makes little sense to wonder about the desired order. In a social order that declares itself autonomous regarding subjectivity, there does not seem to be space for aspirations.

In public opinion, the change of political regime does not produce a substantial change in the "system." On the contrary, it tends to per-ceive a continuity not altered by democracy. Therefore, as in so many other eras, capitalism manages to take on the appearance of a natural process. This automatism enjoys the complicity of memory. The collec-tive memory functions as a process of internalization of the de facto norms. It "learns" that the so-called laws of the market are unalterable norms, whose transgression is automatically punished by the market itself. Once it is internalized that the economic system and the social order are removed from political decisions, participation in politics and the construction of a future have no meaning.

As we understand it, a "naturalization of the social" occurs which leads to ruling out the future as an available and malleable time. It no lon-ger represents a horizon of objectives and social purposes. If social life (the "social system") fundamentally adheres to its intrinsic functional ratio-nales, tomorrow becomes the scene of the opportunities and risks that those functional systems display in their evolution. A scenario of contin-gent decisions. A scenario of individual strategies, not of collective actions.

Nostalgia for the Distant Past

Chileans evaluate the changes that have taken place positively and acknowledge that they are better off than their parents. Access to goods and services, although unequal, allows everyone to improve their standard of living. Consequently, they favor the modernization process underway. At the same time, however, they resent the shortcomings of the economic process. An empirical diagnosis displays a sense of insecurity in the face of misfortunes, helplessness regarding the "logic of the system," mistrust in social relations, of uncertainty vis-à-vis the future, and unease about the "meaning of life." Presenting that situation does not amount to an exercise in catastrophism. We must be aware of the social reality in order to work with it. Undoubtedly, we will build new forms of social coexistence in the future. For the time being, however, the failings invoke the past. But it is no longer the memory of the recent past, doubly cast in doubt by the repression and the flaws in the "economic model," but nostalgia for the distant past.

To the extent that the future has no intelligible meaning nor seems to be a hopeful prospect, a better tomorrow tends to be replaced by a golden past. Latently, an idealization exists of the country of yesteryear, of life in the countryside, the neighborhood, of the fiscal limbo, and the National Health Service. Above all, a yearning for the sociability of the olden days prevails, when there was time for family and friendship, a cordial and unselfish manner, calm in the streets and solidarity among people. Images are sought in the past of familiar customs of friendly coexistence, the complete opposite of the recent past. Instead of remembering rifts and divisions, there is a longing for what is absent: the social bond.

But nostalgia contains a paradox. The dictionary definition, "melancholic sadness caused by the memory of good fortune lost," points to the crux of the matter: life has no replica. If the object of nostalgia is something irreversible, then the yearning for the past fundamentally represents nostalgia for a present that inexorably disappears. It could also be, as Tabucchi asserts[53] in a study on Pessoa, a nostalgia for the possible: evoking what once could have been. Not memory of concrete

---

53   A. Tabucchi, *La nostalgie, l'automobile el l'infini* (Paris: Seuil, 1998).

facts, but rather an almost metaphysical celebration of a past of which only its spirit, its feeling, is retained.

Socializing the Disillusionment

As long as people do not talk about their experiences, do not share their fears and hopes, neither can they develop collective memories. Most importantly, they cannot process the shifts and new meanings that individual memories transact. Just as the interpretation of the "11th" varies according to experiences prior to 1973, the significance of the military government also undergoes numerous reinterpretations. When these reinterpretations cannot be conversed and reflected upon, individual journeys become unintelligible. The person cannot account for and recognize themselves in their life history; the occasional shifts in ideological positions and ethical judgment appear gratuitously or as an outright betrayal. This is reflected in the current Chilean novel, whose characters, according to Cánovas,[54] tend to share a prominent trait: *orphanhood.*

Young people generally think that the anticipated future did not bring changes for them, that democracy did not fulfill its promises. As a result, a great percentage of them do not even register to vote. Their aspirations are concentrated in the personal realm, and in addition, entertain escapist fantasies. A disenchantment prevails, more resigned than rebellious. It is conceivable that this disenchantment arises not only from the experience lived by the youth, but also from the memories transmitted by their parents.

One way of escaping the vertigo of an overwhelming present is to take a step back; to look in the past for the criteria to evaluate the present, rather than in the future. Adopting such hindsight, the parents seem to be the object of conflicting sentiments. On the one hand, objects of envy: they were able to have dreams, they participated in collective projects. On the other, objects of anger: you handed us a damaged country

---

54   R. Cánovas, *Novela chilena: Nuevas generaciones* (Santiago: Universidad Católica, 1997).

and an impossible future. There seems to be a torn-apart consciousness. Chilean youth cannot forget nor wish to relive the past. What should they do with it?

Family socialization offers a "bridge" for the laceration of the present through a reinterpretation of the past. Exploratory studies seem to indicate that many parents tend to refute the golden image of the past. On the contrary, they remember their experience as a deception. They convey a disabused message: in the name of an illusory and abstract cause, they were used (abused) by others and robbed of what really matters, their own lives, their relationships, and their languages. This "memory of deceit" transmits a dualistic vision, which counterposes the "We" of the family and friends, the true country that wants to work in peace, with the "Others," those who introduce illusion and division, the politicos. The tacit message is: children, don't get involved in politics. The circle is completed when the youth ratify this message through their own experience with politics. Then the disenchanted memory of the young people intertwines with the disabused memory of the older folks. We come back to the starting point: the relation between order, time, and memory. On the one hand, memories play a productive role regarding the social order as a source of legitimation or delegitimization. That depends on the degree to which "time" or the "history" of the social order reflects the memories of everyday life. The image of collective time upon which a social order is sustained is usually patchy and unstable and, hence, an insufficient resource for legitimizing the duration of order. Meanwhile, the time of daily life and the memories and hopes generated by it possess the intensity of a vital experience. This emotional charge of temporality and everyday memory can function as a reserve of legitimacy, or even transform itself into the beginning of critique.

Furthermore, the memories and hopes are, in turn, a product of the social order. The basic codes of order operate as criteria for selection and interpretation of the many memories and hopes scattered throughout society. In this way, the social order organizes a general time—such as the history of a nation—in which the individual temporalities can be recognized. The symbolic and cultural dimension of order thus provides containment of the volatile contingency of daily life.

In sum, collective memories build the order and are built by it. In so doing they establish *a mediation between the time of order and the time of everyday experience, between history and biography.* The transformation of the social order and the construction of individual biographies, and above all, the complementarity between both, are inextricably linked to our abilities to recognize and process collective memories and hopes.

V

Order and Memory

The construction of order is intimately connected to the social production of space and time. On the one hand, order is created by delineating its environment, establishing a boundary line between inclusion and exclusion. There is no social and political order without boundaries that separate a "We" from the Others. What is more, the concept of order models the idea of space. It suffices to recall how the image of the human body serves as a metaphor for both the political order as well as for naming the "lungs" or the "arteries" of the city. On the other hand, every construction of order entails the production of a temporal framework. The social order is set inside time, demarcated vis-à-vis a before and an after. It is a task concerning continuity and change through the structuring of events in past, present, and future times. Order lies in the relation established between the past (where did we come from?) and the future (where are we going?).

In the pages that follow, I invite the reader to reflect on the relationship between the political order and the conception of time. Two questions can guide the inquiry. First, in what way does our conception of the political order condition the relationship we establish between past and future? We are interested in the task that politics carries out with regard to time in a dual sense: as "politics of memory," that is, the formulation of a particular vision of the past, and as an action that generates a future horizon. A correlation undoubtedly exists between both moments. The reading of the past is always a self-serving reading, guided by questions from the present and expectations for the future. In other words, the collective memory is not a compiled record of the events that occurred, but rather an interpretation of the experiences in light of the present. Both the individual memory as well as the collective memories are reconstructions. Inversely, the view to the future is also self-interested and envisions the possible opportunities and risks based on certain experiences and orientations. Through this twofold reference to the field of past experiences and the horizons of expectations for the future, the meaning of order begins to define itself.[55]

Second, how do the conceptions of time and the consciousness of temporality influence the idea that we create about the political order? Some conceptions and periods are more aimed at the past, even excessively attached to injustices or grievances of the past, at times of a very distant past (as in the case of certain nationalisms). And certain historical moments exist that tend to perform a type of tabula rasa of the past and value only what is new. It seems, then, that the configuration of collective memories and dreams for the future condition the conception of the political order.[56]

1. Production of a National Memory

In Latin America the construction of order takes the form of the nation state. But this is not found in the origins of the Independence; so various forms compete to shape the territories that free themselves from Spanish rule. The nation state is the final outcome of a long process of creation.

The nation state presents itself today as a unique concept, causing us to forget the conjunction of its constituent moments: state and nation. While the establishment of the state is an eminently political task, the construction of the country becomes a cultural task.[57] The combination of the two moments varies from country to country. In some, political action predominates (France); in others (such as, Germany and Italy,

---

55   R. Koselleck, *Vergangene Zukunft* (Frankfurt: Suhrkamp, 1979). [Spanish version, *Futuro pasado* (Barcelona: Paidós, 1993).]

56   A. Schedler and J. Santiso, *Tiempo y democracia* (Caracas: Nueva Sociedad, 1999).

57   H. Munkler, "Nation as a Model of Political Order and the Growth of National Identity in Europe," *International Sociology* 14, no. 3 (September 1999).

for example) the delay in the politico-state sphere is compensated by the cultural building of the nation.

It is often stated that in Latin America the state creates the nation. In other words, political instrumentation prevails. In fact, the states of the region are built through violence (military or civilian), politics (which leads to the institutions and rules enshrined in the Constitution), administration, and law. The politico-military power is a necessary condition, but not sufficient. In order to strengthen external sovereignty (with respect to other states) and internal sovereignty (obtaining the endorsement or, at least, the obedience of the population) the establishment of a collective identity becomes a priority. This allows for incorporating the population as a "We" distinguishable from "the Others." This is what the idea of the nation provides. For this reason, it takes precedence over other mechanisms of linkage inherited from the colonial era or precolonial tradition.

Nevertheless, the nation does not exist; it must be created. This what the definition of the nation as an "imagined community" refers to.[58] A "We" consciousness—a community—must be created, which serves to undergird the principle of self-determination. In this regard, the formation of a national identity was—in the early nineteenth century—a revolutionary project. It transformed a population into a people and a collective subject of history. Of course, not all of the population was called to belong to the people. The configuration of a national identity serves to incorporate the dominant social groups as well as to differentiate this "people," a cornerstone of the incipient republican order, from the "population" (Indigenous peoples, bandits). It is at once an integration and a differentiation mechanism.

The construction of the nation state intertwines with the reorganization of the temporal structure. The present is delimited through a redefinition of the future and of the past. In one sense, it is essential to design a horizon open to what is new. To build a new state one must break with the inherited temporality and create a new forward perspective. In all of Latin America, independence is undertaken in the name

---

58   B. Anderson, *Comunidades imaginadas: Reflexiones sobre el origen y la difusión del nacionalismo* (Mexico: Fondo de Cultura Económica, 1993).

of the future. Except for the initial reference to monarchic legitimacy, the past is not invoked. On the contrary, in order to preserve the criollo social order, one must relinquish the political past. Two events facilitate this. The universalist ethos of the Enlightenment enabled the creation of future prospects. And the experiences of the United States and France showed the feasibility of a revolutionary break.

The future is conceived of as a process of material and spiritual progress. And the mission of making this progress possible is entrusted to legislation and education. National identity is invoked as a reference in this task: to be a free nation. But a mere invocation of a better tomorrow is too tenuous to unify the disparate expectations about the future. Concrete experiences of something in common is needed to foster a collective identity. And from there, the fact that the building of the nation state entails a reconstruction of the past. It is a matter of seeking and selecting the characteristic traits from the abundant information and experiences of the past that would enable the establishment of a "We." The national identity is invented based on affective values, such as the manner of speaking and eating, the habits and styles of coexistence. But moreover, by incorporating the feast days and popular customs, the scenery and aesthetic tastes. All of this helps in the pursuit of "oneself," but it is culture and history, in particular, that are the basic materials with which to develop a national memory.

As part of this development of a national memory, national museums are created. In the case of Chile, the creation of the National Institute for Higher Education and the National Library, the symbol of written memory, are among the country's first measures in the midst of a war of independence. From their inception, "politics of memory" have existed in the emerging nineteenth-century nation states. How is a national memory created? I will reference a study by Aleida Assman[59] on Germany to describe two strategies that, in my opinion, were widely used in Latin American countries.

---

59   A. Assman, *Arbeit am nationales Gedächtnis* (Frankfurt: Campus, 1993).

The Sacralization of History

In the nineteenth century, the past is dealt with in two very different manners. At the same time that history achieves remarkable progress as a science and institutionalized discipline in the universities, a sacralization of the past takes place. A national memory is not constituted based on simple historical dates; a symbolization of the events is necessary. This is what the monuments and national museums contribute. They provide a dramatization of the past; not just a re-reading of the past but rather a hallowed interpretation. They attempt to determine what the common history is and to tie the national identity to the memory of that common past. It is a delicate operation; nothing less than remaking history with sights trained on the challenges of the present. Building a national history entails "cleansing it" of all turning points, eliminating the alternatives and discontinuities, touching up rivalries and tensions, and redefining adversaries and allies, so that history can be a smooth advance that, as a symmetrical image, announces the infinite progress of the future. The "official history" does not allow itself to be established by decree and thus the disputes of the past can last into the present. Nevertheless, throughout the nineteenth century and a large part of the twentieth, the politics of memory have been successful in transmitting from generation to generation a quite commonly shared idea of "who we are" and to connect that memory to a certain idea of "what we want to and should be."

Among the strategies aimed at transforming historical facts into symbols of the national memory, Assman highlights three features. First of all, repetition. We memorize through repetition. The calendar of national holidays and their ritual commemoration year after year begin to fix in the collective memory certain dates that constitute what is held in common. And the initiatives of the present ensure that they become memorable due to their coinciding with the previously hallowed dates of the past.

Second, superimposition. The tendency is to choose those dates and symbolic figures of the past that can enhance the present. The current moment is superimposed on a determined historical constellation to take advantage of its roots in the collective memory in order to envelop the present day, usually mundane, in a quasi-mythical aura. Mexico provides an early example of such monumentalization of the present.

And I am not only referring to identification with the magnificent pre-Columbian past that is displayed in the Museum of Anthropology. Bernand and Gruzinski describe a curious event in their *Historia del Nuevo Mundo*. In 1539, with the Spanish conquest of the Aztec Empire barely consolidated, there is a performance in Mexico's Plaza Mayor in which invaders along with thousands of Indigenous persons participate: the conquest of Rodas, presenting the struggle of Christians against the Turks. And the same year with the same theme, in Tlaxcala, Franciscans and Indians stage the conquest of Jerusalem, in which the Indians dressed up as Turks end up accepting baptism. "Staged only twenty years after conquering the country, those performances translate the fervor to convert America into a replica of Europe. Assigning the roles of the Europeans to the Indians inscribes in the customs, gestures, and bodies the form of a distant, exotic reality; and further, it attempts to inject into the spirits, and moreover, into the imageries of the vanquished populations, the dreams and obsessions that characterized the sixteenth-century societies: the Crusade, conversion, and henceforth planetary struggle of Christianity against Islam."[60]

Third, the connection between dates and figures of various eras. While historiography is placed in chronological sequences, the politics of memory rely on great leaps. The event of the past is taken out of its historical context and transformed into a timeless myth that legitimates the political goals of the present. In particular, the link to the struggles and heroes of the Independence is a routine resource when exorcising the difficulties currently faced by the country.

The role of monuments and national museums is inserted in these strategies. They are usually forms of exploiting history according to the political objectives of the present. The National Museum makes it possible to link the national identity to a common past and derive the responsibility for the future of the country from that common memory. It is not, then, about a static vision of a distant past, frozen in time, so to speak. The intention, on the contrary, is an updated interpretation with sights set on the future. The hindsight includes a foresight; it speaks as

---

60 C. Bernand and S. Gruzinski, *Historia del Nuevo Mundo* (Mexico: Fondo de Cultura Económica, 1996), 322.

much to what it was as to what it should be. The memory of the past garners a profound sense of what it leads to as a demand for the future. The museum or monument would have no meaning if what they invoke truly existed. Precisely because there is a discrepancy between being and what should be, the National Museum is called on to close that gap. But such a race against time tends to be lost beforehand; particularly when time is accelerating. The distance between the moment it is decided to build a museum or monument and the date it is accessible to the public is usually such that the "place of memory" ends up rotted by the passage of time and the emergence of new challenges and interpretive codes. What had been conceived as an embodiment of the lasting becomes a testament to the transitory.

The Sacralization of Art

A sacralization of art occurs in parallel to the sacralization of history. Constructing the national memory in the nineteenth century additionally hinged on the canonization of what should be considered the classical and representative works of the national spirit. While the respective academic disciplines (history and aesthetics) set in motion and historicize the legacy of the past, the national myths and the canon detemporalize. Artists and their works must be taken out of the historical context in order to remove them from debate and critique, and thus be able to present them as timeless (or even immortal) landmarks of the "national being."

Along the lines of the Assmann study referenced on the German culture, I would underscore two canonization mechanisms. On the one hand, a rigorous selection of those who form part of the national "pantheon." There must be a strict differentiation not only to emphasize and calibrate the excellence of the chosen, but in particular because only a limited number makes their memorization possible. Furthermore, canonization also works with decontextualization. Only to the extent that the figures chosen are pulled out of their historical situations can the discussions and arguments of the time be ignored in order to let the immortal genius shine more brightly. In this fashion, the identification induced with the "classics" allows for creation (invention) of a tradition. The standard is thereby set by which the nation will "measure" its development.

Implementing these devices in Latin American countries faces problems, to be sure. How to establish a national canon that represents "what is ours" without denying the cultural patterns imported from Europe? The European influence and even hegemony is such in the nineteenth century that what is one's own is intrinsically intertwined with the alien and the foreign. As long as the dominant social groups accept the European artistic canons as a universal standard, the enthronement of the national art has a limited scope. It suffices to recall, for example, the allegorical monuments brought from Europe and re-baptized in accordance with the commemoration of the heroes and the national feats. Moreover, the canonization strategy could hardly draw upon "popular art." Valuing the Indigenous heritage would have meant undermining the class differences. It would mean accepting an equality that the political and economic structures of the "oligarchic order" denied on a daily basis.

In spite of these difficulties, the sacralization of art fulfilled its dual function: to serve as "cement" that unites the dominant groups while also serving as a differentiation criterion vis-à-vis the "lowly people." Although it occurred with the support of imported standards, the canonization of "what was cultured" seems to have functioned effectively as a mechanism of national integration as well as a strategy of social distinction.

In short, the sacralization of history and art enabled surrounding the nation with a sacred aura. National memory remained grounded in the image of a holy nation. Religious devotion relocates to the nation under the most diverse forms. We only need to remember the fusion of the Marian devotion (the most famous case must be that of the Virgin of Guadalupe in Mexico) with patriotism. In patriotic fervor, unity in the faith props up the myth of national unity. Indeed, the combination of the cultured and the holy allows for a harmonization of the two sides of the national identity: universalizing social diversity while also blessing social differences.

2. Restructuring of the National Order

The present day is characterized by a profound reorganization of what is national. We only need to recall the two mega-tendencies that drive this restructuring: globalization and individualization. Both processes modify the production of order as well as the temporal framework. The challenges facing reorganization of the social order are linked, in part, to the change in social times.

The Acceleration of Time

The globalization process touches on a crucial point of all construction of order: the limits of inclusion and exclusion. Society becomes opened to transnational flows of finances, technologies, communications, migrations, or lifestyles, not to mention the mafias. Every day we see how national and supranational laws are superimposed—how political decisions take place at different levels, how established traditions are intermingled with the fashions of other latitudes, how people move and cross borders maintaining their former ties and habits. The previous congruence of politics, economy, and culture in the same defined space explodes, shattered to pieces. The various realms are juxtaposed and overlap. Not only have the national borders become porous, all the social boundaries shift: the boundaries of gender and class, between the known and the unknown, between inside and out, between the neighbor and the stranger. The distinction between what is yours and what is someone else's blurs. That means, the motley flow of social living seems to lack a stitch that delimits what we call "society."

This "overflowing" of what is national is accentuated by the restructuring of temporality. A salient aspect of this period is the acceleration of time. Even daily life takes on a dizzying rhythm. Of course, throughout their history, Latin American countries have experienced sequences of cold and hot times. Acceleration in previous eras, however, was steered by the prospect of progress. There was a future horizon that conferred a destination and a sense of movement. By contrast, today that horizon has dissolved, and the very concept of the future seems to be disappearing. In parallel, the past tends to be seen as a bunch of meaningless rubble with no use for the present. A set of obsolete data that would contribute little to understanding the current situation. What is more, the past is often perceived as an encumbrance that hinders us in dealing creatively with the challenges. Therefore, it would be better to forget it.

Thus, cut off from the past and lacking a future, we have no other time than the present: an accelerated "presentism."

This "shrinkage" of the temporal framework makes any notion of order difficult. All construction of order presumes a certain historical background and, as we saw, when it does not exist, that requisite memory of the present must be produced. At the same time, all order demands its duration; it only gains validity and legitimacy, consolidating itself as a lasting order in which it is worthwhile investing in affects and interests. In other words, order requires a future projection. And one of the tasks of modern politics has been precisely to generate time, endow order with a "future." But, insofar as there is no field of valid experiences and horizon of expectations in place that allow one to calculate, foresee, and interpret the social processes, the level of contingency increases. That is, the range of "the possible" is widened, and, consequently, the complexity of the possible combinations, without having the criteria for narrowing down which of those possibilities will become a concrete reality. The result is an order of great contingency and complexity, and therefore, increasingly harder to steer. Under these conditions, it is ever more difficult to perceive order.

The codes by which we classify and order social reality lose their interpretive force. The cognitive maps with which we usually structure social life have been switched. So the processes become opaque and unintelligible. Things function, but we are unable to "ponder" their regulation. In this disordering of the blueprints for interpretation may lie the root cause of the insecurities and uncertainties that mark this turn of century. To the extent that the direction and rhythm of the pursuits appear stripped of discernment and human wishes, the impression of automatism grows. The modernization and globalization processes materialize as movements that are at once blind and irresistible. Neoliberal calls for the "invisible hand" of the market or some other "automatic pilot" acquire plausibility.

The Differentiation of the Temporalities

In recent years, driven by the expansion of the market, a long-standing process has acquired greater visibility: growing individualization. People free themselves of the tutelage of inherited values, habits, and social ties and begin to build their biography assuming their own risk and responsibility. The normative power of traditions is watered down and the "reserves of meaning"—deposited in the family, school, company, and nation—weaken. In this "postmodern climate" the hallowed authorities, social roles and, above all, common interest, no longer provide a solid frame of reference. The milestones, which—like the bell towers in the villages—serve as guiding lights for everyone, disappear. Neither the meaning of life nor the sense of order is provided in advance; they must be developed and negotiated from day to day. In this manner, the disconnection from traditional guidelines leads to the creation of new ties. But they are more flexible and are mobile ties. The old collective long-term identities with clear boundaries and rigid structuring give way to the emergence of light, informal identities of variable geometry. A pluralization of the worlds of everyday life takes place, and people learn to circulate among various "tribes." But this "flexibilization" of all the frames of reference has its price. In the absence of firm referents, it is not easy for people to orient themselves in their lives and in the world. Given that a person individualizes themselves in society, the de-profiling of collective identities hampers the formulation of individual identity.

Moreover, it is well worth remembering the study by Norbert Elias[61] on social self-discipline induced by the centralization of state power. The move from a "state-centric society" toward a polycentric society must affect the type of sociability. The weakening of political centrality can prompt the melting away of a commonality solidified over time and of a more or less shared interpretive code. All these "flexibilization" events alter social temporalities.

Individualization also encompasses the meanings of time. An individualization of time occurs, so to speak. Individual memory predominates, restricted to personal experiences and interpreting the country's history based on those experiences. And the future also tends to be approached from an individual perspective. What establishes the horizons of a future is the design of one's own life project, along with the fears and longings involved in its execution. The promises of tomorrow

---

61   N. Elias, *Über den Prozess der Zivilisation* (Frankfurt: Suhrkamp, 1978).

stem more from one-off strategies than from any collective project. Only the future of one's children or grandchildren transcends the finitude of an individual life. Individual biographies seem to take the place of collective history.

This restriction of the temporal field to the vital course of the "I" arises from the "spirit of the times," but also perhaps from "poor memory." In the case of Chile, we can see a memory injured by the pain of the past and by the disillusionment of what could have been but never was. A stifled memory that does not want to hear any more about those nightmares. A memory that seeks to dissociate a history that, if it once was one's own, ultimately proved to be a history of others. A history for which one does not want to feel responsible. And that compression of the past influences the vision of the future. The feeling of impotence and frustration that recalling the past provokes is projected onto tomorrow. There would be no reason to get involved in crafting a collective project which you could barely influence. The disenchantment learns from the disappointments of the past history and foregoes the "sour grapes." You trust in collective action as long as it is a projection of the "I," the echo chamber of one's own fears and desires.

3. Historical Memory and Future Horizons

Every modern society has a combination of moments of "opening" and of "closure." The social process is continually open to innovation. But the social order cannot open itself up to something different if it does not, at the same time, outline the boundaries that define what is its own. This twofold movement becomes obvious as a result of the globalization process.[62] Innovation fuels a rapid and dramatic opening that thwarts the established limits. While the territorial borders become porous, the social and cultural boundaries that circumscribe "what is ours" come into question. Society is forced to redefine "itself," redefine the form of social coexistence (what is part of "living together" and what is excluded?).

---

62   J. Habermas, *Die postnationale Konstellation* (Frankfurt: Suhrkamp, 1998).

The movement of opening and closure also encompasses the temporal framework. Modern society opens itself to the future; it unceasingly outpaces what currently exists in the pursuit of a better tomorrow. But it does not tolerate a completely open future. It is not possible for everything to be possible. Social living requires a stitch of closure. It is necessary to narrow the range of "the possible," place limits on contingency. Society produces this "closure" in two ways. On one hand, by designing future prospects. These horizons may crystallize into collective dreams about the desired order or into social goals that—more or less implemented (from "development" to "reducing poverty")—are achievable as strategic actions. On the other hand, a "closure" of the past also exists. Society has a determined history. The organization of present community life hinges on what came before: a tradition, certain habits and experiences.

In Latin America utopia plays a special role. It represents a radical opening to the future. Insofar as the desired future slips away over and over again, the horizon tends to be envisaged in an ever more utopian manner: something totally different. Utopia opens a perspective of the future but, at the same time, it generates a closure. As Koselleck shows, the major conceptions of the desired order (from liberalism to socialism) accelerate time, they energize it in light of the horizon to be reached. But they also domesticate it. The utopian future designs a horizon that delimits the possible futures.

The opening and closure of the future are best illustrated by the concept of "progress," which projects a future horizon which helps to guide the opening. Furthermore, the idea of progress illustrates a link between building a future and the social order. The future horizons have also functioned as horizons of meaning. What I mean is: to devise a future horizon is to express an opportunity for meanings—the "meaning of life" and the "meaning of order"—by which the present acquires meaning, becomes intelligible, and can be steered. To the degree that this idea of progress fades, the future remains open, without closure. And without a future horizon, the regulatory principles which allow for interpreting and directing the current process also erode.

One characteristic of the current era seems to consist of the disappearance of any future horizon. There will always be a future, to be sure, like the relentless advance of time. And "futures markets" exist as well as numerous future projections. However, such advances would not be generating a future horizon. It could cause a paradoxical situation. That open future, without a horizon that "closes" it, seems to me to be the reason for a double retraction. Temporality and social order roll back to the present. A certain "presentism" prevails. Community life seems to end with the immediate situation.

The blurring of future horizons and the primacy of the immediate have a twofold consequence. On one hand, contingency increases. The multiplication of factors and their possible combinations and linkages expand "the possible" in such a way that one can no longer foresee which possibilities will really materialize. When (in principle) everything that exists could be different, the social reality seems to evade any human regulation. Then, on the other hand, the future resembles an automatic process that abides by blind forces. The future will bring changes, without a doubt, but we do not know what or how it will change. Accordingly, it is difficult to visualize order as a process shaped by social interaction.

The standing that the demand for social change held decades ago seems to correspond today to the demand for duration. In other words, it is not so much a matter of "opening" and transforming the existing order (this process is already underway) as of placing limits on the possible and creating lasting milestones of community living. How can we once again build some type of "closure" given the current conditions? We have seen the difficulties in developing future horizons. But another path exists: the task of memory. Historical memory also provides a closure. In both individual as well as social life, the past delineates the future. The past has been a constant selection of options; some were chosen and others were discarded. And through these adopted or omitted decisions (deliberately or unintentionally), we shape the alternatives currently available and their significance. Based on a particular past, not just any path is open. Memory provides a filter for processing the possible futures. Ultimately, the development of a historical memory and some future horizons seem to be the same task.

VI

How Do We Reconstruct a "We"?

> What will our collective identity be, the "We" of an
> autonomous society? We are the ones who make our own laws,
> we are an autonomous collectivity of autonomous individuals.
> And we can look at ourselves, recognize ourselves, cross-
> examine ourselves about and by our works.
>
> C. CASTORIADIS

Our society is in the throes of a struggle that pits the demand for democratic self-determination against the naturalization of the social. In its fight
to "be a subject" (individual and collective) of their destiny, people come
up against numerous difficulties. In the previous chapters we addressed
some of them: reformulating the interpretative codes, handling our fears,
the task of remembering. They are facets of the social subjectivity which
encompass affects and emotions as well as the symbolic universes and collective imaginaries. The "politicity" of these elements is revealed in a dual
relation: as forms of everyday experiences that influence the quality of
the democracy, and at the same time, as an expression of the society that
is built by politics. I would propose that, based on the reports on human
development in Chile,[63] we look at some aspects of these relations between
the forms of social coexistence and democratic politics.

---

63 See the reports *Desarrollo humano en Chile 2000. Más sociedad para gobernar
    el futuro* (Santiago: United Nations Development Programme-UNDP, 2000),
    and *Desarrollo humano en Chile 2002, Nosotros los chilenos: un desafío cultu-
    ral* (Santiago: UNDP, 2002).

The argument proceeds in four steps: 1) Let us suppose that the capacity for collective self-determination is linked to the capacity for collective action. In recent years, these societal capacities to act have been centered on the terms of what is called "social capital." One study on the case of Chile suggests that the weakness in the social relation could be the result of cultural change. 2) Indeed, an accelerated process of changes has taken place, in both the practical experiences of coexistence as well as in the imaginaries of that coexistence. 3) The cultural transformations have weakened the image of the "We" that enables forging ties of trust and social cooperation. But, in addition, they have also revealed the difficulty of politics to provide shared meanings about the changes underway. 4) In the final section, I explore some of the challenges that constructing the "We" faces with respect to the social changes.

1. Social Capital in Chile

In the early nineties, Robert Putnam[64] posited that "social capital" would be the mechanism that mediates between people's everyday experience and the economic development and performance of the democratic institutions. Academic circles and development agencies devoted themselves to the study of social capital, understood as the capacity for collective action that people build based on social trust, norms of reciprocity, and civic commitment. Despite the problems raised by the concept,[65] it could be useful in probing the social bond. A set of empirical data comes from

---

64   R. Putnam, R. Leonardi, and R. Y. Nanetti, *Making Democracy Work: Civic Traditions in Modern Italy* (Princeton: Princeton University Press, 1993).

65   A. Portes and P. Landolt, "Social Capital: Promise and Pitfalls of Its Role in Development," *Journal of Latin American Studies* 32 (2000); B. Kliksberg and L. Tomassini, comps., *Capital social y cultura: claves estratégicas para el desarrollo* (Buenos Aires: Banco Interamericano de Desarrollo/Fundación Felipe Herrera/University of Maryland/Fondo de Cultura Económica, 2000); Comisión Económica para América Latina y el Caribe, "Capital social y políticas públicas en Chile, Investigaciones recientes," *Serie Políticas Sociales* (Santiago) 54 (2001).

the *Informe sobre desarrollo humano en Chile 2000*[66] which I can distill into four central themes:

1. First, the quantification of social capital in Chile. The UNDP report offers two approaches. The first centers on the associative potential, for which it designed a national associativity map, that, without being exhaustive, recorded 83,386 organizations, that is, 56 associations per 10,000 inhabitants. In addition, it conducted a national survey in 1999 concerning persons belonging to social organizations. One-third of those interviewed belonged to some social association (a proportion confirmed in the 2002 UNDP report). Among them, more men than women tend to participate, more older adults than young people, and persons of the high socioeconomic group along with those of rural areas had the highest rate of membership. The thematic distribution shows that the interviewees tend to belong mainly to religious, sports, and neighborhood associations.

The second approach sought to quantify the social capital per se. For this provisional measurement an index was created that incorporates the data obtained in the survey around three indicators: relations of social trust, the perception of reciprocity, and the existence of a civic commitment. According to this index, 29 percent of the sample corresponds to the upper bracket; 36 percent of those interviewed possess little or no social capital; and 35 percent are located in the middle bracket. It is difficult to weigh the significance of this data since comparable figures from other countries are not available, nor do temporal series exist for the Chilean case.

2. Second, the distribution of social capital. As in other cases, in Chile a very unequal distribution prevails. While 56 percent of the high socioeconomic group has social capital, only 27 percent of the low stratum does so. It is the persons with a higher level of income and education who demonstrate greater accumulation. In contrast, a lower level of education and income is associated with less social trust and a lesser feeling of reciprocity. In other words, the distribution of social capital

---

66   United Nations Development Programme, 2000, op. cit.

in Chile not only will not diminish, but instead tends to accentuate the social inequalities. This indicates that we should not talk about social capital without also taking relations of domination into account.

3. Third, the historical path of social capital in Chile. This point requires prior clarification. Robert Putnam considers it "stock" accumulated over time. The capital currently available would depend on its historical path ("path dependence" according to North). From this perspective, the author can confirm a considerable decline in the United States in comparison to previous decades.[67] But, would it not be possible for social capital to adopt different modalities? The question refers us back to the historicity of the phenomenon. It is conceivable that, as all historical processes, social capital can modify its form in accordance with the conditions of each period. Therefore, it would be best to approach it rather as a changing flow which adopts different modalities.

Depending on the context and the respective cultural environment, there would be various types of social capital. Today the cultural changes foster more flexible and tentative relations instead of formal organizations. This does not destroy the bonds of social cooperation. Trust, reciprocity, and civic-mindedness can certainly develop as well based on informal ties of a more personal and direct nature. The distinction between formal social capital and informal social capital allows us to account for the "informalization" of the relations. In fact, Chileans have more informal social capital. According to the report, 46 percent of the sample corresponds to the upper bracket of the informal social capital index. Nevertheless, in this case, the distribution is also unequal. Seventy-six percent (76 percent) of the interviewees in the high socioeconomic level have informal social capital, but only 36 percent of the persons of the lower strata do so. Two conclusions on this matter: first, the social groups most in need of social capital in the informal realm are those who have less of it. Second, more attention should be paid to the fact that everyday sociability, despite its waning associativity, may hold a significant potential for trust and cooperation.

---

67   R. Putnam, *Bowling Alone* (New York: Simon & Schuster, 2000).

4. Last, the consequences of social capital for economic development and institutional performance. Once their beneficial effects on development strategies were confirmed,[68] interest in the topic grew. The Chilean study does not address the effects of social capital on the economy. Instead, it validates the other tendency: the political significance of social capital would lie in its contribution to the "social foundation of democracy." According to the survey referenced above, the greater availability of social capital (formal and informal) is associated with greater trust in the ability to influence the country's progress and also with greater democratic participation. Another significant correlation states: those who possess social capital tend to display less political disaffection and show greater confidence in the institutions. In sum, a robust presence of social capital could signify a strengthening of democracy. Were this tendency to be substantiated,[69] the quality of democracy and the quality of community life would go in hand.

As a conclusion for the results presented we can assert that the category of social capital helps to shed light on the overall integration of collective action into the social fabric. However, we should not overestimate its power. I wonder if perhaps we might be seeking to reconstruct in the microsocial realm that social bond that we are no longer able to consider insofar as society. Indeed, many times it seems to be used as a concept equivalent to that of society. But neither the market nor even social capital carries out production and reproduction of that "shared world" of values and norms, of symbols and imaginaries, which enable "living together." Consequently, I would say, social capital is not a shortcut allowing us to focus on the interaction of individuals without a reference to society.

The variety of studies on social capital tend to lead to the same question: How do we produce social capital? By and large, it is answered with

---

68   R. Inglehart, *Modernization and Postmodernization* (Princeton: Princeton University Press, 1997).

69   A. Carrasco and C. García Herrera, "Disposiciones ciudadanas para la profundización democrática. El caso de Santiago," Department of Sociology document (Universidad Católica, 2000).

a circular argument. A strong society creates more social capital while greater social capital gives rise to a strong society. Here I will put forth another argument: the production of social capital presumes a strong "We" imaginary. In other words, it is not easy for people to establish relations of trust and social cooperation if they are not able to see that they share something in common among them. Seen from this perspective, the relative weakness of the social bond in Chile would be related to a weak image of the "We."

2. The Cultural Changes

There can be no doubt: our way of life has drastically changed in recent years. We can speak of a cultural change, understanding culture to mean "ways of living together."[70] I will proceed to mention some trends that have been changing both our practical ways of living together as well as the images that we create of this social coexistence. It has to do with silent and almost imperceptible changes in daily life, but which over three or four decades end up profoundly changing social life. As a result of this transformation of our way of coexisting, the collective imaginaries that used to give meaning to coexistence tend to lose credibility.

An Internalized Globalization

The cultural dimension deployed by the current globalization of capital has been little studied.[71] It would seem that the globalization processes do not form a uniform "global culture," despite how the worldwide

---

70 United Nations Educational, Scientific and Cultural Organization, *Nuestra diversidad creativa* (Madrid: UNESCO, 1997).

71 A. Appadurai, *La modernidad desbordada. Dimensiones culturales de la globalización* (Buenos Aires: Fondo de Cultura Económica, 2001); E. Ortega, *La globalización en la encrucijada* (Santiago: LOM Ediciones, 2002).

profusion of certain brands (from "Barbie" to McDonald's) creates the idea of a widespread standardization. In reality, every society processes, combines, and rearticulates the elements that circulate in the global realm in a particular way. This appropriation entails two things. On the one hand, the internalization and "nationalization" of globalization, from the financial shocks to the custom of fast food. On the other, a new "hybridization"[72] of what is usually summed up as "national culture." Along with the new practices of coexistence, the images we create about them change. As in the "clash of civilizations" five hundred years ago, people's cognitive map has undergone a radical change. In the second chapter I pointed out how a redefinition of the spatial limits (internal/external) takes place and the temporal horizons (before/after) get compressed, leaving people with few symbolic referents to locate their place in the world.

The national society continues to be the customary universe of everyday life. However, people's experiences no longer remain contained in that space. National borders are blurred, temporal distances dissolve. Both the nation's territory as well as its historical horizons are eroded. We must ask ourselves: where does the country end and where does the world begin? How do we draw the lines of inclusion and exclusion that form the boundaries of a social order? Only one thing can be said today: we are a country, but "society" is no longer an obvious fact.

An Accelerated Process of Individualization

One of the most important changes—considering Latin America's communal tradition—is the growing individualization. Individuals are separating themselves from the traditional ties and customs which, at the same time, contained them and protected them. This "going out in the world" forms part of an emancipation process that allows the individual to broaden their horizons of experiences, increase their abilities to participate in social living, and develop their options for self-realization. The opportunities to expand individual liberties are apparent everywhere,

---

72   N. García Canclini, *Consumidores y ciudadanos* (Mexico: Grijalbo, 1995).

especially among the youth. Nevertheless, not all are able to benefit from them. Assuming that no individual is at the margins of society, individualization depends on the options and resources provided by the society in a particular historical era (for example, educational level, social and moral standards, degrees of civic spirit or cynicism). To the extent that our society becomes ever more complex and differentiated, possibilities increase, as do the problems, for the individual's self-determination. Instead of the few classes and social forces of yesteryear, now a proliferation of actors and a variety of value systems and beliefs widen the range of the possible. At the same time, however, that pluralization of normative referents and the competition between interpretive systems hinder the formulation of a collective framework of references. Hence, many individuals live the construction of "themselves" and the pursuit of an authentic "I" as a distressing pressure. Out of that experience of existential insecurity comes the asocial withdrawal of so many people.

The unfinished nature of the individualization can be seen in the empirical study by the UNDP.[73] It is stunning that a large number of Chileans share the sensation that they do not have control over their destiny. Two-thirds of those interviewed affirm that the course of their lives has depended more on external circumstances than on their own decisions. In particular, persons of the lower strata experience social reality as an apparently all-powerful process, which tramples those who do not know how to adapt. If, in addition, they lack social ties that they can fall back on, there is no other choice than to retreat to the private world and to the family. The "no-network individualization" tends to lead to an asocial individualization, a process that not only damages the social fabric, but also corrodes the image of society that people create.

A Market Society

Making the market the organizational principle of social life signifies something more than a reorganization of the economy. It entails a cultural project to the extent that it proposes a deliberate change in the

---

73   United Nations Development Programme, 2002, op. cit.

practices and representations of coexistence. Suffice it to see how the expansion of the market imposes an "individualization" of responsibility and the flexibilization of the social bond which drastically modify our forms of "living together." We see that the consumer's "freedom of choice" is not restricted to the selection of goods and services; it has been incorporated into a new collective imaginary. The image of the individual consumer legitimates the same autonomy to choose the number of children, one's religion or sexual practices. This freedom of choice is even further reinforced by flexibilization. Aside from labor relations, it also facilitates an "informalization" in other areas such as a couple's affective relations or associative affiliation. In this manner, the imaginary of the market and of consumption reinforces a certain self-image of the individual while it also relativizes the normative authority of parents and churches and the role of school-based education in the shaping and transmission of a shared cultural legacy.

The diversity of social life achieves levels previously unheard of, while the nation state weakens. Its transformation has particular relevance for the culture since it was a political (and military) issue. In Chile (as in other countries in the region), it is the state that produces and reproduces a "national culture," giving it substance in the actual lives of the people (education and health policies). The centrality of the state is established in the collective imaginary on this basis. In recent years, the reorganization of the "state-centric" society destroyed the nexus of state and nation. On one hand, the state tends to be reduced to public management. On the other, it is stripped of the symbolic representation of the nation. Accordingly, an imbalance of important magnitudes is produced. The state ceased to embody the collective responsibility while what is national lost its primary anchoring in people's everyday experience.

A Culture of Consumption

One of the most egregious changes would be the shift from a "society of labor" to a "society of consumption." Labor does not disappear, of course, but it changes in meaning within the new social imaginary. Today, the so-called civil society bears the mark of consumption. It is in this cultural framework that the meanings social relations may hold are redefined. In fact, the culture of consumption is even shared by those who are excluded. Through television, advertising, and other devices, including the big-city experience, the culture of consumption has a decisive influence on the way in which people, and especially the poor themselves, define what it means "to be poor."[74]

The consumer culture has profound effects on styles of coexistence. 1) The most conspicuous characteristic lies in the shift from collective action, inherent to the productive world, to the individual strategy typical of consumption. From this, the individual defines "themselves." Related to this self-referencing, 2) the individual identity usually prevails over the collective identity. Consumption is a social act that symbolizes identification and differentiation with respect to others. It then shapes identities, but in a transitory and tentative fashion, without the intensity of the old class identities. To this is added 3) the flexibilization of labor regulations. Deregulation means that job protection as a public good moves to a secondary level in relation to the freedom of the consumer. The seduction and attraction exerted by the goods carry more weight than the legal security of the worker. This alludes to the fact that 4) social imaginaries are currently fed more by advertising than by labor experience. While work produces an objectified world, consumption is the way to display the world of desire and pleasure. Affective experiences thus become a requisite realm in the struggle to "be a subject."

Beyond that, the imaginary of consumption heightens the erosion of people's cognitive maps. 5) Consumption modifies the spatial horizon. In industrial society, the worker is linked to a relatively fixed place, and therefore, immersed in lasting social relations. This local anchoring fosters collective experiences. The consumer, on the other hand, is immersed in the flow of goods, national and imported, which are not limited by their geographical location. The spatial horizon expands while the temporal horizon wanes. 6) Consumption inserts another temporality. While work requires planification of time regarding the projected goal, consumption occurs instantly. The gratifications deferred to the future are replaced by the instantaneous satisfaction of the desire. The eagerness for a direct and immediate experience

---

74   Z. Bauman, *Trabajo, consumismo y nuevos pobres* (Barcelona: Gedisa, 1999).

predominates. Consumption contributes, then, to the acceleration of time and to a growing "presentism," while hampering the processes of learning and maturing. 7) Last, there is a tendency to edge out ethics in favor of aesthetics. Social behavior is no longer guided by a "work ethic" (which values vocation, self-discipline, and deferred gratification) but rather by aesthetic criteria. The manner of perceiving and valuing persons ("appearances") and the objects (the design) tend to form part of a widespread aestheticization of everyday life. This prominence of aesthetics reminds us of another transformation underway.

The Mediatization of Social Communication

The new information technologies and the primacy of the audiovisual world accelerate the change in the "mental maps" that individuals use to classify and order social reality. On one hand, the information technology expansion of the space enables communication without the physical presence of the participants, which changes not only the norms of sociability but also the concept of public space. On the other, a fragmentation of social time occurs. History is broken up into a string of self-contained episodes. The multitude of interpretative codes and the speed with which information and symbols circulate accelerate the obsolescence of past experiences and set up a type of autistic present: a sequence of actions without a historical relation among them.

In this context a dematerialization of the social reality spreads. It might be a less visible tendency than the previous ones, but its effects on the culture are significant. The most illustrative example comes from an area that was, par excellence, the field of material production: the economy. That materiality dropped to second place with the primacy of an intangible value such as the brand. Many of the major companies (like Coca-Cola, Nike, or Disney) focus on "manufacturing" and marketing a brand image more than material goods.[75] While the "real" objects are produced behind the scenes, on the street the promises and images of the "ideal" life reign supreme. Work is relegated to a secondary function,

---

75   N. Klein, *No Logo, La guerra de las marcas* (Barcelona: Paidós, 2001).

while consumption of lifestyles and dreams begins to generate a strange "lightness of being."

The disembodiment emerges as an inherent characteristic of the mediatization of social communication. The rise of an "image culture" revolutionizes experiences and the collective imaginaries. In part, the prominence of the image displaces the former preeminence of the word, altering the type of social conversations and civic deliberations. This does not have to be negative. Television, for example, could play a meaningful role in people not seeing their lives as something already predetermined. But it could also reinforce the "naturalization" of the social reality. The possibilities for producing a virtual reality tend to blur the boundary between the real and the imaginary. The "visual construction of reality"[76] helps to dissolve the relatively shared and lasting "common interest" in the time that it is encapsulated into what is real. And to the degree that the significance of the real becomes lighter (that is, subject to the personal interpretation that each one may give it), reality will no longer be a shared experience.

Summarizing the trends mentioned, I would like to highlight two cultural transformations. On the one hand, the experiences that people get from social harmony have changed. Harmony tends to establish more flexible social relations and, hence, to build a more tenuous and fragile social fabric. And it tends to experience all the ambivalences and ambiguities that affect their daily activities at an unprecedented level. The decision regarding "what to do" not only becomes more difficult, but arises much more often. Furthermore, the descriptions that people usually use about society have changed. Long ago people thought of society as a coherent and cohesive body. Compared to then, now they think that "anything is possible and nothing is certain." No one nor anything provides them with a credible idea about the social body as a whole. And, without that frame of reference, it is not easy to feel you are part of a collective group.

In sum, this brief outline of the changes suggests that the experience and the image of the "We" have undergone a major transformation. It seems to me that, today, there is no profiled figure of the "We." We are

---

76   J. Martín-Barbero, *De los medios a las mediaciones* (Mexico: Gustavo Gili, 1987).

not that "We" that Castoriadis[77] summarized so well in the chapter's epigraph. Constructing an "autonomous collectivity of autonomous individuals" would be precisely the horizon of meaning that guides the struggle for democratic self-determination.

3. The Affective Uprooting of Democracy

Signs of Disaffection

I presume that the difficulties in taking on the social process as something "ours" are linked to the weaknesses of the "We" as a subject of development. Formulated in the positive the assumption would state: people require an imaginary of the "We" in order to experience the processes of change as a result of their own action. Conversely, they create and re-create such a collective imaginary of a "We" based on their concrete experiences of coexistence. Next, I will present some evidence that suggests that the cultural transformations are causing an emotional detachment. Immersed in a process of accelerated changes that they do not control, people are showing signs of disaffection: it seems that they do not have a sense of ownership of these changes.

The emotional detachment is more than a personal matter of each individual: it pertains to a way of living together and would affect democracy in two ways. On the one hand, it pulls the subjective rug out from under democracy. That is, it is left without roots in people's affects and passions. The citizenry will respect the democratic procedures and institutions, but they do not feel an affective commitment. There would be no sense of belonging to a democracy as a "We." It would constitute, on the other hand, a shortfall in democracy because it would not have managed to endow the changes underway with meaning. Democracy—as an experience and social representation of self-determination—would not be generating a shared significance. And the conclusion is evident: a policy that does not help the public

---

77   C. Castoriadis, *El avance de la insignificancia* (Buenos Aires: Eudeba, 1997), 96.

to live and share their everyday experiences as something important, becomes insignificant.

In what follows, I will be drawing from the research for the report *Desarrollo humano en Chile 2002*.[78] I begin with one of the more startling results: signs of disaffection in relation to the so-called economic model. Half of the interviewees declared themselves to be "losers" on that score. The importance of that piece of data lies in the contrast with the economic growth and progress in social welfare during the last decade. How could such remarkable progress be perceived as a loss? It is not that the Chileans are unaware of the achievements; the majority of them state they are in a better situation than that of their parents and believe that their economic situation will continue to improve in the future. In other words, the self-perceived notion of "loser" is not a mere reflection of a certain economic position; it represents a social construct. People do not evaluate the economic (nor the political) system according to the rational calculation of cost-benefit. Numerous factors intervene and, among them, affects. The widespread image of "loser" is related, concretely, to the negative sentiments caused by the economic system. It is striking that 75 percent of those interviewed express insecurity, anger, or loss because of it. The figures seem to confirm the usual allusions to the "pessimism" of Chileans. It would be more appropriate, however, to interpret this tendency as a lack of affective identification with the development achieved. The substantial improvement in the standards of living during these recent years had not elicited an emotional commitment. And that subjective distance is not restricted to progress in the economy.

The alienation seems to refer to the changes in general. Six of every ten people surveyed feel that they have lost more than they have gained with development. Once again, what might they have lost? Reiterating, people do not (only) acknowledge an economic result. Their perception emerges from subjective experiences: from fears and dreams, from experiences and expectations that permeate their daily lives. Thus, possible motives are discovered. It is not surprising that people tend to feel confused in a world that seems to be much less comprehensible

---

78   United Nations Development Programme, 2002, op. cit.

than that of their parents. Added to the perplexity is impotence: six of every ten interviewees believe that their opinion does not count much in the country and that, on the contrary, the people with power take advantage of them. The fear of abandonment grows, suspecting they have been left aside. Perhaps it is the perception that the world is fine, such a perfect closed circle, that you are not needed.

What is the reason for the lack of identification by so many people with the gains achieved? In my view, the critical view of the changes underway could provide an answer. Despite Chile's good socioeconomic variables, only 14 percent of those interviewed assert that "the changes have a clear direction and we know where they are going." In other words, a decade of sustained growth had barely created a future perspective. Instead, one-third of them consider that the changes in Chilean society have no purpose and lack direction. And to top it off, half of those interviewed stated that "in spite of these changes, things are still the same."

In short, it seems that two-thirds of the Chileans interviewed see no sense in the changes in process or do not consider that the changes are anything relevant to their daily lives. The fundamental question remains: What meaning does the country's development have for people's everyday reality? That is the question that politics must answer.

What should have changed but is still the same? The disquiet may reflect the bewilderment inherent to any process of change when the losses are suffered in the flesh without being able to see the future gains. They may be persons who feel they have not left the past behind or have a future that justifies the sacrifices made. It would be a continuation of the malaise that ends up flattening such crucial gains as democracy and greater well-being. Although they are fundamental changes, the democratic transition could have chosen not to launch a different subjective experience. In that case there would have been some disappointment over unfulfilled promises, not concerning living standards as much as the expected change in their way of living ("happiness is coming").

The most disturbing part of the situation is the silence that surrounds it. In people's subjective world, their emotional deficiencies are not being verbalized. There is a discomfort without clear substance or precise target. Now, that lack of words not only shrouds popular opinion in silence, democracy would also be devoid of discourse. What I mean is, the Chilean transition did not generate a narrative that provided a credible interpretation of what was done. We do not have a "story" that places the changes in perspective. And actions without words are like dogs without collars.

In conclusion, it seems that in many cases people are not embracing the country's development as something of their own. That would convey a deficiency not only of the governments that led the transition but also of democracy itself. With the understanding that one of its functions is to develop social significance in relation to civic conviviality, the results mentioned suggest that the democratic process was not implemented very well. Aside from its good institutional performance, it did not know how to produce the codes of interpretation and meaning that enable the citizenry to appropriate the social reality. On the contrary, the self-referred operation of the practical systems looks more like a true expropriation of the social significances. People may feel expropriated and attribute that loss of meaning to democracy.

The Weakness of the Collective Imaginaries

What is our social imaginary? What ideas do we have about our ways of coexisting? I am parting from the following premise: every society recognizes itself through a social imaginary.[79] Only through that space projected beyond itself can a society constitute itself as a collective order. This imaginary synthesis of society is embodied by various forms of "imagined community," among them, the state and the nation, which not only encompass material forms, but also represent symbolic forms of the "We." Through them the population feels part of a collective order. Hence, these collective imaginaries are as real as unemployment or the quality of education. More precisely, the latter are inseparable from the ideas and images that people have about the social order. However, it seems that we are witnessing an overall weakening of the social imaginaries. In the case of Chile, for example, the fragile experience of

---

79   C. Castoriadis, *L'institution imaginaire de la societé* (Paris: Seuil, 1975); R. Chartier, *El mundo como representación* (Barcelona: Gedisa, 1996).

society, previously described, is associated with a weak imaginary of the "We." An indication of that would be a certain hollowing out of "what is Chilean" as well as the fragility of the democratic imaginary.

Let us first look at the strange levity of the "We" exhibited in a rather detached identification regarding what is national. Six of every ten interviewees stated that it would be difficult to say what is Chilean or that you must not speak about that. Their wariness does not imply that these persons are not loyal to Chile. They may very well feel Chilean and yet have emptied "what is Chilean" of content. The qualitative studies indicate that even the icons of "Chilean identity" (flag and national anthem, national heroes and official history) seem to have lost relevance as signs of identity. The source of this weakening lies in the dictatorship which divided the society to such an extent that it undermined the idea of what is Chilean as a "common home." The return to democracy reestablished a certain basic consensus, but not an imaginary of "we Chileans." What is more, I would say that the silencing of the past conflicts hindered a post-dictatorship imaginary. By not wanting to remember, for fear of reliving the collapse of the national community, we lack "bricks" to rebuild that community. In fact, according to the previous UNDP report,[80] half of those interviewed declare that "talking about the past damages our conviviality," and two-thirds of the people surveyed believe that in Chile "there is more that divides us" than what unites us.

The affective distance is not only due to politico-historical reasons. The changes would have a major impact on the contemporary experience of Chileans. Views on what is national are related to the way in which people assess the changes in the country. The persons more skeptical about what is Chilean are usually those who do not see a purpose to the changes or believe that things remain the same. Those who experience abandonment and impotence on a daily basis, those who lack social ties and future prospects, would have no reason to feel they are part of a nation. Why should those who do not feel welcome and acknowledged by society commit themselves to what is Chilean? The reciprocity relation also functions inversely: a washed-out imaginary of

---

80   United Nations Development Programme, 2000, op. cit.

"we Chileans" inhibits the concrete construction of the bonds of trust and cooperation that shape a "We" in people's daily endeavors.

The tendency for a disidentification, partial but significant, is likewise expressed in relation to democracy. Just as important as the weakening of "we Chileans" is that of "we citizens." Some evidence suggests that this second imaginary of the "We" still lacks a firm foothold. A successful transition presumes proper functioning of the institutions and democratic procedures. But it is not a sufficient condition. In addition, it demands that the founding values of a "community of citizens" be part of a "public spirit." Taking Chile as an example, one can see how difficult the challenge is. Twelve years after the re-establishment of democratic rule, citizen participation is limited, not only due to electoral shrinkage (40 percent of the potential electorate), but also because of a political disaffection. Similar to the withdrawal from life in society, there is a withdrawal from political life. A significant number of people (27 percent of those interviewed) seem to live by the motto that "everyone must fend for themselves because politics is useless."

The weakness of democracy as an imaginary of the civic "We" is revealed by the limited support sparked by the democratic government. According to various studies, not even half of the Chileans interviewed contend that it is a system preferable to any other. Instead, almost one-third declare themselves to be indifferent to the country's political system. The values of democracy—from popular sovereignty to the opinion of minorities—do not represent shared premises. The indifference has to do with the known distrust in democratic institutions. Apart from this pervasive trend, we should mention the negative image of democracy held by many Chileans. Half of those interviewed conceive of democracy as either "a game of chance in which many play but few win," or (to a lesser degree) as "a supermarket from which everyone takes what they need." This elitist and consumer view reflects a characterization that is not very amenable to collective commitments.

The reason for this dislocation seems to lie in the patchy connection that people's everyday lives have with the very idea of democracy. Democracy is not managing to root itself in the everyday reality of the population. An illustrative fact: seven of every ten interviewees believe that in discussions one must "avoid conflicts so that things don't escalate." That is, there is a fear of experiencing democracy as a form of processing and resolving conflicts. I would say that, in general, we do not have an image of democracy that helps to give meaning to our everyday experiences. Democracy is not operating as a symbolic representation of the society which helps to reveal it to be a product of social interaction. Framed in another way: it seems that many citizens do not manage to appropriate the social process as something belonging to them because they lack a democratic imaginary that situates them as a collective subject of the changes.

Perhaps that can explain the current deterioration of democracy in the region. Its poor quality may be expressing not only an institutional malfunctioning, but rather its ineffectiveness as a collective imaginary in which society can recognize itself. It is possible that the weak image of democracy may be none other than the counterpart of another imaginary: the current organization of society as a natural order. This naturalization, based on a society-market image as a self-regulated order, is reflected in the figure of the citizen-consumer who evaluates and chooses among the existing offers. The society-market imaginary can create a credible reflection of coexistence, but does not include its diversity. The famous "invisible hand" of the market promises a balance among the forces; something different from the establishment of a common framework. What is held in common is something built, the product of a deliberate act. That is what the democratic imaginary contributes: the construction of a "world held in common" by all, through which each person can feel and reflect on their everyday experience as a shared diversity. In short, it allows for focusing on the autonomy of the individual along with their social integration.

4. Politics as a Cultural Task

We should meditate on two timely events in 2002. As the Argentine crisis shows, the efficiency of public administration is a necessary condition of good governance. But the electoral defeat of Jospin following a successful administration suggests that politics does not end with good governance. To "govern differently" we must pay attention to the cultural changes, that is, take into account people's new ways of relating and envisioning themselves. From the transformation described, it follows that we can no longer conceive of "society" as a predetermined realm, with fixed boundaries of inclusion and exclusion. In a globalized world there is no defined sphere of interests and opinions, whose conflicts would be processed and decided through democratic politics. The various imbalances of the social order have an impact on the representative function of democracy. Nevertheless, instead of focusing on the "crisis of representation," I think it would be more fruitful to highlight the productive dimension of politics—the production of society. What Paul Klee said about art is valid here: it does not reproduce what is visible, it forms the visible. Is that not democratic self-determination? An action is political to the extent that it builds a social link. This construction of the social through the struggle for collective self-determination is the way in which society establishes itself as a subject. In light of this self-constitution of the "autonomous society," we can assess a policy according to its potential for transformation; that is, its capacity to generate experiences and imaginaries of "We" which allow people to broaden their possibilities for action. This is what politics as a cultural task is about.

Politics is facing a great cultural challenge: to name and interpret the social changes underway. Owing to the dispute among different interpretations, the "common meaning" was produced regarding what these transformations signify. The political struggle spotlights the problems and risks these changes prompt, while also deciding on the goals to be achieved. To close, I will present four battlefronts that allow us to interpret the changes as a struggle to establish a public "We."

Social Subjectivity Versus Naturalization

The first conflict consists of the confrontation with the naturalization of the social. Meaning, the process which freezes coexistence in an immovable and distant "system." To fight against naturalization is to fight against de-subjectification; against the objectification of interpersonal relations in an abstract and self-regulated system. The sacralization of the "logic of the system" drives out social subjectivity. Exploited as a function of the systems, human beings tend to live against the grain. In many cases, people's daily lives are affected by emotions and sentiments that they do not know how to name. And without a name, there is no way to reflect and converse and share the pains and sorrows. There is no way to build trust between people, and therefore, there would be no subjective base upon which to build social cohesion. Under these conditions, social harmony is reduced to strategies of adaptation to a process of alien and hostile changes. It is true that people always try to adapt; that is inherent in the history of the species. But adaptation is not necessarily positive; it becomes reflexive when one becomes aware that the state of affairs is reversible.

People as subjects, individual and collective, who control their future, oppose naturalization. The political challenge lies in restoring— as a practical experience and as an ideal image—a citizen "We" with abilities to shape the direction of the country and their lives. In this struggle to "be a subject," the legend of popular sovereignty, found in the origin of democracy, is revived. It does not matter that "the people" does not exist as an empirical fact. What counts is the principle of sovereignty: social coexistence as an order constructed by society itself. This cornerstone of democracy is still valid and continues to be its utopia.

We combat the naturalization of the social by reintroducing subjectivity into social living.

Being a subject means being recognized in one's subjective experience. One of the principal tasks of a cultural policy consists of naming people's fears and desires, of embracing their hopes and fears. It is in this realm, as I understand it, where "people's concrete problems" lie. Therefore, it is of little use to resolve material problems if, at the same time, politics does not take responsibility for the subjective experiences of people in day-to-day living. The challenge lies in the mediation between that subjective perception and the social reality and flaws at the macrosocial level. This marks the difference with a populist policy, which embraces the social subjectivity, splitting it off from its material conditions, and with a technocratic policy, solely concerned with the operation of the functional systems.

Democratic Imaginary Versus Social Fragmentation

The transformation of Chilean society leads to an accelerated diversification of factors and actors. Social diversity could represent one of the country's greatest riches, as long as it is included in an order. Without integration mechanisms, the diversity of the society results in fragmentation. What I mean is, the socioeconomic inequalities could reach such a level that they cause not only the bonds of solidarity to burst, but also basic rights. Here we have a second divide: the tendencies for dispersion are countered by a policy of integration. It is not enough, however, to repeatedly invoke "social capital" and "civil society." There are no panaceas, we have already seen that. The idyllic aura of civil society evaporates when two-thirds of the interviewees conceive of their relations with others as a competitive race. And the accumulation of social capital is questioned by a third of those interviewed, who assert that "the only thing that matters is meeting your needs and those of your family." The dissociative dynamics of "negative individualism" are powerful, and they are even more so since they rest on a limitless process such as the market. And it will not be the contraction of economic growth that curbs it as long as the imaginary of the market predominates. In order to place limits on its centrifugal forces, the force of gravity exerted by a "We" is required.

A strengthening of the social bond is a response to the threats of social dismantling. These bonds of trust and cooperation are built and strengthened when individuals learn that they share something in common. From that another cultural challenge of politics arises: to help every individual to feel part of a community. Well then, that is what democracy does as an imaginary of the "We." More precisely, the image of a coordinated plurality of numerous "We's." This offers that imaginary of a "shared world" through which the public can experience social diversity as the expression of a collective order.

Public Space Versus Privatized Withdrawal

How robust is democracy as an inclusive imaginary of the "We" among us? The threat originates not only from the market mechanisms that foster fragmentation of the social fabric, but equally from the "privatization" of behaviors. It is not a minor tendency considering that one-third of those interviewed agree with the statement that "if things are going well in my house, the situation of the country is not very important to me." If that is true, how can we consolidate the democratic imaginary and undertake practical experiences of society when so many people retreat from social living? It is no coincidence that Chileans hold family as the most important thing in their lives. In the face of the overpowering advance of the "system," the only thing left is to take refuge in the family. But the demands for emotional support, moral foundations and meaning in life increase to such a degree that they overload the family. And the same people who glorify the towering place of family sense the precarity of the refuge. Six of every ten interviewees assert that the family is "a source of tensions and problems" or, directly, "an institution in crisis." It becomes apparent that family life is undergoing a great transformation that we can deal with only if we address it in the broader context. When we approach the family as an institution included in the change in social life, we can see the relation that the growing "privatization" has with the transformation of the public space. The overload on family life does not seem unrelated to the decline in spaces of encounter and social conversation.

The tendency toward a privatized withdrawal can be combated by strengthening the public realm as a place where the individual acquires the force of the collective. The same democratic imaginary, just referenced, is built based on the experiences lived by the population in the public space. It is here where people come to the fore and learn to communicate and relate to others. Through public debate, they name and share their experiences and begin to develop a plurality of "We." What happens, however, when the audiovisual industry barely allows the words to be heard? There are new languages—image and music—that condition views on the world. In many cases, the privatized withdrawal to the home is accompanied by the use of new communication styles. And that can modify the experiences of the "We." Could politics translate and process these new forms of experiencing and imagining our "living together"?

Politics is facing the challenge posed by the new public spaces, such as shopping centers and, in particular, television. The latter radically expands mass access to a shared sphere while also playing a leading role in the shaping of the "matters of general interest." A redimensioning of what is public is taking place which we should neither ignore nor overestimate. In fact, in contrast to television's influence on the public agenda, the impact of the "public actors" on the definition of "what is public" is limited. One reason highlighted by Jesús Martín-Barbero is the importance of the "visual production of the real" in our times. The meanings of the social reality tend to be pre-defined and, more often, respond to audiovisual technical demands than to public discussions. The television example suggests that, as with the market, proper functioning of the public debate requires regulations. Public space must also be defended and promoted by institutions that help to generate gatherings and conversations, foster agreements and respect dissent.

Future Horizons Versus Permanent Present

Last, I would like to call attention to the struggle around time.[81] As with space, time plays a central role in the construction of a sovereign society. Today, the social withdrawal and political retraction are heightened by a temporal retreat. We live in the present as if it were the only existing time. The meteoric acceleration of the rhythm of daily life is driven by the trends of the era: the simultaneity created by globalization, the mediatization of social communication, the speed of images and "live" reality, the flexibilization of labor, and the immediate satisfaction of consumption. These changes tend to hollow out the principal long-term staging area: institutions. The slow pace of democratic institutionality seems obsolete in the face of the rhythm that television and the opinion polls stamp on the public debate. They postpone reality and accelerate the urgency of problems, inducing the public's impatience. If, in its inception, representative democracy had been justified by the need to distance the government from the impatience and volatility of public opinion, now that distance is melting away. Pressured for immediate responses, politics tends to lose any medium or long-term strategies.[82]

---

81 J. Santiso, "Wall Street and the Mexican Crisis: A Temporal Analysis of Emerging Markets," *International Political Science Review* 20, no. 1 (1999), and "La democracia como horizonte de espera y campos de experiencia: el caso chileno," *Revista de Ciencia Política* (Santiago) 21, no. 2 (2001).

82 P. Rosanvallon, "Les utopies régressives de la démocratie," in various authors, *France, les révolutions invisibles* (Paris: Calman-Lévy, 1998).

Compared to market time—contingency—the time of politics is that of perspective. In reality, democratic politics is at stake in the handling of time. "Only the control of time allows people to stop thinking they are playthings of happenstance. Only the control of time allows them to access a form of existence in which they collectively decide their destiny."[83] It is a task of politics to counteract the urgency of the immediate reality by means of a historical time. The historicity weaves together discontinuities and duration, the lessons learned with future horizons. Horizons which are not projections of goals nor plans to implement; but rather "constructs" or faith in the meaning we attribute to the journey taken and the promises of a better tomorrow. Seen thus, doing politics consists of producing the horizons of meaning that enable putting things into perspective.

In the midst of the postmodern climate, I will defend a benefit of modernity: perspective. This requires, as Zaki Laïdi puts it, first, taking a step back. We must break ourselves loose from the daily routine in order to lift our sights beyond the immediate. Second, perspective presumes a vantage point from which to observe. There is no neutral optic; every perspective is positioned, self-serving. Third, this entails a project: that is, an intentionality regarding the future. Perspective prepares an intentional action in relation to a "world to be created." But, when reconstruction of the space (achieved by Renaissance painting) gives way to the symbolic construction of the future, the perspective becomes a narrative history. Creating a perspective is to create an account that situates the present in relation to the past and the future. Establishing that new vista could be the principal cultural challenge for politics in contemporary Chile: to recount the "country project" being born (which wants to and could be born) out of the process of transition. It would mean telling the story of the "We" that we wish to become.

---

83   Z. Laïdi, *Le sacre du présent* (Paris: Flammarion, 2000), 94.

About the Author

Norbert Lechner (Karlsruhe, Germany, 1993–Santiago de Chile, 2004) was a German researcher and political scientist who became a Chilean national. He received his PhD in political science from the University of Freiburg and went on to become one of the most outstanding theorists of his generation. He lived and worked in Chile starting in 1971, where he presented his ideas as a professor and researcher both at universities and international organizations such as UNESCO and UNDP. Lechner was director of the Latin American Faculty of Social Sciences (1988–94) and author of numerous articles and books that have left a deep mark on the social sciences of Latin America, including *La crisis del Estado en América Latina* (1977), *La conflictiva y nunca acabada construcción del orden deseado* (1984), *Los patios interiores de la democracia* (1990), and *Las sombras del mañana. La dimensión subjetiva de la política* (2002), for which he won the Santiago Municipal Prize in the essay category in 2003.

About the Editors

Velia Cecilia Bobes is professor-researcher at the Latin American Faculty of Social Sciences, FLACSO-Mexico, and has a PhD in social sciences with a specialty in sociology from the Center for Sociological Studies of El Colegio de México. She is member of the Mexican Academy of Sciences and the National System of Researchers (Level II). She has been coordinator of the master's program in social sciences and the doctorate program in research. Currently she is director of the *Latin American Perfiles* magazine. She has taught courses in social theory and political sociology and directed theses at master's and doctorate levels. She has published books, articles, and chapters on civil society, citizenship, and migration issues. Her most recent books are *Política migratoria y derechos de los migrantes en México* (editor) (Mexico City: FLACSO, 2018); *El cambio constitucional en Cuba* (edited with Rafael Rojas and Armando Chaguaceda) (Madrid: Fondo de Cultura Económica, 2017); *Política migratoria en México: Legislación, imaginarios y actores* (coauthored with Melisa Pardo) (Mexico City: FLACSO, 2018); *Cuba ¿Ajuste o transición? Impacto de la reforma en el contexto del resta- blecimiento de las relaciones con los Estados Unidos* (editor) (Mexico City): FLACSO, 2015.

Francisco Valdés-Ugalde (1953) is professor at the Institute for Social Research, Autonomous National University of Mexico. He also teaches at the Facultad Latinoamericana de Ciencias Sociales-México. From 2010 to 2018, he was Director General of the Latin American Faculty of Social Sciences-Mexico (FLACSO-Mexico). He received his PhD from the Autonomous National University of México. He has been a member of the Superior Council of FLACSO and is currently its President. He is a member of the Mexican Academy of Sciences and has taught or conducted research at several universities, among them Columbia University, Harvard University, Brown University, the University of Connecticut, the University of California-San Diego, the University of Salamanca, and the Research Institute José Ortega y Gasset in Madrid. He is or has been a contributor and/or member of the editorial boards of a number of journals, including *Revista Mexicana de Sociología* (director, 2007–10), *The Journal of American History*, and *Perfiles Latinoamericanos*. He is also a regular columnist for the Mexican newspaper *El Universal*.

In 2001 he was Director General of the Instituto Nacional de Estudios Históricos de la Revolución Mexicana of the Ministry of the Interior, Mexico. He has written extensively on political science, as well as Latin American and Mexican politics. His books include: *Democracy in Latin America: The Failure of Inclusion and the Resurgence of Authoritarianism*, (Berlin: De Gruyter, 2023); *Ensayo para después del naufragio. Democracia, derechos y Estado en tiempos de ira* (to be published in 2023 by Penguin Random House); *El Estado y los derechos humanos en América Latina: México, Ecuador and Uruguay* (coauthor) (Mexico City: FLACSO, 2020); *Entre el pesimismo y la esperanza. Los derechos humanos en América Latina. Metodología para su estudio y medición* (coauthor) (Mexico City: FLACSO, 2015); *Obras. Norbert Lechner* (coeditor) (Mexico City: Fondo de Cultura Económica); *América Latina en los albores del siglo XXI* (coauthor), Mexico City: FLACSO, 2012; *La regla ausente; Conflicto constitucional y democracia en México* (Barcelona: GEDISA-FLACSO-UNAM, 2010); *Izquierda, sociedad y democracia ¿hay un futuro democrático para América Latina?* (editor); *Nuevo Horizonte*, (Mexico City: Editores-Friedrich Ebert Stiftung, 2009); *Libertad, coordinación social y justicia. Debates fundamentales sobre liberalismo y colectivismo* (coauthor) (Mexico City: UNAM & FLACSO, 2007); *Reforma del Estado y coordinación social* (editor) (Mexico City: Instituto de Investigaciones Sociales-UN- AM-Editorial Plaza y Valdés, 1999); *Autonomía y legitimidad: los empresarios, la política y el Estado en México* (Mexico City: Siglo XXI Editores-Instituto de Investigaciones Sociales, UNAM, 1997).

About the Translators

Victoria J. Furio earned a secondary education degree in French and Spanish in 1973 and went on to direct the Mutuality in Mission program and the Interreligious Task Force on Central America. Following fifteen years in Latin America devoted to human rights and development, she has worked as an NGO conference interpreter and translator since 1998.

Mariana Ortega-Breña is a translator, editor, and writer specializing in history, social sciences, and cultural studies. She has worked for a variety of NGOs, governmental institutions, publishers and universities, including the Organisation for Economic Cooperation and Development (OECD), the International Network on Migration and Development (INMD), Mexico's Instituto Nacional de los Pueblos Indígenas (INPI) and Instituto Nacional de Antropología e Historia (INAH), Penguin Random House, Fondo de Cultura Económica (FCE), Université Paris-Sorbonne, and the University of California, among others

Index

utopias
  critiques of   24
  democracy and   85, 91, 93
  disenchantment and   195, 198
  of good order   62–63, 72
  historical memory and   295
  indeterminacy and   146–147
  Latin American   295
  liberalism and   23
  Marxism and   23, 85, 174
  need for certainty and
      173–174, 176
  need for order and   136
  secularization and   165
  temporal acceleration
      and   264

V

Venezuela   35, 76, 151
Ventós, Rubert de   199–200
voluntarism   51, 153, 189, 253

W

Weber, Max   45, 82, 107, 174, 182,
    192–193, 227
welfare state   10, 19, 25, 38, 40, 46,
    48, 79, 97, 135, 155
Wenders, Wim   71

Z

Zermeño, Sergio   15–16, 18, 20, 33

About the Latin America Research Commons

Latin America Research Commons (LARC) is the first open-access publishing press dedicated to the publication of monographs in Spanish and Portuguese. It is an editorial project that originated in the Latin American Studies Association (LASA), and its main goal is to ensure the widest possible dissemination of original monographs and journals in all disciplines related to Latin American studies. It is oriented to making sure that scholars from around the world are able to find and access the research they need without economic or geographic barriers.

In Translation: Key Books in Latin American Studies is a LARC series dedicated to publishing classic Latin American books which have never been translated before and to reaching new readers.

www.ingramcontent.com/pod-product-compliance
Lightning Source LLC
Chambersburg PA
CBHW020454270326
41926CB00008B/604